International Human Rights: Advances in Laws and Practice

International Human Rights: Advances in Laws and Practice

Edited by
Ada Miller

STATES
ACADEMIC PRESS
www.statesacademicpress.com

Published by States Academic Press,
109 South 5th Street,
Brooklyn, NY 11249, USA

ISBN: 978-1-63989-297-6

Cataloging-in-Publication Data

International human rights : advances in laws and practice / edited by Ada Miller.
p. cm.
Includes bibliographical references and index.
ISBN 978-1-63989-297-6
1. Human rights. 2. International law and human rights. 3. Intervention (International law). 4. Political development. I. Miller, Ada.
K3240 .H86 2022
341.48--dc23

For information on all States Academic Press publications visit our website at www.statesacademicpress.com

STATES
ACADEMIC PRESS

Contents

Preface

The world is advancing at a fast pace like never before. Therefore, the need is to keep up with the latest developments. This book was an idea that came to fruition when the specialists in the area realized the need to coordinate together and document essential themes in the subject. That's when I was requested to be the editor. Editing this book has been an honour as it brings together diverse authors researching on different streams of the field. The book collates essential materials contributed by veterans in the area which can be utilized by students and researchers alike.

Human rights are a wide variety of values or capabilities that are thought to enhance human agency or protect human interests. It is claimed equally for all present and future individuals and is declared universal in character. In order to safeguard the collective well-being, people everywhere need to achieve diverse values or capabilities. It is observed that this need is often ignored by social as well as natural forces. This leads to exploitation, oppression, persecution and other forms of deprivation. Human rights and their associated national and international legal processes are deeply rooted in these observations. This book is a compilation of chapters that discuss the most vital concepts and emerging trends in the field of human rights. It includes contributions made by international experts. This book is a vital tool for all researching and studying this field.

Each chapter is a sole-standing publication that reflects each author's interpretation. Thus, the book displays a multi-facetted picture of our current understanding of application, resources and aspects of the field. I would like to thank the contributors of this book and my family for their endless support.

Editor

PART I

INTRODUCTION

1

International law and domestic human rights litigation in Africa

Magnus Killander[*] & Horace Adjolohoun[**]

Summary

Lawyers and judges in civil law Africa are reluctant to make use of international human rights law despite the monist constitutional framework. In contrast courts in dualist common law countries have made extensive references to international human rights law in their jurisprudence. However, direct application of human rights treaties is rare. The main reason for this is not whether a constitutional framework is monist or dualist, but the fact that international human rights treaties have influenced the national bills of rights. The main role of international human rights law, in the form of case law and other interpretation by supervisory bodies, should be to aide national courts to interpret constitutionally recognised rights.

1 Introduction

The objective of this book is to discuss the role international law plays in domestic human rights litigation and to reflect on what role international law should, in the authors' view, play. The role of international law in domestic courts is an area which has received much attention from academia and the legal profession.[1] Many country-specific or comparative studies have been published.[2] Human rights feature

---

* Head of research, Centre for Human Rights, Faculty of Law, University of Pretoria, South Africa; magnus.killander@up.ac.za. Associate editor, *Oxford Reports on International Law in Domestic Courts* (ILDC), editor (Africa), Oxford Reports on International Human Rights Law; http://www.oxfordlawreports.com; editor-in-chief, *African Human Rights Law Reports*, http://www.chr.up.ac.za.

** Research fellow, Centre for Human Rights, Faculty of Law, University of Pretoria, South Africa (based in Benin); sathorace@yahoo.fr

1 An online service, International Law in Domestic Courts (ILDC), www.oxfordlawreports.com, has been established to further research and to provide easy access to relevant case law for litigators.

2 See eg D Sloss (ed) *The role of domestic courts in treaty enforcement* (2009); B Conforti & F Francioni (eds) *Enforcing international human rights in domestic courts* (1997); MA Waters 'Creeping monism: The judicial trend toward interpretive incorporation of human rights treaties' (2007) 107 *Columbia Law Review* 628-705; Y Shany 'How supreme is the supreme law of the land? Comparative analysis of the influence of international human

prominently in many of these studies. Much of the research in this area is empirical, focusing on one or more specific countries,[3] including in Africa.[4]

This introductory chapter outlines the legal framework and judicial practice across Africa. We find that international human rights law is not optimally used and provide recommendations as to how courts could make use of international human rights law in a more systematic manner. We also set out recommendations on how to convince judges to engage with international human rights law in a more constructive way than is currently the case in many African countries.

2 Revisiting the monism-dualism dichotomy

The relationship between international law and domestic law is often portrayed in terms of the monism-dualism dichotomy. African civil law countries have traditionally been seen as monist and common law countries as dualist.[5] However, as will be shown below and in the chapters that follow, courts in many traditionally dualist countries in Africa use international law to a larger degree than explicitly monist countries such as those of Francophone Africa. In fact courts in most civil law countries oppose the direct applicability of international law and make little use of international law in interpreting constitutional provisions.

---

rights treaties upon the interpretation of constitutional texts by domestic courts' (2006) 31 *Brooklyn Journal of International Law* 341-404; G van Ert *Using international law in Canadian courts* (2008); M Kirby 'Domestic courts and international human rights law: The ongoing judicial conversation' (2009) 27 *Netherlands Quarterly of Human Rights* 291-307.

3 For a theoretical discussion see eg J Nijman & A Nollkaemper (eds) *New perspectives on the divide between national & international law* (2007).

4 T Maluwa 'International law as an aid in the interpretation and application of law in municipal legal systems in Africa' in B Ajibola & D van Zyl (eds) *The judiciary in Africa* (1998) 47-63; ME Adjami 'African courts, international law, and comparative case law: Chimera or emerging human rights jurisprudence' (2002) 24 *Michigan Journal of International Law* 104-166; OB Tshosa *National law and international human rights law - Cases of Botswana, Namibia and Zimbabwe* (2001); M Killander 'The role of international law in human rights litigation in Africa' in E Quansah & W Binchy (eds) *The judicial protection of human rights in Botswana* (2009); F Viljoen *International human rights law in Africa* (2007) 529-585; C d'Orsi 'Les spécificités du droit international en Afrique Sub-saharienne avec une particulière référence à l'intégration du droit international dans l'ordre juridique interne des pays d'Afrique Sub-saharienne' (2005) 58 *Revue hellénique de droit international* 593-615; MC Djiena Wembou 'Les normes internationales relatives aux droits de l'homme et leur application dans la législation interne des États africains: Problèmes et perspectives' (1999) 11 *African Journal of International and Comparative Law* 51-66.

5 With common law countries we here include those with a Roman Dutch common law heritage (South Africa, Namibia, Botswana, Lesotho, Swaziland and Zimbabwe). It should also be noted that Mauritius and the Seychelles have mixed legal systems based on French civil law and English common law.

2.1 Monism in the civil law tradition: Between asserted theory and judicial restraint

Monist theory provides that international law and national law are manifestations of a single conception of law. Municipal courts are bound to directly apply international law without any recourse to adoption by courts or transformation by the legislature.[6] This section will first consider the position in Francophone African countries,[7] before briefly considering the position in other civil law countries in Africa.

Relevant provisions of Francophone African constitutions are modelled on, if not couched word for word in, the terms of the 1958 French Constitution's article 55: 'Treaties or agreements duly ratified or approved shall, upon publication, prevail over Acts of Parliament, subject, with respect to each agreement or treaty, to its application by the other party.'[8]

Upon ratification and publication at the domestic level, international treaties become part and parcel of the law of the land. Moreover, in cases of conflict, municipal law has, according to the constitutions, a subordinate position. International treaty law thus enjoys normative precedence over domestic law, though as shown below practice does not reflect the constitutional provisions.

Whether international law also takes precedence over constitutional law is debatable. The French *Conseil d'Etat* has made it clear that 'supremacy conferred on international law [by article 55 of the French Constitution] does not apply, within the domestic order, to provisions of constitutional nature'.[9] In most Francophone countries in Africa the question should not arise as their constitutional councils or courts examine the conformity of international treaties with the Constitution before ratification. If the Council finds that a treaty conflicts with the Constitution it may only be ratified after the Constitution has been amended.[10] Many constitutions make reference to international human

---

6 J Dugard *International law: A South African perspective* (2005) 47.

7 That is countries with a French or Belgian (Burundi, Rwanda & DRC) colonial heritage.

8 See the constitutions of Benin (art 147), Burkina Faso (art 151), Burundi (art 292), Cameroon (art 45), Central African Republic (art 69), Chad (art 222), Congo-Brazzaville (art 185), Côte d'Ivoire (art 87), DRC (art 215), Guinea (art 79), Mali (art 116), Mauritania (art 80), Niger (art 132), Rwanda (art 190), Senegal (art 91) and Togo (art 140).

9 '[L]a suprématie ainsi conférée aux engagements internationaux ne s'applique pas, dans l'ordre interne, aux dispositions de nature constitutionnelle', *M Sarran, Levacher et autres*, Conseil d'Etat, Assemblée, 30 October 1998, http://www.rajf.org/spip.php?article233 (accessed 30 April 2010). This view was confirmed in a subsequent pronouncement by the Court of Cassation in *Pauline Fraisse, Bulletin d'information* 520 du 15/09/2000, 2 June 2000, http://www.courdecassation.fr (accessed 30 April 2010).

10 Algeria (art 165), Benin (art 146), Burkina Faso (art 150), Cameroon (art 44), Central African Republic (art 68), Madagascar (art 118), Mali (art 90).

rights instruments in their preambles.[11] The Constitution of Benin goes further and explicitly incorporates the African Charter on Human and Peoples' Rights as an integral part of the Constitution.[12]

The status of customary international law in the legal order is not set out in the constitutions of Francophone African countries.[13] We are not aware of any cases in which courts from these countries have relied on customary international law.[14]

Treaties must be published at the national level to enter into force in the domestic sphere. As Sow Sidibé points out, 'publication determines the date of entry into force and creates a presumption of awareness of the treaty towards everyone'.[15] Unfortunately, the adoption of this rule by most civil law countries in Africa has opened the door for uncertainty. Judges are known to have denied applicability of ratified treaties for lack of publication in, for example, Benin[16] and Côte d'Ivoire.[17]

The constitutions of most Francophone countries provide for the condition of reciprocity of application by the other party. It is widely recognised that the requirement of reciprocity does not apply to human rights treaties.[18] The Constitution of Burundi explicitly states that reciprocal application is relevant only for bilateral treaties.[19]

Judicial practice in these countries stands at odds with the international law-friendly constitutional framework. Direct applicability of international law in domestic courts in civil law countries is in practice avoided by the courts, though sometimes invoked by counsel.[20] On the

---

11 Viljoen (n 4 above) 531.

12 Art 7.

13 N Mouelle Kombi 'Les dispositions relatives aux conventions internationales dans les nouvelles constitutions des États d'Afrique francophone' (2000) 8 *African Yearbook of International Law* 246. In France international customary law is generally recognised as part of the law of the land see Nguyen QD *et al Droit international public* (1987) 314.

14 French courts have relied on international customary law in some of the few cases where it has been raised by the parties to a case see E Decaux *et al* 'France' in PM Eisemann (ed) *L'intégration du droit international et communautaire dans l'ordre juridique national* (1996) 277-279. On the (non-)application of French courts of the Universal Declaration of Human Rights see E Decaux 'A report on the role of French judges in the enforcement of international human rights' in Conforti & Francioni (n 2 above).

15 'La publication détermine la date d'entrée en vigueur du traité et crée un présomption de connaissance du traité par tous.' A Sow Sidibé 'Communication introductive generale' in *Actes du colloque international sur l'application du droit international dans l'ordre juridique interne des Etats africains francophones* (2003) 54, http://democratie.francophonie.org/rubrique.php3?id_rubrique=828 (accessed 30 April 2010).

16 Decision DCC 03-009, Cour constitutionelle, 19 February 2003, http://www.cour-constitutionnelle-benin.org/courconsbj.html (accessed 30 April 2010).

17 *Arrêt Mailland*, Cour sûpreme, 16 March 1966, as cited in Sow Sidibé (n 13 above) 54.

18 See with regard to France, E Lambert Abdelgawad & A Weber 'The reception process in France and Germany' in H Keller & A Stone Sweet (eds) *A Europe of rights: The impact of the ECHR on national legal systems* (2008) 116.

19 Art 292.

20 A former member of the African Commission on Human and Peoples' Rights has noted that she sometimes invoked international law as an advocate in Congo, but that 'judges and magistrates have not taken into account these provisions when making

rare occasions that courts refer to international law it is usually to reinforce constitutional provisions.[21] Courts take a narrow view of what should be seen as a self-executing, directly applicable treaty provision. This position is perhaps best illustrated by the judgment of the Senegalese Court of Cassation in the *Habré* case.[22] The Senegalese government had not taken sufficient measures to provide for jurisdiction over international crimes, including torture, perpetrated outside Senegal. The Court of Cassation held that the relevant provisions of the Convention against Torture (CAT) were not self-executing and that Mr Habré could therefore only be prosecuted if Senegal adopted implementing legislation to give the courts jurisdiction.[23]

The French judiciary has recently started to take a wider approach to what should be considered as self-executing provisions of a human rights treaty. The Court of Cassation held in 2005 that article 3(1) of the Convention on the Rights of the Child (CRC), regarding the best interests of the child, was self-executing and could therefore be directly applied by the courts.[24] It remains to be seen whether Francophone domestic courts in Africa will follow suit and give a more generous interpretation to what would constitute a self-executing provision of an international human rights treaty. The previous reluctance of the French judiciary to directly apply the CRC was 'based on the idea that that Convention only provided for obligations of the state parties but did not create individual rights.'[25] The refusal of French courts to apply international treaty provisions has also been based on perceived lack of specificity.[26]

As opposed to its counterparts in other parts of Francophone Africa, the Constitutional Court of Benin has a broad human rights mandate. Importantly the Court can also be accessed directly by individuals who have had their rights violated. However, despite its status as a specialised human rights court its practice is quite unprincipled especially with regards to the African Charter. This is despite the fact that the Charter is

---

decisions or formulating opinions'. (1996) *African Legal Aid Quarterly* 34 quoted in Viljoen (n 4 above) 546.

21 See eg the judgment of the Supreme Court of Chad in *Société des Femmes Tchadiennes Transitaires v Ministère des Finances*, Cour supreme, 024/05, (2005) AHRLR 104 (ChSC 2005), 13 December 2005.

22 For a detailed discussion of the *Habré* case see chapter 11.

23 It is noticeable that when the Committee against Torture received a complaint about the lack of implementation of CAT following the court's decision the Committee itself recognised that CAT is not self-executing. See *Guengueng et al v Senegal*, Committee against Torture, CAT/C/36/D/181/2001, 19 May 2006 para 7.13.

24 *X v Y and anor*, Cassation appeal, Information Bulletin of the Court of Cassation No 626 of 1 October 2005, No 810; ILDC 770 (FR 2005), 14 June 2005.

25 See the analysis of O de Frouville & C Nivard of *X and Y and anor* (n 24 above) at www.oxfordlawreports.com.

26 Arrêt n° 199, Cour de cassation, Chambre commerciale, 25 January 2005 - (dealing with art 11 of the ICESCR, 'right to an adequate standard of living').

an integral part of the Benin Constitution.[27] The lack of elaboration of the reasons for the Court's decisions is one problem.[28] Some have argued that this is perhaps due to the influence of the French civil law tradition on judicial opinion writing.[29] While most African civil law countries stick to this colonial legacy, recent pronouncements by the Constitutional Council of France bring about increasing legal discussion and argumentation.[30] This might be due to the influence of the jurisprudence of the European Court of Human Rights, which has also opened up French courts to the use of international jurisprudence.[31]

There have been no reported cases of reliance on the findings of the African Commission or human rights treaty bodies in the case law of African Francophone countries. The use of comparative jurisprudence is also rare. A recent decision by the Supreme Court of Rwanda is revolutionary among African civil law jurisdictions.[32] In addition to referring to the Convention on the Elimination of All Forms of Discrimination Against Women (CEDAW), the Court referred to case law from South Africa, the US and Canada. The jurisprudence of the military courts in the Democratic Republic of the Congo is also interesting, both for their direct application of the Rome Statute on the International Criminal Court and their citing of international case law.[33]

This is not to say that Francophone African countries do not use foreign jurisprudence. In fact, for example administrative law is largely based on case law.[34] However, judges stick to French cases such as *Jand'heur*[35] and *Dame Lamote*.[36] These cases are what the judges know,

---

27 See chapter 7 of this book. See also A Rotman 'Benin's Constitutional Court: An institutional model for guaranteeing human rights' (2004) 17 *Harvard Human Rights Law Journal* 281-314.

28 HS Adjolohoun 'The right to reparation as applied under the African Charter by Benin's Constitutional Court' unpublished LLM dissertation, Centre for Human Rights, University of Pretoria, 2007, 31.

29 Rotman (n 27 above) 100.

30 F Malhiere 'Les présupposés théoriques de la brièveté des décisions du Conseil Constitutionnel' 7ème Congrès français de droit constitutionnel AFDC Paris, September 2008, http://www.droitconstitutionnel.org/congresParis/comC7/Malhiere TXT.pdf (accessed on 30 July 2009).

31 Cf Lambert Abdelgawad & Weber (n 18 above) 128.

32 See RS/Inconst/Pén.0001/08/CS, Supreme Court, 26 September 2008. Thanks to Tom Mulisa for summarising the judgment, which is written in Kinyarwanda. It should be recognised that because of the many Rwandan lawyers trained in exile common law approaches may have more impact there than in other civil law countries.

33 For a summary and analysis of two of these cases in English see Ituri District *Military Prosecutor v Kahwa Panga Mandro*, First instance decision, RMP No 227/PEN/2006; ILDC 524 (CD 2006); *Military Prosecutor v Bongi Massaba*, Criminal trial judgment and accompanying civil action for damages, RP No 018/2006; RMP No 242/PEN/06; ILDC 387 (CD 2006). See also Avocats sans Frontières *Etude de Jurisprudence: L'application du Statut de Rome de la Cour Pénale Internationale par les juridictions de la République Démocratique du Congo*, March 2009.

34 Cf G Braibant *Le droit administratif français* (1988) 34.

35 *Jand'heur,* Cour de cassation, chambres réunies, 13 February 1930.

what they learnt to apply, what they best understand. It will thus not be surprising that, even where counsel leaves the judge with a copy of the relevant international instrument or case, the judge would not apply it and instead look at domestic or French case law in addition to the relevant domestic legislation.

Portuguese-speaking African countries have largely followed the approach of Francophone Africa as set out above. The Constitution of Mozambique, for example, makes it explicit that norms of international law 'have the same force in the Mozambican legal order as have infra-constitutional legislative acts'.[37] The Mozambican Constitution further provides in article 43 that the Bill of Rights in the Constitution shall be interpreted 'in harmony with the Universal Declaration of Human Rights and with the African Charter on Human and Peoples' Rights'.[38] The Angolan Constitution provides that '[t]he fundamental rights provided for in the present Law shall not exclude others stemming from the laws and applicable rules of international law.'[39] From a constitutional stand-point, Portuguese-speaking African countries are as international law-friendly as their Francophone counterparts. However, in practice it is just as difficult to bring human rights cases before the courts.[40]

Application of international human rights law in Mozambique can be illustrated with the case *President of the Republic of Mozambique v Bernardo Sacarolha Ngomacha*.[41] In this case the Supreme Court held that traditional authorities were obliged to consider constitutional principles and international human rights law when taking their decisions. The Court held that the traditional authorities had breached article 3 of the CRC and articles 8, 23 and 24 of the ICCPR when forcing a six-year old girl to leave her family to live with a man until she gave birth to a daughter so as to compensate him for the death of one of his children.

In a recent electoral dispute in Angola, the complainant argued that the Angolan electoral laws were not in conformity with SADC standards. The Constitutional Court held that it could not make a finding on this claim as the complainant had not submitted the relevant standards and had not specified which provisions had been violated. However, despite this finding the Court went on to hold that the electoral laws complied

---

36 *Ministre de l'agriculture c Dame Lamotte*, Conseil d'Etat, Rec Lebon 110, 17 February 1950.

37 Art 18.

38 See also art 21(2) of the Constitution of Angola.

39 Art 21(1).

40 See eg Afrimap *Mozambique: Justice sector and the rule of law* (2006).

41 *President of the Republic of Mozambique v Bernardo Sacarolha Ngomacha*, Supreme Court (Tribunal Supremo), criminal section I, Proc.5/2004-A. Discussed in Afrimap (n 40 above) 131-132.

with the Norms and Standards for Election in the SADC Region adopted by the SADC Parliamentary Forum in March 2001.[42]

Above we have dealt with countries with a French, Belgian or Portuguese colonial heritage. These are not the only countries in Africa which would fall under the civil law banner.[43] Italy colonised Eritrea, Libya and Somalia and has influenced the legal systems of these countries, though Islamic law dominates Libya and Somalia and the Eritrean legal system has been heavily influenced by Ethiopia which, though briefly occupied by Italy, was never colonised. Ethiopia has adopted codified laws which to a large extent was drafted by Europeans and reflect continental civil law.[44]

Article 9(4) of the Ethiopian Constitution provides that ratified treaties are part of the law of the land. However, in practice there is a requirement of publication in the *Federal Negarit Gazette*.[45] In a landmark judgment in November 2007, the cassation bench of the Federal Supreme Court held that the best interests of the child as set out in the CRC overrode the provision in Ethiopian legislation that a parent should always have priority to custody over his or her child.[46]

The legal system of Egypt is based on the French civil law as well as Islamic law.[47] With regard to international law, the Egyptian Constitution provides that ratified and published treaties 'have the force of law'.[48] As opposed to the situation in many other civil law countries in Africa, treaties are not considered superior to legislation and a treaty can thus both amend legislation and be amended by legislation.[49] International law is mainly used as an interpretative tool and the Supreme Constitutional Court has held that courts should interpret the constitutional human rights provisions in light of international human rights treaties.[50]

In conclusion, African civil law countries have a monist constitutional framework but their judicial cultures create dualism in practice. Admittedly, the fact that these countries have extensive bills of rights makes it likely that the question of direct application rarely arises.

---

42 Processo de reclamação do acordão nº13/08, Acordão Nº 21/2008, 21 July 2008, http://www.tribunalconstitucional.ao (accessed 5 May 2010). Thanks to Geraldine Geraldo for drawing our attention to this case.

43 It should also be recognised that most countries have pluralistic legal systems with civil law existing side by side with customary law, Islamic law etc.

44 T Kumenit 'An overview of the most important features of the Ethiopian legal system', www.ialsnet.org/meetings/enriching/kumenit.pdf (accessed 5 May 2010).

45 RM Aberra 'Ethiopia' in C Heyns (ed) *Human rights law in Africa* (2004) 1080.

46 *Tsedale Demisse v Kifle Demisse*, Appeal decision, Cassation file no 23632; ILDC 1032 (ET 2007), 6 November 2007.

47 MS Abdel Wahab 'An overview of the Egyptian legal system and legal research', http://www.nyulawglobal.org/globalex/Egypt.htm (accessed 5 May 2010).

48 Art 151.

49 N Bernard-Maugiron 'Egypt' in Heyns (n 45 above) 1040. This is also the position in Namibia as discussed below.

50 Bernard-Maugiron (n 49 above) 1040.

However, an increased use of the findings of international human rights monitoring bodies in interpreting constitutional provisions would enrich the jurisprudence on human rights recognised in the constitutions. The first measure must, however, be to address constraints on the access to justice to remedy violations of nationally recognised human rights.

2.2 Dualism in the common law tradition: Growing trends to monism?

Dualist theory provides that international law and domestic law are separate legal systems.[51] If international law is not transformed into national law through legislation, national courts cannot apply it. In Africa, dualism is generally associated with common law countries, the countries once colonised by Britain. Justice Ocran of the Supreme Court of Ghana notes that 'national judiciaries with a common law background start with an uphill task [in the application of international law]: the dualist position bequeathed to us by our colonial masters still sticks to us like an albatross around our necks.'[52] This colonial heritage leads some observers to call for a break from the inherited strict dualism because of its peculiarity to English political and legal history.[53] However, the description of English legal system as the epitome of dualism is arguably exaggerated. Firstly, most would argue that customary international law form part of the law of the land in common law countries.[54] Secondly, unincorporated international treaties play an increasingly important role, though the courts may not directly apply them. Kerr LJ of the English Court of Appeal held in *Maclaine Watson v Department of Trade* that 'a court must be free to inform itself fully of the contents of a treaty whenever these are relevant to the decision of any issue which is not in itself a non-justiciable issue.'[55] Higgins argues that this approach allow courts to use whatever is needed from unincorporated treaties, including

---

51 G Gaja 'Dualism – a review' in Nijman & Nollkaemper (n 3 above) 52.

52 M Ocran 'Access to global jurisprudence and problems in the domestic application of international legal norms', keynote address at the 2nd West African Judicial Colloquium, 8 October 2007, Accra, Ghana, http://www.brandeis.edu/ethics/pdfs/internationaljustice/WAfricaColloq.pdf (accessed 18 January 2010).

53 See eg E Egede 'Bringing human rights home: An examination of the domestication of human rights treaties in Nigeria' (2007) 51(2) *Journal of African Law* 280.

54 Dugard (n 6 above) 50. This is made explicit in the constitutions of Malawi (s 11) and South Africa (s 232). For a critique of the position that customary international law form part of the law of the land in Commonwealth countries see S Beaulac 'Customary international law in domestic courts: Imbroglio, Lord Denning, stare decisis' in CPM Waters (ed) *British and Canadian perspectives on international law* (2006) 379-392.

55 *Maclaine Watson & Co Ltd v Department of Trade and Industry*, High Court Chancery Division, 80 ILR 39, 29 July 1987, quoted by R Higgins 'The role of domestic courts in the enforcement of international human rights: The United Kingdom' in Conforti & Francioni (n 2 above) 37-58 40.

'international case law arising under them', as long as the court does not purport to enforce the treaty obligation.[56]

This approach is similar to how international law is used by courts in many African common law countries as discussed below.

2.2.1 Direct application

A few common law countries have adopted monism with regard to treaties in their legislative framework. In Namibia, international law is directly applicable unless otherwise provided by the Constitution or an Act of Parliament.[57] The Namibian Supreme Court has seemingly gone beyond this 'weak' monism by providing that article 14(3)(d) of the ICCPR took precedence over conflicting provisions in the Legal Aid Act.[58] However, in general, in common with African civil law countries as discussed above, 'the UN human rights instruments are not receiving the prominence one would have expected. The courts still expect the legislator to provide a legal framework for the implementation of treaty principles.'[59]

Section 231(4) of the South African Constitution provides that courts can apply a 'self-executing provision' of a treaty even if the treaty has not been enacted into law.[60] The Constitutional Court of South Africa has

---

56 Higgins (n 55 above) 41. Increasingly English courts have made use of international human rights law in statutory interpretation and development of the common law, Higgins 47-48. However, it is clear that the real impetus to use of international human rights law in the UK was the incorporation of the European Convention on Human Rights through the Human Rights Act 1998. For more recent developments see S Besson 'The reception process in Ireland and the United Kingdom' in Keller & Stone Sweet (n 18 above) 31-106.

57 Art 144 of the Constitution.

58 *Government of the Republic of Namibia & Others v Mwilima & Others*, Supreme Court Decision, SA 29/01; ILDC 162 (NA 2002), [2002] NASC 8, 7 June 2002.

59 N Horn 'International human rights norms and standards: The development of Namibian case and statutory law' in N Horn & A Bösl (eds) *Human rights and the rule of law in Namibia* (2008) 144. The lack of consideration of international human rights law in sensitive cases, such as controversial equality cases, as discussed by Zongwe in chapter 8, is particularly noticeable. However, as noted above the Supreme Court in *Mwilima* (n 58 above) applied the legal aid provision in the ICCPR despite that the persons on trial were the Caprivi separatists which Zongwe places among the 'unpopular minorities'.

60 The recently adopted Constitution of Swaziland has a similar a similar provision, s 238(4). However, this provision was not applied when the court had occasion to do so in *Jan Sithole NO (in his capacity as a Trustee of the National Constitutional Assembly (NCA) Trust and Others v Prime Minister of the Kingdom of Swaziland and Others* (Civil Case No. 2792/2006) [2007] SZHC 1 (6 November 2007); cf Killander (n 4 above) 12. On South African courts and international law see the chapter of Ngidi. See also eg J Dugard 'South Africa' in Sloss (n 2 above); EM Ngolele 'The content of the doctrine of self-execution and its limited effect in South African law' (2006) 31 *South African Yearbook of International Law* 141-172; S Rosa & M Dutschke 'Child rights at the core: The use of international law in South African cases on children's socio-economic rights' (2006) 22 *South African Journal on Human Rights* 224; Dugard (n 6 above) 336-340, with further references.

not explicitly discussed section 231(4), but held in *Grootboom* that 'where the relevant principle of international law binds South Africa, it may be directly applicable'.[61] In *Zealand* the Constitutional Court based a right to compensation for unlawful imprisonment on section 12 of the Constitution dealing with freedom and security of the person, even though there is no provision in the Bill of Rights which provides for compensation for violations of its provisions.[62] The Court added that 'South Africa also bears an international obligation in this regard in terms of article 9(5) of the ICCPR.'[63] The recent finding by the Western Cape High Court in a similar case that the 'ICCPR is not a self-executing legal instrument' is unfortunate.[64] In this case it was held that article 9(5) of the ICCPR was not applicable in a case of judicial immunity and that it was up to the legislature to adopt legislation to incorporate the right to compensation for unlawful detention provided for in article 9(5) of the ICCPR.

The Constitution of Malawi provides that treaties entered into before the commencement of the Constitution in 1994, such as many of the main international human rights treaties, are part of the law of the land, while later treaties requires incorporation.[65] The Supreme Court of Appeal recently made it clear that in both cases the applicability of the treaty provision is subject to legislation in force at the time, but that in case of conflict, 'the courts will try as much as possible to avoid a clash'.[66] In Zimbabwe human rights treaties ratified before an amendment to the Constitution in 1993 are arguably part of the law of the land.[67]

Nigeria is the only common law country to have domesticated the African Charter.[68] Despite this, there are surprisingly few cases before Nigerian courts that make use of the provisions of the African Charter. However, it must be noted that the Charter proved very useful as a backup for the suspended constitutional provisions during the military

---

61 *Government of RSA and others v Grootboom and others* (CCT11/00) [2000] ZACC 19; 2001 (1) SA 46 (4 October 2000); ILDC 285 (ZA 2000) para 26.

62 *Zealand v Minister of Justice and Constitutional Development and Another* (CCT54/07) [2008] ZACC 3 (11 March 2008).

63 Art 9(5) provides for 'an enforceable right to compensation' in cases of unlawful arrest.

64 *Claassen v Minister of Justice and Constitutional Development and Another* [2009] ZAWCHC 190 (8 December 2009).

65 T Trier Hansen 'Implementation of international human rights standards through the national courts in Malawi (2002) 46 *Journal of African Law* 31-42.

66 *In the matter of the Adoption of Children Act Chapter 26:01 of the Laws of Malawi and in the matter of Chifundo James (an infant)* MSCA Adoption Appeal No. 29 of 2009; ILDC 1345, 12 June 2009.

67 In *Kachingwe and ors v Minister of Home Affairs and Commissioner of Police*, Final appeal judgment, No SC 145/04; ILDC 722 (ZW 2005) 18 July 2005 the Supreme Court of Zimbabwe held (at para 64) that 'in all probability' the contention was right, 'but determination of that point of law is not necessary for the determination of this case'.

68 AO Enabulele 'Implementation of treaties in Nigeria and the status question: Whither Nigerian courts' (2009) 17 *African Journal of International and Comparative Law* 326-341.

regimes of the 1990's. The Supreme Court of Nigeria held in *Abacha v Fawehinmi* that the African Charter has a status higher than ordinary laws, but lower than the Constitution.[69] How this plays out with regard to socio-economic rights, which are recognised as justiciable rights in the African Charter, but only as directive principles in the Nigerian Constitution, is considered by Durojaye.[70] He also considers the potential impact of the new Fundamental Rights Enforcement Procedure Rules issued by the Chief Justice in December 2009,[71] which eases procedural requirements for human rights litigation.

The Constitution of Uganda has no provision on the relationship between international and domestic law. However, the provision in article 45 that the Bill of Rights is not exhaustive forms a basis for applying rights not explicitly mentioned. This approach was approved by one of the judges in the Ugandan Constitutional Court in *Uganda Law Society & Anor v The Attorney General*,[72] to include right to appeal, which is not included in the Ugandan Bill of Rights, among the rights protected by the Constitution.[73] The Constitution of Ghana has a similar provision providing that the rights set out in the Bill of Rights 'shall not be regarded as excluding others not specifically mentioned which are considered to be inherent in a democracy and intended to secure the freedom and dignity of man.'[74] Tanzanian courts have held that the Constitution incorporates the Universal Declaration of Human Rights.[75]

It is clear that direct applicability is only relevant in a small number of cases. Constitutional bills of rights are now in place in all African countries. The increasing number of rights covered is a clear indication of the impact of international human rights law.[76] This indirect domestication makes it less likely that international human rights treaties need to be directly applied, but further reinforces the importance of treaties and case law, resolutions, etc. associated with them for interpretation of the constitutional provisions. National legislation regarding, for example, refugees and children, often reflects international treaties in these areas in a way that incorporate treaty provisions.

---

69 *Abacha and ors v Fawehinmi*, Appeal to Supreme Court, SC 45/1997; ILDC 21 (NG 2000); (2001) AHRLR 172 (NgSC 2000), 28 April 2000.

70 See chapter 9.

71 Available at www.accesstojustice-ng.org/articles/New%20FREP%20Rules%20.pdf (accessed 5 May 2010).

72 *Uganda Law Society & Anor v The Attorney General* Constitutional Petitions No 2 & 8 of 2002 [2009] UGCC 1 (5 February 2009) http://www.ulii.org/ug/cases/UGCC/2009/1.html (accessed 15 November 2009).

73 See chapter 6.

74 Constitution, 1992, art 33(5). See chapter 3.

75 See chapter 4.

76 On constitutional human rights provisions see C Heyns & W Kaguongo 'Constitutional human rights law in Africa' (2006) 22 *South African Journal on Human Rights* 673-714. Constitutions of African countries are available on www.chr.up.ac.za.

2.2.2 Interpretation

The role of international law in interpretation relates to the interpretation of constitutional provisions, statutory interpretation and the development of the common law and customary law. The South African Constitution includes provisions on the role of international law with regard to the interpretation of the Bill of Rights and statutory interpretation. The provision in section 39(1)(b) that courts 'must consider international law when interpreting the Bill of Rights' is the most important provision on the influence of international law on domestic law in the South African Constitution. The Constitution of Malawi provides that in interpreting the Constitution courts shall, 'where applicable, have regard to current norms of public international law'.[77] The Interpretation Act of Botswana provides that 'as an aid to the construction of the enactment a court may have regard to ... any relevant international treaty'.[78]

With the exceptions above, African common law countries do not have constitutional or statutory provisions including international law as relevant to the interpretation of the constitution or statutes. However, this should not prevent courts from using international law. The common law provides that 'wherever possible the words of a statute will be interpreted so as to be consistent with a treaty obligation'.[79] Courts should apply this principle not only to statutory interpretation, but also to constitutional interpretation, thereby paving the way for striking down legislation which violates international law by a properly construed bill of rights.[80] An expansive reading of the bill of rights would, for example, be needed in socio-economic rights cases in states that do not recognise such rights as justiciable in their bill of rights.

In discussing the role of international law in interpretation it is clear that courts need not necessarily apply case law, resolutions, etc emanating from international monitoring bodies and courts.[81] A domestic court may decide not to follow such guidance. However, the court must try to convince a prospective international monitoring body that its approach is better than that proposed by the international quasi-judicial body or court; or that the international body should allow national divergence under doctrines such as the margin of appreciation. What is important is that national courts consider not only treaty

---

77 S 11(2)(c).

78 See chapter 3 of this book.

79 Higgins (n 55 above) 42. Cf the 1988 Bangalore Principles, adopted at a judicial colloquium of commonwealth judges, which provided that '[i]t is within the proper nature of the judicial process ... for national courts to have regard to international obligations ... for the purpose of removing ambiguity or uncertainty from national constitutions, legislation or common law.' Quoted in Waters (n 2 above) 646.

80 Cf the 1998 Bangalore Principles as discussed by Waters (n 2 above) 646-647.

81 However, domestic courts would be advised to follow the interpretation of international courts with jurisdiction over the country in question such as the African Court on Human and Peoples' Rights or sub-regional courts.

provisions, but also all relevant case law, resolutions, etc. Examination of case law shows that, in most cases, there is not much reference to international case law, resolutions, general comments, etc.[82] Courts should include discussion of such materials as it would provide a better basis for their decisions. International instruments themselves often do not provide much aid to the interpretation of the provisions of a bill of rights couched in similar terms.[83] Case law from other countries should also be examined as international human rights law is not only developed at the international level but also domestically through the jurisprudence on the contents of bills of rights.

As illustrated by the chapters of Ambani[84] and Kabumba,[85] international human rights law plays an increasingly important role in constitutional interpretation in Kenya and Uganda, though the cases which have gone beyond citing treaty provisions are limited. Courts in Botswana, Ghana, Tanzania and Zambia made progressive use of international law in human rights litigation in some cases in the 1990's, but as illustrated by the chapters of Quansah,[86] Murungu[87] and Hansungule,[88] in recent years there are fewer cases which reflect a consideration of international human rights law handed down in these countries. However, the establishment of specialised human rights chambers such as has been done recently in Ghana might be one way to counteract such trends. In Nigeria the new Fundamental Rights Enforcement Procedure Rules explicitly provides for a greater reliance on international human rights law, not only the African Charter, which, as noted above, has been domesticated in Nigeria.[89]

2.3 Confronting practices: Is the dichotomy (monism/dualism) useful?

Countries of monist tradition behave according to dualist principles whereas dualist countries, overlooking common law transformation prerequisites, sometimes apply or draw inspiration from international human rights law in adjudicating human rights matters. A more interesting enquiry than establishing whether a country is monist or dualist is to establish whether a provision of a treaty is self-executing. It is

---

82 It is in particular noticeable that the African Commission's case law is rarely discussed in cases decided by African domestic courts. However, see the judgment of the Gambian Supreme Court in *Sabally v Inspector General of Police and Others* (2002) AHRLR 87 (GaSC 2001).

83 For extensive use of international case law see eg the Zimbabwean case of *Kachingwe* (n 67 above).

84 See chapter 2. For a discussion of Kenyan cases see also Killander (n 4 above) 18-20.

85 See chapter 6.

86 See chapter 3.

87 See chapter 4.

88 See chapter 5.

89 Fundamental Rights Enforcement Procedure Rules (n 71 above).

true that self-executing provisions could only be directly applied in countries which provides for this possibility which in Africa includes all civil law countries, Kenya, Namibia, South Africa, Swaziland and arguably with regard to many human rights treaties, Ghana, Malawi, Uganda and Zimbabwe.[90] However, the self-executing nature of a treaty may also be relevant in interpreting a bill of rights to be in line with the treaty provision.

Treaties may be self-executing wholly or just in some of their provisions where 'they lend themselves to judicial or administrative application without further legislative implementation'.[91] The UN Committee on Economic, Social and Cultural Rights notes that, with regard to the provisions of the Covenant on Economic, Social and Cultural Rights, courts should

> avoid any a priori assumption that the norms should be considered to be non-self-executing. In fact, many of them are stated in terms which are at least as clear and specific as those in other human rights treaties, the provisions of which are regularly deemed by courts to be self-executing.[92]

As noted above it is clear that few of the rights entrenched in human rights treaties do not have constitutional equivalents. The number of cases in which courts need to directly apply international human rights law are not many. Instead the question in most cases is: How should courts interpret a right set out in the national bill of rights? International human rights law has much to add in such an inquiry, though seldom through the specific wording of a treaty. Instead, case law, resolutions, general comments, etc should inform courts. Here persuasiveness is the key term, but courts should also try to avoid findings which if taken before an international body with jurisdiction over the case is likely to lead to a finding of a violation of international human rights. A well-functioning regional human rights system is important to create this effect.[93]

Interpretation also has its limitations and cannot function as a substitute for implementing legislation. Indeed, most international

---

90 With regard to Malawi and Zimbabwe see the constitutional provisions cited above indicating that treaties ratified before 1994 and 1993 respectively have the force of law. On Ghana and Uganda see above with regard to their non-exhaustive bills of rights. Kenya is the latest addition to this list after the adoption of a new constitution in August 2010. The new Constitution provides that ratified international treaties form part of the law of Kenya.

91 V Leary *International labour conventions and national law* (1982) 39.

92 CESCR General Comment 9 'The domestic application of the Covenant' (1998).

93 As noted with regard to France and the European Convention on Human Rights: 'The most important factor driving change [increasing use of references to the European Convention] has been the explosion of repetitive violations found in Strasbourg. The desire to reduce exposure to more condemnations is changing the very basis of France's relationship with the Convention.' Lambert Abdelgawad & Weber (n 18 above) 128.

human rights treaties require implementing legislation.[94] States are often given some leeway by monitoring bodies as to how to implement a treaty. However, the situation may arise that national legislation must be repealed or amended. An important question is how to approach domestic opposition to reforms inspired by international human rights law.[95] One important avenue to address such opposition is education.

3 Increasing the use of international human rights law by domestic courts

The limited use of international human rights law by national courts in Africa stems from a number of reasons.[96] These include limited access to relevant international human rights documents, lack of adequate case reporting, both at the national and international level, attitudes of judicial officers and their lack of exposure to international human rights law and poorly drafted pleadings that do not bring out the relevant issues. In addition, lack of access to justice in many countries due to, among others, the high cost of litigation and cumbersome procedural rules, hinders human rights litigation.

The role that national judges are vested to play by a treaty is important. The abundant and accurate application of OHADA[97] and CIMA[98] law by national judges in Francophone Africa is a result of the role they are given by the treaties and an effective training system. No such attention is given to international human rights law, which largely remains unknown, difficult to access and interpret, and sometimes in conflict with domestic law.

It does not make sense to disconnect lawyers' behaviour and judges' attitudes with regard to the use of international law and human rights in litigation. Both are from the same background and go through the same initial training. They share similar, if not identical, legal and procedural knowledge.

A range of factors may determine the use of international law by lawyers in African courts. It is obvious that for parties and their counsel to use international law in litigation, they must first be aware of existing

---

94 See eg CESCR, concluding observations/comments, 5 June 2002, E/C.12/1/Add.78, para 9.

95 Opposition to the proposed new family law in Mali is a case in point, see ST Diarra 'Muslim conservatives blocking new family law' *IPS* 19 May 2010, http://allafrica.com/stories/201005191339.html (accessed 21 May 2010).

96 Cf Hon Justice Philip Waki in 'The processes and the challenges encountered by national courts in applying international human rights law: Kenyan experience', unpublished paper presented at the Judicial Colloquium on the Domestic Application of International Human Rights Norms, Nairobi, 27 February–1 March 2006.

97 *Organisation pour l'Harmonisation en Afrique du Droit des Affaires* (Organisation for harmonisation of business law in Africa), http://www.ohada.org.

98 *Conférence Interafricaine des Marchés d'Assurances* (Inter-African Conference on Insurance Markets), http://www.cima-afrique.org.

treaties, case law, etc. This pertains to the extent to which international law forms part of legal training. International law is nowadays commonly part of the curriculum of law faculties. Constitutional law and human rights are equally taught, but international human rights law as such is often not a specialisation field in law faculties.[99] Lack of reliance on international human rights law in relevant cases may also be a result of that lawyers knowing through experience that judges will not accept international law arguments.

In Francophone Africa, lawyers are generally trained to make legal arguments from the Napoleon Code, French civil and criminal procedure, or business law. Once admitted to the Bar, very few of those lawyers feel it necessary to seek further training and qualifications in human rights law. Attention is rather given to continuing training offered by the regional OHADA School, ERSUMA,[100] which is in charge of training all legal practitioners in the treaty law.

Significant initiatives have been implemented with a view to influencing judges to become friendlier to international human rights law. For instance, the Francophone Africa Supreme Courts Association has organised human rights courses for judges at National Schools of Judicial Training in Benin, Burkina Faso and Senegal. Seminars with judges from both sides of the civil law-common law divide have been arranged in West Africa.[101] In Uganda, a Judicial Studies Institute which provides human rights training was established under the auspices of the judiciary in 2004.[102] The East African Magistrates and Judges Association with its headquarters in Arusha, Tanzania, has as one of its objectives to 'promote and protect human rights'.[103] The Southern African Chief Justices Forum holds annual conferences which includes discussions on human rights issues.[104] The ILDC Africa project has organised workshops with judges in East Africa and Nigeria and with practising lawyers from Southern and West Africa.[105] Publications on human rights law for magistrates and judges have also been prepared in some countries.[106]

---

99 Though consider eg the LLM in Human Rights and Democratisation in Africa (University of Pretoria) and the UNESCO Chairs in human rights established at universities in several African countries, see http://www.unesco.org/africa/portal/chairs.html (accessed 6 May 2010).

100 *Ecole Régionale Supérieure de la Magistrature* (regional higher school of judicial training).

101 The West African Judicial Colloquia, Dakar, Senegal, January 2006, Accra, Ghana, October 2007, http://www.brandeis.edu/ethics/pdfs/internationaljustice/WAfrica Colloq.pdf.

102 Judicial Studies Institute of Uganda website: http://www.judicature.go.ug/Uganda/index.html (accessed on 16 July 2009).

103 As above.

104 See http://www.venice.coe.int/SACJF/default.htm.

105 See http://www.chr.up.ac.za.

106 See eg Ministère de la Justice (Niger) *Manuel des droits de l'homme à l'usage des magistrates* (2009).

To ensure more reliance on international law, ratified treaties should be published and widely disseminated, judicial officers and lawyers provided with knowledge and skills, which would help change attitudes and improve the quality of pleadings and judgments. Countries which have not already done so should provide a constitutional or legislative mandate for courts to consider international human rights law in addition to implementing legislation consistent with their international obligations. Such a constitutional mandate could be modelled on article 48 of the Constitution of Seychelles which provides that the Bill of Rights

> shall be interpreted in such a way as not to be inconsistent with any international obligations of Seychelles relating to human rights and freedoms and a court shall, when interpreting the provisions of this Chapter, take judicial note of:
> (a) the international instruments containing these obligations;
> (b) the reports and expression of views of bodies administering or enforcing these instruments;
> (c) the reports, decisions or opinions of international and regional institutions administering or enforcing Conventions on human rights and freedoms;
> (d) the Constitutions of other democratic states or nations and decisions of the courts of the states or nations in respect of their Constitutions.

4 Overview of the chapters

The contributions to this book, by academics and practitioners from across the continent address the themes set out above. This introduction is followed by country studies on the use of international law by courts in eight African countries: Benin, Botswana, Côte d'Ivoire, Ghana, Kenya, Tanzania, Uganda and Zambia. Ambani discusses how Kenyan courts are still being kept hostage of a dualistic mindset that has no relevance to Kenya. He shows that courts in some instances have used international human rights law in creative ways and that the new Constitution should provide renewed impetus to the application of international human rights law in Kenya. Quansah shows how courts in Botswana and Ghana have to some extent used international law for interpretative purposes. He concludes that 'the non-incorporation of international treaties into national law in both countries has not adversely affected the protection of the guaranteed human rights.' Murungu considers how Tanzanian courts have made use of international law and also considers the first case decided by the new Tanzanian human rights commission. Hansungule shows how most judges in Zambia still avoid the use of international law, but that the government is increasingly incorporating international treaties into national law. Kabumba shows how Ugandan courts have not only made quite extensive use of international law as an aid to interpretation but even directly applied international human rights treaties which by some judges have been interpreted as forming part of the Constitution. The chapter of Tanoh and Adjolohoun discusses the reasons for the lack of human rights litigation in Côte d'Ivoire and the constraints of the human rights litigation system in Benin which is often portrayed as a model for the rest of Francophone Africa.

The chapters in the last part of the book do not aim to give a comprehensive overview of how courts deal with international law in the countries under review. Instead they focus on specific themes. Zongwe shows how, despite the international law friendly constitutional framework in Namibia, courts in controversial equality cases neglect to consider international law and instead rely on comparative case law from selected countries. Marone examines the *Habré* case in Senegal as an example of the reluctance of Francophone African courts to apply international human rights law. She also shows how the reaction to the outcome of this case helped reform the Senegalese legal system in relation to accountability for international crimes. Durojaye discusses the problem facing right to health litigation in Nigeria as socio-economic rights are only recognised as non-justiciable directive principles in the Constitution. Ngidi gives examples of how children's rights litigators have used international law arguments in South African courts to bolster the protection of children's rights in the country. Finally Esom shows that international law also has a role to play before National Human Rights Institutions which under certain circumstances can function as alternatives to court enforcement.

5 Conclusion

Viljoen states that 'the norms of customary international human rights law are by and large contained in the constitutions of African states'.[107] This is also, in general, the case with international human rights treaties. All African states have bills of rights in some form or another.[108] Not all of these bills of rights cover all the rights recognised in the UN covenants and the African Charter. However, domestic courts do not often need to look to international treaties to find the right that have been violated in a specific case. The question of direct application is thus less important than how courts approach the issue of interpretation. In interpreting constitutional and legislative provisions protecting human rights, judges should take note of how similar provisions have been interpreted in other jurisdictions, whether by foreign courts or by international courts or quasi-judicial bodies. In order to achieve this lawyers and judges must have access to relevant material. Training and cross-border networking also play an important role.

The development of international human rights law is not the sole domain of international courts and quasi-judicial bodies. Domestic courts (and quasi-judicial bodies) also have a role to play. Access to courts remains a challenge in many African countries. However, when a litigant manages to bring a human rights case, courts should take the opportunity

---

107 Viljoen (n 4 above) 530.

108 Heyns & Kaguongo (n 76 above).

to engage not only in the application of domestic law but also in the development of international human rights law. This can only be done by engaging with how a right has been interpreted elsewhere.

PART II

COUNTRY STUDIES

2

Navigating past the 'dualist doctrine': The case for progressive jurisprudence on the application of international human rights norms in Kenya

J Osogo Ambani*

Summary

Prior to the enactment of the 2010 Constitution, Kenya subscribed to the common law doctrine of dualism. While this in itself was not retrogressive, its practice led to the relegation of the often fairly progressive international human rights instruments. Significant entitlements ratified by the state remained in abeyance simply because they had not been domesticated. What was even more curious was the fact that the state had stuck with this doctrine notwithstanding that the factors responsible for it in the United Kingdom - its cradle - have never operated in Kenya. This situation called for review. This chapter argues that two options are available. First, the people of Kenya could seize the opportunity of the 2010 Constitution to write a legal dispensation that recognises international law as a direct source of law. Second, the judiciary would have to reconsider an initial position affirming dualism. Moreover, given the new constitutional order, there is no reason why norms which have attained the status of customary law should not apply even where their transformation into municipal law has not taken place.

1 Introduction and context

Intergovernmental organisations such as the United Nations (UN), the International Labour Organisation (ILO) and the African Union (AU) have invariably enacted human rights norms. Often, these hallowed rules, set at the international level, constitute ideal standards which national jurisdictions are expected to keep stead of. In fact, states that ratify such norms no longer have a mere moral obligation to implement them – they now also have a legally enforceable duty to do so.

* LLM (UP), LLB (UoN); Lecturer at the Catholic University of Eastern Africa; ambaniosogo@yahoo.com.

The law of treaties further presupposes that international standards ratified by states should be observed in good faith.[1] Many human rights treaties have taken it a notch higher by expressly requiring member states to adhere to their stipulations.[2] Clearly, the international stage has gained prominence and it is now an additional standard setting forum over and above national jurisdictions.

This change of human rights strategy in terms of the forums and institutions involved certainly calls for a realignment of structural and doctrinal items on the municipal front. It is submitted here that as Kenya charts the new constitutional course,[3] an item that may require immediate consideration is the previous practice of the dualism doctrine.[4] As shown below, prior to the 2010 Constitution, successful reliance by individuals or groups on international human rights instruments before the domestic courts of Kenya was hardly guaranteed largely due to the premise that the state, being of common law tradition, was dualist.[5] By this is meant that, at least in the municipal domain, international law could not automatically apply without undergoing the process of transformation. Herein lay the knotty obstacle that bedevilled the realisation of human rights in Kenya.

This chapter first traces the dualist doctrine to its cradle, the United Kingdom. It then discusses the doctrine through the eyes of Kenyan judicial precedents, and how it has impeded the realisation of human rights in the past, before suggesting reforms, anchored on the 2010 Constitution.

2 The dualist doctrine: The tradition and the cradle

Dualism is the flipside of the coin that is monism of which it has been written:[6]

> In 'monist' states, following French constitutional law, once a treaty has been ratified and published 'externally', it becomes part of internal law. At least in theory, no legislative action is needed to lower the second storey level of international law norms to the ground floor level of national law.

On the other hand, the dualist doctrine 'is based upon the perception of two quite distinct systems of law', operating separately, and holding that 'before any rule or principle of international law can have any effect within the domestic jurisdiction, it must be expressly and specifically

---

1 According to art 18 of the Vienna Convention on the Law of Treaties, states have an obligation to uphold agreements they adhere to in good faith.

2 See for instance art 4 of the Convention on the Rights of the Child.

3 On 27 August 2010 Kenya enacted the new Constitution of Kenya.

4 This statement should not be taken to imply that monism or any other related doctrine is necessarily a better system.

5 Again, this is not to say that in other systems individuals will always rely successfully on international human rights instruments. Kenya's special history and context ought to be judged on its own merits.

6 F Viljoen *International human rights law in Africa* (2007) 531.

"transformed" into municipal law.'[7] Viljoen concurs that international law and national law are fundamentally different in a dualist legal system and 'domestic law-making (enabling legislation) is required to "transform" or "incorporate" ("domesticate") international law into national law'.[8] By 'transformation' is meant the 'amendment of existing laws or the adoption of new domestic legislation' in line with a ratified treaty.[9] The process of 'incorporation' entails the wholesale inclusion of an international instrument in national law.[10]

For most of Commonwealth Africa, the concept of dualism thrives. Under dualism treaties are not counted as part of municipal law until transformation or incorporation has occurred. The aim is to put check on executive prerogatives so that only those treaties solemnised by national legislative structures have legal effect. This is in tandem with the system of parliamentary sovereignty, 'which has been developed as a cherished bulwark against the exercise of executive prerogatives'.[11] Indeed:[12]

> English law in general favours 'dualism', that is, a position in which the two systems of law (national and international) co-exist, but function separately; each has distinct purposes and the subjects of international law are typically sovereign states, not individual persons. This co-existence does not guarantee harmony between the two systems.

Loveland argues that this position is 'entirely consistent both with the traditional Diceyan theory and the political outcome of the 1688 revolution'.[13] The rationale for this doctrine is written in Britain's own history, thus:[14]

> The 1688 revolution produced an agreement between William of Orange and Parliament which provided that the constitutional role of the King's government was to govern within the laws made by Parliament. The government itself could not create new laws simply by coming to an agreement with foreign countries. If one allowed that to happen, one would essentially be saying that it is government rather than Parliament that is the sovereign law-maker, as the government could bypass the refusal of the House of Commons and/or the House of Lords to consent to its proposed laws.

It follows then that, at least in the common law, 'when new obligations are created by treaty, legislation is needed for them to become rules of national law'.[15]

---

7 MN Shaw *International law* (1997) 104.
8 Viljoen (n 6 above) 18.
9 As above.
10 As above.
11 Viljoen (n 6 above) 535-536.
12 AW Bradley & K Ewing *Constitutional and administrative law* (1993) 326.
13 I Loveland *Constitutional law, administrative law and human rights: A critical introduction* (2006) 35.
14 Loveland (n 13 above) 35-36.
15 Bradley & Ewing (n 12 above) 326.

3 Dualism: The erstwhile Kenyan imitation

The doctrine of dualism evolved in England to check the prerogatives of the Crown in foreign affairs, especially the power to make law by entering into agreements with foreign states. Thus, the House of Commons needed to validate such solemn commitments before they could apply in England as law. The system of parliamentary democracy is thus a natural habitat for this doctrine.

It is usually argued that the president in Kenya inherited all the prerogatives of the Crown in relation to the state on attainment of republican status in 1964.[16] A likely bequest was the prerogative enabling the conduct of foreign relations in particular the signing of treaties on behalf of the state. Should this be the case, it was true in Kenya, like in England, that

> the Government is free to negotiate treaty and other relations with foreign nations, though the common law rule requiring incorporation by Parliament into domestic law applies, if such incorporation is necessary. [17]

The original judicial authority for this principle (dualism) in Kenya was expressed in the case of *Okunda v Republic*[18] where the High Court limited the sources of law in Kenya to those listed under the Judicature Act:[19]

> The jurisdiction of the High Court, the Court of Appeal and of all subordinate courts shall be exercised in conformity with:
> The Constitution;
> Subject thereto, all other written laws ...;
> Subject thereto and so far as those written laws do not extend or apply, the substance of the Common Law, the Doctrines of Equity and the Statutes of General Application enforced in England on the 12th August 1897 and the procedure and practice observed in courts of justice in England at that date; but the Common Law, Doctrines of Equity and Statutes of General Application shall apply so far as the circumstances of Kenya and its inhabitants permit and subject to such qualifications as those circumstances may render necessary.

The Court held that international law, not being one of the listed sources, was not an independent force of law. Unless domesticated through either a constitutional amendment or an Act of Parliament, international law had no legal effect in Kenya.

In a 2001 case, *Pattni & Another v Republic*,[20] the High Court, again, established that international norms, much as they could be of persuasive value, are not binding in Kenya save for where they are incorporated into the Constitution or other written laws. While making reference to the Universal Declaration of Human Rights (UDHR), the International Covenant on Civil and Political Rights (ICCPR)[21] and the African

---

16 YP Ghai & JPWB McAuslan *Public law and political change in Kenya* (1970) 254.
17 Ghai & McAuslan (n 16 above) 256.
18 *Okunda v Republic* [1970] EA 512.
19 Chapter 8, Laws of Kenya, s 3(1).
20 *Pattni & Another v Republic* [2001] KLR 262.
21 Acceded to by Kenya on 1 May 1972.

Charter on Human and Peoples' Rights (African Charter),[22] Githinji, Osiemo and Otieno JJ ruled that:[23]

> Although those instruments testify to the globalization of fundamental rights and freedoms of an individual, it is our Constitution as a law which is paramount. That is not to say, however, that Court (sic) cannot in appropriate cases, take account of emerging international consensus of values in this area.

While the Court conceded some ground in the latter decision by demonstrating willingness to 'take account of emerging international consensus of values' in the human rights realm, this apparently could only happen 'in appropriate cases' bearing in mind that at all times the Constitution is paramount.

Three verifying questions have been suggested to test the extent to which international human rights norms have been domesticated in African states: First, whether international human rights norms are part of domestic law; second, where such norms feature in the hierarchy of the municipal national legal order, in case they are applicable; and third, whether domestic courts apply them in their decisions.[24]

The two precedents discussed above indicate that in the old constitutional order there was a genuine temptation on the part of Kenyan courts to answer the first question in the negative. According to this view international human rights norms did not form part of Kenya's domestic legal order. Norms enacted outside Kenya had first go through either the process of incorporation or transformation to have legal effect municipally. This is illustrated by the transformation of the Convention on the Rights of the Child and the African Charter on the Rights and Welfare of the Child into Kenyan law. In this regard, the Children Act is 'An Act of Parliament to ... give effect to the principles of the Convention on the Rights of the Child and the African Charter on the Rights and Welfare of the Child and for connected purposes.'[25]

Even though international human rights norms generally could not have automatic legal influence, in some instances, courts referred to them.[26]

The Court of Appeal in the case of *Mary Rono v Jane Rono* recognised that both customary international law and treaty law can be applied by courts, even in the absence of implementing legislation, 'provided that

---

22 Ratified by Kenya on 10 February 1992.

23 *Pattni* (n 20 above) 262.

24 Viljoen (n 6 above) 530.

25 See, Preamble. Cf *Wambua v Wambua* (2004) AHRLR 189 (KeHC 2004); *SO v LAM* [2009] eKLR, civil appeal 175 of 2006, Court of Appeal, 30 January 2009.

26 In addition to the cases discussed here see also eg *Kenya v Minister For Home Affairs and ors, ex p Leonard Sitamze*, First instance, Miscellaneous Civil Case 1652 of 2004; ILDC 1094 (KE 2007), 18 April 2007; *Lemeiguran and ors v* Attorney *General of Kenya and ors*, First instance (by way of Originating Summons), Misc Civil App No 305 of 2004; ILDC 698 (KE 2006); (2006) eKLR, 18 December 2006.

there is no conflict with existing state law'.[27] In this sense, courts could rely on these norms as 'an aid to interpretation' of either the Constitution or ordinary laws ('interpretative guidance') but not 'as the basis of a remedy'.[28] Waki JA recognised this utility:[29]

> I have gone at some length into international law provisions to underscore the view I take in this matter that the central issue relating to discrimination which this appeal raises, cannot be fully addressed by reference to domestic legislation alone. The relevant international laws which Kenya has ratified, *will also inform my decision*. (Emphasis added).

In a subsequent 2008 decision, *Re The Estate of Lerionka Ole Ntutu (Deceased),*[30] Rawal J took occasion to explain that the position arrived at in the *Rono* decision was inevitable given principle 7 of the Bangalore Principles on the Domestic Application of International Human Rights Norms, which states:

> It is within the proper nature of the judicial process and well established functions of national courts to have regard to international obligations which a country undertakes – whether or not they have been incorporated into domestic law – *for the purpose of removing ambiguity or uncertainty from national constitution – legislation or the common law*.

The reliance on Bangalore Principles further illustrates that courts were in some instances willing to be influenced even by soft law provisions.

In the *RM v AG* case,[31] Nyamu and Ibrahim JJ were of the view that courts ought to apply international norms only in instances where they are not in conflict with municipal law. According to the judges:[32]

> Where the national law is clear and inconsistent with the international obligation, in common law countries, the national court is obliged to give effect to national law. And in such cases the court should draw such inconsistencies to the attention of the appropriate authorities since the supremacy of the national law in no way mitigates a breach of an international legal obligation which is undertaken by a country…

It follows that the place of international human rights norms was, until the 2010 Constitution, beneath the Constitution (which is paramount), lower than ordinary state laws, and, perhaps, at best, would be useful where legislation were in abeyance or in removing ambiguities or uncertainty from municipal legislation. This low rank is usually not enviable, even in the quite progressive jurisdictions where there is direct enforcement of international human rights norms. This is because even if theoretically international law may occupy a lower step on the ladder,

---

27 *Rono v Rono* (2005) AHRLR 107 (KeCA 2005) para 22.

28 See generally Viljoen (n 6 above) 540.

29 Para 24.

30 *Re The Estate of Lerionka Ole Ntutu (Deceased)* (2008) eKLR.

31 *RM v Attorney-General* (2006) AHRLR 256 (KeHC 2006).

32 Para 22.

below ordinary national law, this possibility has potential to negate totally the role of international law.[33]

4 Case for progressive jurisprudence on the application of international human rights norms in Kenya

The scenario that has obtained in Kenya easily puts to test Oppenheim's expression that:

> [S]tates show considerable flexibility in the procedures whereby they give effect within their territories to the rules of international law ... while the procedures vary, the result that effect is given within states to the requirements of international law is by and large achieved by all states.[34]

Indeed, there did not seem to be concerted efforts by judicial and legislative authorities to establish a consistent and beneficial jurisprudence on domestic application of international human rights norms. The result was that those within the borders of the state would be forced to forego even the entitlements which have been voluntarily ratified on the international scene. It did not help matters that the relegated international norms in the realm of human rights are often progressive and have a richer menu of entitlements. It is perhaps in this light that the Committee on Economic Social and Cultural Rights noted with concern with regard to Kenya 'that the Covenant rights have not been incorporated into the domestic law and therefore are not directly applicable in the courts of the State party'.[35] The Committee thus recommended that:[36]

> The State party includes economic, social and cultural rights in its new Constitution, with a view to incorporating the Covenant rights into domestic law and ensuring their direct applicability in the courts.

To remedy the anomaly caused by the dualism doctrine, Kenya may need to seize the now quite progressive constitutional provisions to secure cogent parliamentary statutes, practice and conventions guaranteeing direct application of international human rights norms on the municipal domain. The major innovation of the 2010 Constitution is the provision that international treaties ratified by the state are a source of law in Kenya.[37] In addition, the Constitution mandates the president to 'ensure that the international obligations of the Republic are fulfilled through the actions of the relevant Cabinet Secretaries'.[38] These

---

33 Viljoen (n 6 above) 538.

34 Shaw (n 7 above) 104 quoting R Jennings & A Watts (eds) *Oppenheim's international law* (1992) 54.

35 See para 9 of the Concluding observations of the Committee on Economic, Social and Cultural Rights with respect to Kenya adopted at the Committee's forty first session in Geneva, 3-21 November 2008.

36 As above.

37 The Constitution of Kenya article 2(6).

38 Article 132(5).

provisions should be understood to amend the Judicature Act (discussed above) by introducing an additional source of law in its traditional hierarchy of sources which includes the Constitution, Acts of Parliament, common law, doctrines of equity and customary law. It is suggested that in this hierarchy of sources of law, the place of international law should be either at par with Acts of Parliament or even higher.

The Constitution further stipulates that the general principles of international law form part of the law of Kenya.[39] It is arguable that such principles would entail the acceptance and applicability of norms that have attained customary international law status in the municipal courts. Customary international law norms are usually inferred from a combination of state practice (*usus*) and the acceptance of an obligation to be bound (*opinio juris sive necessitatis*).[40]

It is instructive that the common law tradition does not bar the application of customary international law. Rules of custom may have legal effect in England and therefore the entire common law.[41] English courts have on occasions held that customary international law is part of the common law of England[42] more so where the custom in question is not in conflict with express provisions of municipal law. On this approach:[43]

> There is no need for any 'transformation': a national court may directly apply the customary international rule, provided that this would not be contrary to statute or a prior decision binding on the court.

Should this thinking be accepted, a host of human rights instruments/stipulations such as parts of the UDHR[44] and CRC[45] which are now considered customary international law may find automatic application in Kenya. Already, the case of *Waweru v Republic*,[46] recognised that certain environmental principles 'do constitute part of international customary law' and that 'courts ought to take cognisance of

---

39 Constitution article 2(5).

40 J Dugard *International law: A South African perspective* 29.

41 It is important to mention that the jurisprudence on this aspect is rather confusing, and the rule is not necessarily a predictable one. See *R v Keyna* (1867) 2 Ex.D 63; *West Rand Gold Mining case* (1905) 2 KB 391. See generally Shaw (n 7 above) 104-108.

42 Bradley & Ewing (n 11 above); See also *Trendtex Trading Corpn v Central Bank of Nigeria* (1977) 1 QB 529 (CA); *Triquet v Bath* (1764) 3 Burr 1478; *Buvot v Barbuit* (1737).

43 Bradley & Ewing (n 12 above).

44 See, for instance, A Eide & G Alfredsson 'Introduction' in A Eide & G Alfredsson (eds) *The Universal Declaration of* Human *Rights: A common standard of achievement* (1999), where it is suggested that parts of the UDHR could have attained the status of customary international law.

45 According to some scholars, the near universal endorsement on the CRC may imply the universality of the treaty. See, for instance, T Kaime 'The Convention on the Rights of the Child and the cultural legitimacy of children's rights in Africa: Some reflections' (2005) 5 *African Human Rights Law Journal* 222; M Brading 'Reconciling universality of children's rights and cultural diversity' in *International Yearbook of Regional Human Rights Master's Programmes* (2006) 308.

46 *Waweru v The Republic* (2007) AHRLR 149 (KeHC 2007).

them in all relevant situations'. Going by this position, customary international law should now have a pride of place in the legal system.

It is however, advisable that both treaty law and customary international law be expressly made sources of law. Express reference to customary international law is advantageous because:[47]

> As long as international human rights treaties do not enjoy universal ratification, treaties will be an incomplete means of attaining the goal of universal respect for human rights. Customary international law fills this gap, as it binds those states not party to a treaty – provided that the relevant norm has become a rule of customary international law.

Thus, even where the executive declines to ratify significant international human rights instruments, those human rights items that have crystallised into customary international law shall continue to bind the state.

To further ensure that Kenya upholds her international obligations, which in most cases constitute ideal standards, stipulations akin to those provided for in article 29(6) of the Draft Bill of the Constitution of Kenya 2002[48] ought to be secured and preserved somewhere in the legal system:

> The Republic shall fulfill all its international obligations in respect of human rights and for that purpose:
> The Republic shall report on time to international human rights bodies on the implementation of human rights treaties;
> Draft reports intended for submission by the Republic to international bodies shall be published in Kenya for two months and facilities shall be provided for the public to discuss and debate them before the reports are revised and submitted;
> The Republic shall facilitate the submission of alternative drafts by civil society organizations to international human rights bodies; and
> The comments and recommendations of international bodies shall be disseminated to the public and the Government shall make a statement to Parliament on how it intends to implement those recommendations.

This chapter makes the case for express abrogation of the *Okunda* philosophy to yield ground for more direct application of international human rights norms in Kenyan courts in accordance with the new constitutional dispensation. This suggestion finds vindication in the fact that the realities in England that necessitated dualism – such as the 1688 revolution – are not present in Kenya. Kenya is not a parliamentary system. On the contrary, the 2010 Constitution installs a presidential system of government akin to that in the United States. Under the new scheme, executive authority of the state is vested in the president, the deputy president and the cabinet.[49] It is an additional constitutional

---

47 Viljoen (n 6 above) 26-27.

48 This was a Draft Constitution released by the Constitution of Kenya Review Commission in 2002. The draft was later to undergo a lot of processes including a national constitution conference, and other amendments before being rejected at the referendum in November 2005.

49 Article 130(1).

safeguard that the president holds no other state or public office.[50] Similarly, a Cabinet Secretary is not required to be a member of parliament.[51] In addition, the nature and character of prerogative powers in England, which are at the core of the doctrine under review, are not identical to those in Kenya. For instance, the president may not have all the prerogatives of the crown in England. As Ghai and McAuslan succinctly point out, even at independence, there was a thick cloud of uncertainty regarding what exactly comprised prerogative powers:[52]

> The government has inherited all the prerogative powers that the Queen could exercise in relation to Kenya in 1964. It is not immediately clear what additional powers are bestowed by this provision. It has been held that since the prerogative is part of common law, and Kenya, during her dependent status had received the common law, the Queen's prerogative powers were in some respect as extensive as in Britain, with minor exceptions, though in other respects they were even wider. But the prerogatives that the President can exercise on behalf of the Government are those that belonged to the Queen in relation to an independent Kenya, which were not as extensive ... Again, the prerogative, being part of the common law, is liable to be replaced or repealed by written law. Thus, many of the former prerogatives are either regulated by law, or have been repealed.

According to Ojwang, the monarch's representatives in Kenya, believed to have bequeathed these powers, did not exercise the prerogatives in the common law sense.[53] The colony and the protectorate were only extensions of the area of effectiveness of British sovereignty, which itself revolved around the authority of the monarch. The colonial time thus created a condition in which the prerogative must bear an appearance somewhat different from the common law understanding. Both Mitullah and Ojwang are in agreement that at the end of colonialism, most of the powers held by the monarch as prerogatives were defined and specifically sanctified in the independence Constitution:[54]

> The formal enactment of common law prerogatives effectively changed their character into a wholly novel species of prerogatives. They ceased to belong to the unwritten common law, and their scope was delimited by written law; such that they appear to fetter the sovereign's discretion. If this interpretation is taken, then it must be the case that the prerogative had been transformed from common law character to constitutional prerogatives, or a special category of prerogative powers.

The resulting constitutional prerogatives – even in the new dispensation – are susceptive to other checks such as judicial review and

---

50 Article 131(3).

51 Article 152(3).

52 Ghai & McAuslan (n 15 above) 255.

53 See JB Ojwang *Constitutional development in Kenya: Institutional adaptation and social change* (1990).

54 WV Mitullah 'Exercise of executive powers in Kenya: The case of the prerogative of mercy', in M Odhiambo, O Ambani & WV Mitullah (eds) *Informing a constitutional moment: Essays on constitution reform in Kenya* (2005) 7.

not just parliamentary supervision which necessitated dualism in England.

While it is conceded that, initially, the Constitution's 'laconic provisions' and silences 'with respect of questions relating to diplomatic matters, international relations, war and peace'[55] in effect left the governing principles to be shaped in accordance with common law practices – the conclusion that the character of Kenya's prerogative power is no longer identical to Britain's is inevitable. In the absence of the revolution and in the wake of quite dissimilar prerogatives and constitutional structures, nothing warrants dualism in Kenya.

5 Conclusion

This contribution discussed the impact the dualism doctrine has had on domestic application of international human rights norms. It has also advanced the case for a consistent and progressive philosophy on the application of international law in Kenya. There are two openings for progressive jurisprudence in this regard. First, Kenya should seize the prevailing transitional moment heralded by a new constitutional order to wholesomely acknowledge international (human rights) law as one of the sources of law municipally. In this respect, the state could do more than take the cue from South Africa where international law is an interpretive tool.[56] Second, courts of superior record should expressly overrule the *Okunda* philosophy. The new philosophy would then put into consideration the emerging significance of the international scene in human rights norm setting. There is need to reckon that the common law tradition does not bar direct municipal application of customary international law and further that the factors which necessitated dualism in England are not present in Kenya.

For Kenyans to effectively realise the fairly generous entitlements ratified by their state on the international stage, someone may need to bury the tradition called dualism.

---

55 As above.

56 Cf the chapter 10 of this book. See also JD Bessler 'In the spirit of ubuntu: Enforcing the rights of orphans and vulnerable children affected by HIV/AIDS in South Africa' (2008) 31 *Hastings International and Comparative Law Review* 50-51.

3

An examination of the use of international law as an interpretative tool in human rights litigation in Ghana and Botswana

Emmanuel K Quansah*

Summary

The constitutions of both Ghana and Botswana do not expressly define the relationship between international law and national law. However, both countries subscribe to the dualist approach to the incorporation of international law into national law. In the context of this scenario, the courts in both countries in adjudicating human rights issues have tried, whenever possible, to rely on relevant international human rights instruments even where such instruments have not been incorporated into national law. This has been on the basis that such international instruments do not derogate from or conflict with the constitution or national law. From the discussion of the case law on human rights adjudication in the two jurisdictions, it would seem that although the judges do not have a clear mandate to apply international law, they have tried, where necessary to rely on such law in determining human rights issues. The non-incorporation of international treaties into national law in both countries has not adversely affected the protection of the guaranteed human rights. In fact the absence of incorporation of treaties seems to have emboldened the judiciary to use such treaties where relevant to solidify the national legal framework for the protection of such rights. In the light of the constitutional constraints and political apathy towards incorporation of international treaties faced by the courts in these two countries, one will conclude that their report card looks quite good.

1 Introduction

The 1992 and 1966 constitutions of Ghana and Botswana respectively do not spell out in clear terms the relationship between international and national law. International lawyers have traditionally used the concept of monism and dualism to describe the relationship between international

* Professor of Law, University of Botswana; quansahe@mopipi.ub.bw.

law and national (domestic) law.[1] Monism treats international and national law as part of the same legal order and consequently, national law must always conform to the requirements of international law. This should happen whether or not the relevant national institution has taken any formal steps to incorporate international law into the national law in accordance with the requisite constitutional provision. In contrast, dualism views international and national law as distinct from each other; the former only penetrating the national legal order by explicit consent, in the form of legislation, of the relevant national institution (incorporation) or by transformation.[2] When there is a conflict between the two laws, national courts should apply the national law at the expense of international law.[3]

Ghana and Botswana subscribe to the dualist approach to the incorporation of international law into domestic law. It is therefore the expectation that the executive/legislature will take the requisite steps to incorporate international treaties, protocols etc to which the countries are party into the national legal order in order to aid the enforcement of the various human rights guaranteed by the respective constitutions.[4] However, the empirical evidence shows that the relevant authorities are reluctant to incorporate such international instruments into the national

1 See for example, J Dugard *International law: A South African perspective* (2005) 47; I Brownlie *Principles of public international law* (1998) 31-33; M Dixon *Textbook on international law* (2000) 82-85; OB Tshosa *National law and international human rights law: Cases of Botswana, Namibia and Zimbabwe* (2001) 3-13; RF Oppong 'Re-imagining international law: An examination of recent trends in the reception of international law into national legal systems in Africa' (2007) 30 *Fordham International Law Journal* 296 at 297 and T Ginsburg *et al* 'Commitment and diffusion: How and why national constitutions incorporate international law' (2008) *University of Illinois Law Review* 201 at 204-206.

2 For the distinction between incorporation and transformation, see the Australian case of *Nulyarimma v Thompson; Buzzacott v Hill, Downer & Commonwealth of Australia* (1999) 165 ALR 621 at para 84.

3 For the pros and cons of the debate, see JG Starke 'Monism and dualism in the theory of international law' (1936) 16 *British Yearbook on International Law* 66.

4 Chapter 5 of the Ghana Constitution incorporates and entrenches 'Fundamental human rights and freedoms', including both civil and political rights and economic, social and cultural rights. These rights are binding both on the state and on private individuals and institutions. Chapter 6 provides 'Directive principles of state policy', which have been held by the Supreme Court to be justiciable under the appropriate circumstances where they link up with particular rights which are recognised under Chapter 5 (see *NPP v Inspector-General of Police* [1993-94] 2 GLR 459 at 494). In general, the directive principles provide guidance for the executive, courts and others on interpretation of the Constitution and other law. Similarly, Chapter II of the Botswana Constitution protects 'Fundamental rights and freedoms of the individual' which are mainly civil and political rights. In both jurisdictions the human rights provisions are justiciable. See s 33 of the Ghana Constitution and s 18 of the Botswana Constitution. See generally, CM Fombad, 'The protection of human rights in Botswana: An overview of the regulatory framework' in CM Fombad (ed) *Essays on the law of Botswana* (2007) 1-31 and OB Tshosa 'Judicial protection of human rights in Botswana and the role of international humanitarian law' in EK Quansah & W Binchy (eds) *Judicial protection of human rights in Botswana: Emerging issues* (2009) 61.

legal order which would enable national courts to enforce and implement them in human rights litigation that comes before them.[5] This situation notwithstanding, the courts of the two countries have valiantly tried on a number of occasions to utilise the provisions of international instruments in adjudicating human rights issues.[6]

This chapter will accordingly examine firstly, the formal status of international law in the legal order of the two countries and the practical implication thereof; secondly, it will examine the extent to which international law is applied and used as an interpretation tool in human rights litigation. Thirdly, it will show the extent to which the courts in the two countries rely on different international and foreign case law to decide human rights cases; and finally, it will conclude by assessing whether the reluctance of the relevant authorities to incorporate international human rights instruments into national law has hampered the protection of human rights in the two countries.

2 Ghana

2.1 International law and the Ghana Constitution

The hierarchy of laws established by article 11 of the 1992 Constitution does not expressly mention international law as part of the laws of Ghana. However, the article includes amongst such laws, 'enactments made by or under the authority of parliament; any orders, Rules and Regulations made by any person or authority under a power conferred by this Constitution…'. Article 75(1) vests in the president the power to execute or to cause to be executed treaties, agreements or conventions in the name of Ghana, subject to ratification by an Act of Parliament supported by the votes of more than one-half of all members of parliament. Consequently, international law in the form of treaties, conventions and protocols may become part of the laws of Ghana if the appropriate constitutional procedure is adhered to. As stated earlier, Ghana subscribes to the dualist approach to the relationship between international law and national law. As such for international law to become part of national law the requisite legislative or executive action needs to be taken to incorporate ratified international treaties into national law before they can be applied by the courts. This position was

5 For Ghana, see Open Society Initiative for West Africa *Ghana: Justice sector and the rule of law* (2007) 4. A plea for incorporation of international law into national law in Ghana was made as far back as 1991 by Prof EVO Dankwa in 'Implementation of international human rights instruments: Ghana as an illustration' (1991) 3 *Proceedings of the Third Annual Conference of The African Society of International and Comparative Law* 57. See also K Appiagyei-Atua 'Ghana at 50: The place of international human rights norms in the courts' in H Bonsu *et al* (eds) *Ghana since independence: History, development and prospects* (2007) 118. The situation is similar in Botswana as discussed below.

6 See M Killander 'The role of international law in human rights litigation in Africa' in Quansah & Binchy (n 4 above) 7.

expressly stated by Ampiah, JSC in *NPP v Attorney-General* (*CIBA* case) when he said:[7]

> [L]aws, municipal or otherwise, which are found to be inconsistent with the Constitution cannot be binding on the state whatever their nature. International laws, including intra African enactments, are not binding on Ghana until such laws have been adopted or ratified by the municipal laws ... This is a principle of public international law which recognizes the sovereignty of States as prerequisite for international relationship and law.

It has been suggested that incorporation of international instruments into the national law of Ghana may take one of four forms,[8] namely through (1) direct incorporation of rights recognised in an international instrument into the Constitution, an Act of Parliament or a Bill of Rights in the national legal order as exemplified by Chapter 5 of the Constitution; (2) transformation or incorporation through a statement embodied in the preamble of a piece of legislation to the effect that the legislation is intended to give effect to a specific international instrument; (3) 'inferred implementation', whereby a new legislation or an amendment of existing legislation is made to give effect to treaty obligations; and (4) legislation which gives indirect effect to treaty commitments without necessarily and directly making reference to that particular international treaty. Unfortunately, incorporation of international instruments into national law has not taken any clear cut pattern.

Since the attainment of independence in 1957, Ghana has become party to numerous international, African and regional human rights instruments.[9] However, in practice, it incorporated very few of the instruments that it ratified into national laws. Amongst those incorporated, the following may be mentioned: Convention on the Rights of Children (CRC)[10] largely incorporated into the Children's Act 1998[11] and the Juvenile Justice Act 2003;[12] the OAU Convention Regarding Specific Aspects of Refugee Problems in Africa,[13] the UN

---

7 *NPP v Attorney-General* [1996-97] SCGLR 729 at 761.

8 See Appiagyei-Atua (n 5 above).

9 Some of the instruments acceded to include: UN Convention Relating to the Status of Refugees (1958), Convention on the Prevention and Punishment of the Crime of genocide (1963), International Convention on the Elimination of All Forms of Racial Discrimination (1966), OAU Convention Regarding Specific Aspects of Refugee Problems in Africa (1975), Convention on the Elimination of All Forms of Discrimination Against Women (1980), African Charter on Human and Peoples' Rights (1984), Convention on the Rights of the Child (1990) and the Rome Statute on the International Criminal Court (1999). For a full list of international instruments of which Ghana is a signatory, see the annex to *Ghana: Justice sector and the rule of law* (n 5 above). See also Appiagyei-Atua (n 5 above).

10 Acceded to on 5 February 1990.

11 Act 560.

12 Act 653.

13 Acceded to on 19 June 1975.

Convention Relating to the Status of Refugees (1951)[14] and the UN Protocol Relating to the Status of Refugees (1967).[15] These are reflected in the Refugee Law 1993.[16] The UN Protocol to Prevent, Suppress and Punish Trafficking in Persons (2000) is incorporated in the Human Trafficking Act of 2005.[17]

In some cases where there has not been a formal incorporation of a particular international instrument, existing laws have been amended to incorporate relevant portions of such international instrument that the country has ratified. For example, the Criminal Code Act of 1998[18] amended the Criminal Code 1960[19] by inserting a new section 69A into the Code criminalising female genital mutilation as a second-degree felony punishable by a minimum three-year imprisonment. Also the 1998 Act inserted a new section 314A criminalising customary or ritual enslavement of any kind, including the *trokosi* practice[20] which had generated international condemnation, and provides for a minimum punishment upon conviction of three years in prison.

Furthermore, even where formal incorporation has not been made, international law principles may still operate in human rights litigation in terms of article 40 of the Constitution. This article obliges the government, *inter alia*, to 'promote respect for international law, treaty obligations and settlement of international disputes by peaceful means' and to adhere to the principles enshrined in the treaties of all international organisations of which the country is a member. In terms of article 73, the government shall conduct its international affairs in consonance with accepted principles of public international law and diplomacy in a manner consistent with the interest of Ghana. Thus in the *CIBA* case[21] the Supreme Court held that the principles of international instruments relating to fundamental human rights are enforceable to the extent that they fit into the provisions of article 33(5) of the Constitution which allows the courts to rely on other human rights principles in

---

14 Acceded to on 18 March 1963.

15 Acceded to on 30 October 1968.

16 PNDCL 305.

17 Act 694. However, Ghana has neither signed, acceded to nor ratified the protocol.

18 Act 554. These amendments to the Criminal Code may be seen as fulfilling some of the terms of the International Covenant on Civil and Political Rights (ICCPR) which the country ratified in 2000 without reservation. The enactment of the Domestic Violence Act 2007 (Act 732) would also seem to be an attempt at implementing some aspects of the UN Declaration on the Elimination of Violence against Women.

19 Act 29.

20 This is a form of ritual slavery that has been practised for several hundred years by the Ewes of Tongu and Anlo in the Volta Region and Damgbes of Greater Accra Region of Ghana. Under this practice, a family must offer a virgin daughter to the gods to atone for the 'sins and crimes' of a relative, who in most cases may be long dead. Girls between the ages of eight and fifteen are usually offered for such atonement and they may live at a particular fetish shrine for the rest of their lives. This amendment was geared to a further implementation of the CRC.

21 n 7 above.

addition to those specifically set out in Chapter 5 of the Constitution dealing with 'fundamental human rights'. Atuguba JSC said:[22]

> As to the enforceability of international instruments relating to fundamental human rights, I think that the matter can easily be resolved by recourse to article 33(5) ... It cannot be contended that the principles of those instruments do not fit into this provision, and they are therefore to that extent enforceable.[23]

In the light of the above *dictum* and the cited provisions of the Constitution, the door is open for the courts, in appropriate circumstances, to apply international instruments relating to human rights which have not been expressly incorporated into national law in order to determine human rights issues.

2.2 Application of international law in human rights litigation

The enforcement of the guaranteed human rights under the Ghana Constitution is placed under the jurisdiction of the High Court.[24] Article 33(1) of the Constitution provides that any person alleging that a provision of the Constitution on fundamental human rights and freedoms has been, is, or is likely to be contravened in relation to him or her, may apply to the High Court for redress. Where the case involves interpretation and enforcement of the Constitution, the Supreme Court is vested with jurisdiction under articles 2(1) and 130. It is under these provisions that human rights litigation may be brought before the courts for adjudication.

As stated above, although there is no express stipulation in the Ghana Constitution for the application of international law in litigation before the courts, there have been occasions when international instruments have been relied upon in determination of cases. In *New Patriotic Party v Inspector General of Police*[25] the plaintiffs brought an action before the Supreme Court challenging the provisions of sections 8, 12 and 13 of the Public Order Decree 1972 which provided, *inter alia*, that the holding of all processions and meetings and the public celebration of any traditional custom shall be subject to obtaining prior police permit. Section 12 of the Act empowered a superior police officer to stop or to disperse such a procession or meeting whether a permit had been obtained or not. Section 13 made it an offence to hold such processions, meetings and

22 At 788.

23 See also the *obiter dictum* of Sophia Akuffo JSC in *Adjei-Ampofo v Attorney-General* [2003-2004] 1 SCGLR 411 at 418.

24 See *Edusei v A-G* [1996-97] SCGLR 1. Apart from the constitutional provisions, section 15(1)(d) as amended by the Courts (Amendment) Act, 2000 (Act 620) also vests in the High Court jurisdiction to enforce the 'fundamental human rights and freedoms' guaranteed by the Constitution. This discussion will be confined to post 1992 decisions since the courts attitude towards human rights before the inception of the 1992 Constitution was a dismal one. See Appiagyei-Atua (n 5 above).

25 *New Patriotic Party v Inspector General of Police* [1993-94] 2 GLR 459 (SC); (2001) AHRLR 138 (GhSC 1993).

public celebrations without such police permission. Plaintiffs contended that these provisions were inconsistent with and in contravention of the Constitution, particularly article 21(1)(d)[26] and consequently void and unenforceable. They further claimed that under the provisions of the Constitution no permission was required either from the police or other public authority for the holding of a rally, demonstration, procession or the public celebration of any traditional custom by any person, group or organisation. The Supreme Court unanimously held that certain sections of the Public Order Decree, including those stated above, were inconsistent and in contravention of article 21(1)(d) of the Constitution. In the course of the judgment, Archer CJ said:[27]

> Ghana is a signatory to this African Charter and member states of the OAU and parties to the Charter are expected to recognise the rights, duties and freedoms enshrined in the Charter and to undertake to adopt legislative and other measures to give effect to the rights and duties. I do not think the fact that Ghana has not passed specific legislation to give effect to the Charter means that the Charter cannot be relied upon.

In *Republic v Gorman and Others,* the Supreme Court relied partly on the UN Convention on Narcotic Drugs and Psychotropic Substances to deny bail to the accused persons. The Court said: [28]

> The Constitution adopts the view of human rights that seek to balance the rights of the individual as against the legitimate interests of the community. While the balance is decidedly tilted in favour of the individual, the public interest and the protection of the general public are very much part of the discourse on human rights in our Constitution.

In *Adjei-Ampofo v Attorney-General*[29] it was noted, albeit *obiter*, that:

> The reference to 'others' referred to in article 33(5) could only be those rights and freedoms that have crystallized into widely or generally accepted rights, duties, declarations and guarantees through treaties, conventions, international or regional accords, norms and usages. One may venture as an example, the right of women to reproductive health, which forms part of the 1995 Beijing Declaration and Platform for Action, to which Ghana is a signatory.

In that case, the plaintiff argued that a certain section of the Criminal Code as subsequently amended was void for contravening the well-known international and constitutional doctrines of void-for-vagueness and void-for-over-breadth. He contended that even though these doctrines were not expressly provided for under the 1992 Constitution, they were inherent in all democratic institutions such as Ghana's Constitution and consequently applicable in Ghana. The Supreme Court was therefore obliged by the terms of article 33(5) not only to consider the letter of the Constitution but the spirit as well. The Attorney-General

---

26 The said article deals with freedom of assembly including freedom to take part in processions and demonstrations.

27 At 466.

28 *Republic v Gorman and Others* (2004) AHRLR 141 (GhSC 2004) para 37.

29 *Adjei-Ampofo* (n 23 above).

raised a preliminary objection, *inter alia,* that the international doctrines which the plaintiff alleged were contravened did not form part of the Constitution which the plaintiff acknowledged in his statement of claim. The Attorney-General therefore submitted that the Court lacked jurisdiction to hear the case. The Supreme Court unanimously upheld the preliminary objection by stating that the plaintiff had failed to specify the particular provision of the Constitution with which the amended provision of the Criminal Code was in conflict. The Court added that it is only where it is seized with the interpretation of a particular provision of the Constitution that it will endeavour to ascertain the spirit behind it and reinforce it accordingly. However, the *obiter dictum* made by the Court in the course of its ruling indicates its preparedness to use international human rights standards as an interpretational tool.

In *Issa Iddi Abass & Others v Accra Metropolitan Assembly & Another*, the Court, though it referenced international human rights conventions, did not rely on any specific provisions of a treaty in deciding the case.[30]

The above cases reveal courts' preparedness to go beyond the traditional use of unincorporated treaties as aids to interpretation. The courts appear to suggest that unincorporated treaties may create enforceable rights in national law. The cases thus attach national significance to the international act of ratifying treaties.[31]

2.3 Reliance on foreign case law in human rights litigation

The trend of relying on international or foreign case law in human rights litigation is evident from analysis of the cases reported in the various law reports.[32] In *New Patriotic Party v Inspector-General of Police*, for instance, Hayfron-Benjamin JSC said:[33]

> In rendering my opinion I have considered and applied the views - both of the majority and the dissenting - contained in the judgments of the United States Supreme Court which show the principles and policy considerations involved. In my respectful opinion, they constitute useful guides to the interpretation of our Constitution, 1992 - particularly the charter on fundamental human and civil rights.

In *Asare v Attorney-General*[34] Date-Bah JSC in discussing the objective purposive approach to constitutional interpretation, relied on the American case of *Theophanous v Herald Weekly Time Ltd*[35] Again in *Adofo v*

---

30 *Issa Iddi Abass & Others v Accra Metropolitan Assembly & Another*, unreported, Misca 1203/2002 (24 July 2002) cited by Appiagyei-Atua (n 5 above).

31 See Oppong (n 1 above) 315.

32 See particularly, the Supreme Court of Ghana law Reports (SCGLR).

33 *NPP v Inspector-General of Police* (n 25 above) para 57. His Lordship also relied *inter alia*, on the *dicta* of Douglas J delivering the majority opinion of the US Supreme Court in *Saia v New York* 334 US 558 at 560-561 at paras 48 and 50; Lord Atkin in *Berton v Alliance Economic Investment Co Ltd* [1922] 1 KB 742 at 759 at para 54

34 *Asare v Attorney-General* [2003-2004] SCGLR 823.

35 *Theophanous v Herald Weekly Time Ltd* (1994) 182 CLR 104.

Attorney-General & Anor[36] he relied on President Wilson of the United States in a passage quoted from him by the US Supreme Court in *Evans v Gore*[37] to find that constitutional arrangements such as those prevailing in Ghana cannot work to their purpose unless there is a court system in place to resolve matters impinging on the liberty of the individual and the powers of government.

The above sample cases clearly demonstrate that the Ghana courts have no qualms in relying on foreign case law when necessary in order to determine human rights issues. Without empirical evidence it is not clear which foreign country's cases dominate the reference.

3 Botswana

3.1 International law and the Botswana Constitution

Similar to the provisions of the Ghana Constitution, the Botswana Constitution does not contain any provision delineating the role of international law within the national legal order. Instead, section 24(1) of the Interpretation Act 1984 provides that:

> For the purpose of ascertaining that which an enactment was made to correct and as an aid to the construction of the enactment a court may have regard to any text-book or other work of reference, to the report of any commission of inquiry into the state of the law, to any memorandum published by authority in reference to the enactment or to the Bill for the enactment, *to any relevant international treaty, agreement or convention and to any papers laid before the National Assembly in reference to the enactment or to its subject-matter,* but not to the debates in the Assembly. (Emphasis added)

Although this provision allows the courts to construe national law by reference to international treaties etc, it does not expressly authorise international law as part of national law. Furthermore, like Ghana, Botswana also subscribes to the dualist approach to the relationship between international law and national law.[38] This position was acknowledged by Horwitz AJ at first instance in the seminal case of *Dow v Attorney-General*[39] where the plaintiff challenged the constitutionality of sections 4 and 5 of the Citizenship Act 1982.[40] Having relied upon certain

36 *Adofo v Attorney-General & Anor* [2005-2006] SCGLR 42.

37 253 US 245 (1920).

38 See Tshosa (n 1 above) 71-72. The author however, argues (at 64) that the inter-relationship between customary international law and national law is governed by the classical monist theory, ie rules of customary international law are deemed to be automatically applicable in national law.

39 *Dow v Attorney-General* [1991] BLR 233. For a commentary on the case, see EK Quansah 'Unity Dow v Attorney-General of Botswana - One more relic of a woman's servitude removed' (1992) 4 *African Journal of International and Comparative Law* 195 and EK Quansah 'Unity Dow v Attorney-General - The sequel' (1993) 5 *African Journal of International and Comparative Law* 189.

40 The said sections allowed Botswana citizenship to be traced through one's father but if born out of wedlock through one's mother.

international instruments such as UN Declaration on the Elimination of All Forms of Discrimination against Women (1967) and the Convention on Rights of the Child (1989) in declaring sections 4 and 5 of the Citizenship Act 1982 (as amended) as *ultra vires* the Constitution, he observed as follows:[41]

> I am strengthened in my view by the fact that Botswana is a signatory to the OAU Convention on Non-Discrimination [African Chater on Human and Peoples' Rights]. I bear in mind that signing a convention does not give it power of law in Botswana but the effect of the adherence by Botswana to the Convention must show that a construction of the section which does not do violence to the language but is consistent with and in harmony with the Convention must be preferable ...

In *Bojang v The State,*[42] the Court opined that:[43]

> But even assuming that the right to legal representation is part of the customary international law, can it be seriously contended that such right to legal representation as embodied in international instruments, automatically forms part of the municipal laws of Botswana without any act of legislative incorporation? I doubt it. I find nothing in the laws of this country to the effect that international law or for that matter, provisions of international conventions can dispense with the theory of incorporation to operate directly on individuals.

The Court of Appeal in *Good v Attorney-General,*[44] referenced international conventions protecting the rights of individuals, including non-citizens, and reiterated the same position as follows:[45]

> Botswana is a signatory to a number of international treaties. It is trite and well recognized that signing such a treaty does not give it the power of law in Botswana and its provisions do not form part of the domestic law of this country until they are passed into law by Parliament. Those treaties do not confer enforceable rights on individuals within a state.

Customary international law, based on the received Roman-Dutch common law, is automatically part of national law. In *Republic of Angola v Springbok Investments (Pty) Ltd*[46] the applicant, a sovereign state, applied to the High Court to set aside an attachment by the defendant of funds standing to the credit of its bank account. The applicant argued that such funds were immune from attachment on the basis that it was a sovereign state and therefore, in international law, it enjoyed immunity from the jurisdiction of the Botswana courts. There is no Botswanan statute dealing with sovereign immunity. The question therefore arose as to whether the customary international rules of sovereign immunity form

---

41 At 245. This observation was endorsed by the Court of Appeal when it heard the case on appeal. See *Attorney-General v Dow* [1992] BLR 119 at 154.

42 *Bojang v The State* [1994] BLR 146.

43 At 157 per Gyeke-Dako J.

44 *Good v Attorney-General* [2005] 2 BLR 337.

45 Per Tebbutt JP at 345-346.

46 *Republic of Angola v Springbok Investments (Pty) Ltd* [2005] 2 BLR 159 (HC).

part of Botswana law. Kirby J, having surveyed the position in England, South Africa and Zimbabwe, opined as follows:[47]

> The position in this country is thus similar to that which obtains in Zimbabwe, where there is also no act and to that which obtained in the United Kingdom and South Africa before their acts were introduced. All three countries have moved away from the formal view (the doctrine of transformation) that all aspects of international law require to be introduced by statute, or by specific decisions of judges, or by long-standing custom, before they become part of the law of a country. Instead they have embraced the doctrine of incorporation, which holds that the rules of international law, or the *jus gentium*, are incorporated automatically into the law of all nations and are considered to be part of the law unless they conflict with statutes or the common law. Under this doctrine the rules of international law may be developed by the courts in line with changes in the world ... I have no doubt that the rules of international law form part of the law of Botswana, as a member of the wider family of nations, save in so far as they conflict with Botswana legislation or the common law, and it is the duty of the court to apply them.

He consequently held that the bank account was immune from attachment under customary international law.

Botswana, like Ghana, has only incorporated a limited number of treaties into national law.[48] Of these, the following may be mentioned: the Wildlife Conservation and National Parks Act, 1992 giving effect to the 1973 Convention on International Trade in Endangered Species of Wild Fauna and Flora (CITES);[49] the Waste Management Act 1998 giving effect to the 1989 Basel Convention on the Control of Transboundary Movements of Hazardous Wastes and Their Disposal;[50] Diplomatic Immunities and Privileges Act 1968 giving effect to the Vienna Convention on Diplomatic Relations;[51] Settlement of Investment Disputes (Convention) Act 1970, giving effect to Convention on the Settlement of Investment Disputes between States and Nationals of other States;[52] and the Geneva Conventions Act 1970, giving effect to (1) Geneva Convention for the Amelioration of the Condition of the Wounded and Sick in Armed Forces in the Field, (2) Geneva Convention for the Amelioration of the Condition of Wounded, Sick and Shipwrecked Members of Armed Forces at Sea, (3) Geneva Convention relative to the Treatment of Prisoners of War and (4) Geneva Convention

---

47 At 162.Relying on *dicta* from *Chung Chi Cheng v R* [1938] 4 All ER 786 (PC). See also *Bah v Libyan Embassy*, Application to Industrial Court, case no IC 956/2005, ILDC 154 (BW 2005); [2006] 1 BLR 22 (HC), 28 November 2005 at 25 and OB Tshosa, 'Immunity of diplomatic missions in Botswana in light of Amadou Oury Bah v Libyan Embassy' (2008) 7 *University of Botswana Law Journal* 173.

48 For treaties, protocol etc to which Botswana is a signatory, see http://www.agc.gov.bw/treaty_register_30th_March_2009.pdf (accessed 22 March 2009). As of this date some 269 treaties, conventions, protocols and statutes had been signed by Botswana.

49 Acceded to on 14 November 1977.

50 Acceded to on 20 May 1998.

51 Acceded to on 11 April 1969.

52 Acceded to on 15 January 1970.

relative to the protection of Civilian Persons in time of War.[53] As can be seen from this list, none of these incorporated instruments deal with core human rights. However, the recently enacted Children's Act, 2009[54] is geared towards incorporating the provisions of the CRC

3.2 Application of international law in human rights litigation

Section 18(1) of the Botswana Constitution, like article 33(1) of the Ghana Constitution confers on the High Court jurisdiction to hear and determine violations of the fundamental human rights provisions set out in the Constitution. However, the courts have not been seized with many human rights cases in which international human rights instruments have been at the core of the dispute. Rather there have been cases where courts mention such instruments in passing or relied on them to justify some conclusion which the court has come to in deciding allegations of human rights infringements under the Constitution. In *Attorney-General v Dow*[55] the majority of the Court of Appeal upheld the trial court's reliance on international law[56] and the country's obligations thereunder in the face of the state's objection. Amissah JP opined that:[57]

> Botswana is a member of the community of civilised states which has undertaken to abide by certain standards of conduct, and, unless it is impossible to do otherwise, it would be wrong for its courts to interpret its legislation in a manner which conflicts with the international obligations Botswana has undertaken. This principle, used as an aid to construction as is quite permissible under section 24 of the Interpretation Act, adds reinforcement to the view that the intention of the framers of the Constitution could not have been to permit discrimination purely on the basis of sex.

Aguda JA, who was part of the majority, went further and stated:[58]

> I take the view that in all these circumstances a court in this country, faced with the difficulty of interpretation as to whether or not some legislation breached any of the provisions entrenched in Chapter II of our Constitution which deal with fundamental rights and freedoms of individual, is entitled to look at the international agreements, treaties and obligations entered into before or after the legislation was enacted to ensure that such domestic legislation does not breach any of the international conventions, agreements, treaties, and obligations binding upon this country save upon clear and unambiguous language. *In my view this must be so whether or not such international conventions, agreements, treaties, protocols or obligations have been specifically incorporated into our domestic law.* (Emphasis added).

The learned Justice of Appeal then went on to explain that if parliament had incorporated an international agreement into domestic

---

53 All acceded to on 29 March 1968.

54 Act 8 of 2009, yet to come into operation.

55 n 41 above.

56 Particularly, the African Charter on Human and Peoples' Rights, the European Convention on Human Rights and the Convention on the Elimination of All Forms of Discrimination against Women.

57 At 154.

58 At 170.

law, there would be no problem since such a treaty would be treated as part of the domestic law for purposes of adjudication in a domestic court. If it had not been incorporated into domestic law, a domestic court must accept the position that the legislature or the executive will not act contrary to the undertaking given on behalf of the country by the executive. However where the country has not in terms become party to an international agreement it may only serve as an aid to the interpretation of a domestic law, or the construction of the Constitution.[59]

In *Bojang v The State*,[60] a review application founded on a magistrate's failure to inform an accused of her fundamental constitutional right to legal representation, the High Court noted that due to the paucity of case law at the time to guide it in resolving the issue before it,[61] it had to seek guidance not only from comparative judicial pronouncements, but also from human rights treaties that protect the right to legal representation.[62] In the course of his ruling, Gyeke-Dako J recognised that the embodiment of laudable human rights principles in various human rights instruments[63] reflected a universal acceptance of the right to legal representation as an important factor in the concept of a fair trial.[64] Similarly, in *Kgolagano v Attorney-General*[65] the accused was charged with murder and there was a two-and-a-half year delay in bringing him to trial. At the commencement of the trial, his attorney invoked section 10(1) of the Constitution and argued that the applicant had been denied the right to trial within a reasonable time. In determining whether the delay in question was unreasonable, Gyeke-Dako J again sought assistance and guidance from comparative case law in Zimbabwe and the United States interpreting similar clauses as well as international human rights instruments. With respect to the latter he opined:[66]

> The right to be tried within a 'reasonable time' is also guaranteed by section 11 of the Canadian Charter or Rights and freedoms and also by article 6(1) of the European Convention for the Protection of Human Rights and Fundamental

---

59 At 171. Similar references were made to international instruments by Aguda JA in the case of *Petrus & Anor v The State* [1984] BLR 14 at 37, a case which dealt with the constitutionality of corporal punishment as prescribed by s 301(3) of the Criminal Procedure and Evidence Act.

60 n 42 above.

61 For an update of the case law on the point, see EK Quansah 'Judicial attitudes to the fair trial provisions in the Botswana Constitution' in Fombad (ed) (n 4 above) 65 at 67, 70. See also DDN Nsereko 'The right to legal representation in Botswana' (1988) *Israel Yearbook on Human Rights* 21.

62 Bojang (n 42 above) at 152 per Gyeke-Dako J.

63 He referred to such international instruments as the Universal Declaration of Human Rights (art II), International Covenant on Civil and Political Rights (art 14(3)(d)), European Convention on Human Rights (art 6(3)(c), American Convention on Human Rights (art 8(2)(e)) and the African Charter on Human and Peoples' Rights (art 7(1)).

64 At 157.

65 *Kgolagano v Attorney-General* [1997] BLR 914 (HC).

66 At 923-924.

> Freedoms. This right is also embodied in the African Charter on Human and People's Rights.

However, in *Kanane v The State*,[67] a case dealing with homosexual practice, the Court of Appeal made reference to a number of foreign cases but it surprisingly neither mentioned nor discussed any international human rights instrument. It has been pointed out that the Court could at least have taken note of the jurisprudence of the UN Human Rights Committee with regard to the International Covenant on Civil and Political Rights (ICCPR) to which Botswana is a party.[68]

In *Good v Attorney-General*[69] the Court of Appeal after referencing the ICCPR and the African Charter on Human and Peoples' Rights refused to apply them to the issue in the case as they have not been incorporated into national law. Tebbutt JP opined that:[70]

> The rule of law is also the cornerstone of the domestic law of the country and its application is not dependent upon some concept of a quality of law inherent in the articles of international treaties or conventions, which were not in existence when the Botswana Constitution was framed.

One may question the correctness of this *dictum* not only because it throws into doubt the relevance and value of the international human rights system on which the national regime is substantially built, but it also suggests that international instruments such as the Universal Declaration of Human Rights, which came into existence before Botswana became an independent State with its own Constitution in 1966, are not relevant. This certainly is not the case. For as remarked by Amissah JP in *Dow*'s case,[71] the antecedents of the Constitution of Botswana with regard to the imperatives of the international community were greatly influenced by the European Convention for the Protection of Human Rights and Fundamental Freedoms (1950) as well as the UN's Universal Declaration of Human Rights (1948).

The performance of the Botswana courts in relying on international law in human rights litigation has been appropriately summed up as follows:[72]

---

67 *Kanane v The State* [2003] 2 BLR 67. For commentary on the case, see EK Quansah 'Same-sex relationship in Botswana: Current perspectives and future prospects' (2004) 4 *African Human Rights Law Journal* 201, KN Bojosi 'An opportunity missed for gay rights in Botswana: *Utjiwa Kanane v The State*' (2004) 20 *South African Journal on Human Rights* 466, and MM Chilisa 'Two steps back for human rights: A critique of the *Kanane* case' (2007) 1 *The Botswana Review of Ethics, Law and HIV/AIDS* (2007) 45.

68 See Killander (n 6 above) 17 referring to *Toonen v Australia,* communication 488/1992, UN Doc CCPR/C/50/D/488/1992 (1994).

69 n 44 above. For a commentary see BT Balule '*Good v Attorney General* (2): Some reflections on the national security dilemma in Botswana' (2008) 7 *University of Botswana Law Journal* 153.

70 At 357.

71 n 41 above at 152-153.

72 Tshosa (n 1 above) 201.

> When interpreting the various human rights norms in the Bill of Rights, Botswana courts have not actively and consistently referred to and relied upon similar provisions in international human rights instruments and international norms generally. Their interpretation has mainly been based on national law and jurisprudence. Admittedly, there are instances where reliance has been placed on human rights treaties such as the UDHR, ICCPR, ECHR and ACHPR as well as international customary law ... But, even in these instances such reference has been cursory. It has also occurred in few and isolated cases. Moreover, it has not been consistent and uniform.

The discussion above bears ample testimony to this conclusion.

3.3 Reliance on foreign case law in human rights litigation

The Botswana courts have constantly utilised foreign case law in determining human rights issues. In *Attorney-General v Dow*,[73] 56 foreign cases were cited and in *Bojang v The State*[74] 37 cases were cited. This sustained reliance on foreign case law is confirmed by a 2008 study of the phenomenon with regard to constitutional issues that invariably involve human rights.[75] The study revealed that of the 46 reported decisions in the Botswana Law Reports between 1993 and 2006, 379 cases were cited, making an average of eight cited cases per judgment. Of these cited cases, 253 were judgments of foreign courts, meaning that on average six foreign cases were cited per judgment. A breakdown of the jurisdictions from which the foreign cases were cited yields very interesting results. The three most commonly cited jurisdictions are South Africa, from where 125 cases, that is 49% or almost half of the foreign cases cited came from, England comes next with 50 cases (almost 20%) and the US with 37 cases (almost 15%). Other jurisdictions are international cases (12 of which were cited), Canada (8 cases), Namibia (6 cases), Australia (4 cases), Germany (2 cases), Nigeria (2 cases), Zimbabwe (2 cases) and one case each from Ghana, Sierra Leone, Lesotho and Zambia.[76]

This attitude to foreign case law may be partly attributable to the slow growth of legal jurisprudence in Botswana and partly to the educational background of the judges who sit on the bench of the superior courts. Despite Botswana's strong links with the South African legal system,[77] there appears to have been a deliberate attempt during the apartheid days to avoid appointing South Africans to the Botswana bench despite the common Roman-Dutch heritage.[78] Only those who were considered to have 'acceptable political opinions' were appointed. Nevertheless, the study shows that almost half of the judges that have sat in the superior

---

73 n 41 above.

74 n 42 above.

75 See CM Fombad 'A study on the use of foreign precedents by constitutional judges in Botswana' (unpublished, 2008). (On file with the author).

76 Fombad (n 75 above) 18.

77 See for example, GJ van Niekerk 'The use of South African law in the courts of Botswana' (2004) 37 *Comparative and International Law of Southern Africa* 312.

78 See B Othlogile *A history of the higher courts of Botswana 1912-1990* (1995) 86.

courts of Botswana until the mid-1990s have been trained in the Roman-Dutch law and the other half, English law. Consequently, generally the predisposition by judges with a Roman-Dutch background is to resort to South African and other Roman-Dutch authorities whilst those with an English law background rely on English authorities.[79]

4 Comparative attitude of judges in the two jurisdictions

From the discussion so far, although the judges in the two jurisdictions do not have a clear mandate to apply international law in human rights litigation, they have tried, when necessary, to rely on such law in order to determine human rights issues. The reliance on international law has been rather tangential as it has not been the crucial issue for determination in the human rights cases that have come before the courts. In Ghana, the provisions of articles 40 and 73 of the Constitutional could have been relied upon to apply international instruments in human rights litigation. In Botswana the provisions of section 24 of the Interpretation Act could have been utilised more.

However, the question which needs to be asked is why the judges should strive so hard to apply international law to human rights litigation when there is no obligation to do so. The answer may lie in the increasing realisation that national sovereignty, in the light of contemporary interdependence of nations, should not always be held paramount. As pointed out by Amissah JP in *Dow*'s case, Botswana being a civilised nation should as far as possible interpret its legislation in compliance with its international obligations.[80] In the *CIBA* case in Ghana, Archer JSC noted:[81]

> The court could not ignore the fact that the attainment and enjoyment of fundamental rights had become prime instruments of international relations. The struggles, exploits and demands of oppressed peoples in Africa, America and elsewhere provided helpful examples to guide the interpretation of the fundamental rights provisions of the Constitution.

Furthermore, the Vienna Convention on the Law of Treaties explicitly provides that '[a] party may not invoke the provisions of its internal law as justification for its failure to perform a treaty.'[82] Also, in every treaty there is reference to a means for parties to undertake certain steps to ensure compliance with the provisions of the treaty. For example, the

---

79 See for example, *Archibald* v *Attorney-General* [1991] BLR 169. For a commentary on the case, see CM Fombad '*Archibald* v *Attorney-General* in perspective: The role of actuarial evidence in the assessment of the dependents' damages for loss of support in Botswana' (1999) 11 *African Journal of International and Comparative Law* (1999) 245-261.

80 n 41 above.

81 n 7 above.

82 Article 27. See also Appiagyei-Atua (n 5 above).

International Covenant on Civil and Political Rights (ICCPR) provides under article 2(2) as follows:[83]

> Where not already provided for by existing legislative or other measures, each State Party to the present Covenant undertakes to take the necessary steps, in accordance with its constitutional processes and with the provisions of the present Covenant, to adopt such legislative or other measures as may be necessary to give effect to the rights recognized in the present Covenant.

Consequently, the first line of defence of human rights is the national courts and it behoves on the judiciary to do all it can to fortify this defence. International instruments are some of the effective arms in its armoury to do this.

Furthermore, the concept of the 'global village' justifies the use of international law in the national setting in the absence of an obligation to do so. This concept has internationalised judicial decision-making into 'judicial globalisation'.[84] Through conferences, workshops, judicial training programmes, seminars and other peer-to-peer interactions, judges are exposed to decisions of international tribunals, other domestic courts, etc, involving the application of international human rights and comparative norms. These experiences should therefore reflect in their decision-making.[85]

Lastly, applying international law within national jurisdictions will enable the norms contained in international human rights instruments to be more widely recognised and applied by national courts.[86] This accordingly will make international human rights a concept that ordinary people can identify with and utilise to promote their rights, interests and dignity as human beings. Furthermore, where judicial power is exercised in accordance with international human rights standards it will help safeguard the democratic constitutional order and promote human rights and good governance. [87]

The attitude of the judges in the two jurisdictions reveals a preparedness to go beyond the traditional use of unincorporated treaties as aids to interpretation. Some cases suggest that unincorporated treaties may create enforceable rights in national law.[88] However, it has been asserted that:[89]

> [T]he fact of unincorporation may be a manifestation of parliamentary resistance to the treaty. By giving effect to it absent a national implementing measure, the

83 See also A Seibert-Fohr 'Domestic implementation of the International Covenant on Civil and Political Rights pursuant to its article 2 para 2' (2001) 5 *Max Planck Yearbook of United Nations Law* 399-472.

84 See PA Panganiban 'Judicial globalization' http://www.cdi.anu.edu.au/CDIwebsite_19982004/philippines/philippines_downloads/PhilJudgolbal.pdf (accessed 11 May 2010).

85 See Appiagyei-Atua (n 5 above).

86 As above.

87 As above.

88 See Oppong (n 1 above) 315.

89 As above.

> judiciary may be indirectly setting itself up against the will of an elected branch of government or upsetting the balance of power between the various organs of government.

Notwithstanding this caveat, one may conclude that the judiciary in the two jurisdictions has not, by their attitude towards unincorporated international treaties etc, upset in any pronounced way the balance of power existing between the organs of government. Even if it has, the respective executives have begrudgingly accepted it without much fuss.

5 Has the non-incorporation of international treaties hampered the protection of human rights in the two jurisdictions?

The constitutions of both countries guarantee fundamental human rights which are predominantly civil and political rights although the Constitution of Ghana contains some social, economic and cultural rights. As indicated above, both countries adopt the dualist approach to international treaties incorporation into national law. Both countries however, have a poor record of incorporating international treaties which they have ratified. It has been said for example, that the implementation of treaties in Ghana has been beset with problems. The treaties are scattered across different ministries and it is difficult to find a comprehensive list of all the treaties ratified by Ghana.[90] These handicaps notwithstanding, it is abundantly clear from the discussion above, that the non-incorporation of international treaties into national law in both countries has not adversely affected the protection of the guaranteed human rights. A cursory look at the law reports emanating from the two countries shows that the enforcement of the fundamental human rights provisions in the respective constitutions has been vigorously sustained. Many cases have been heard and determined without necessarily relying on international treaties.[91] In fact the absence of incorporation of treaties seems to have emboldened the judiciary to use such treaties where relevant, to solidify the national legal framework for the protection of

---

90 See *Ghana: Justice sector and the rule of law* (n 5 above) 21. For Botswana, the Attorney General's Chambers is the custodian of the various treaties, protocols etc signed by that country.

91 For Ghana, see for example, *NPP v Attorney-General* (n 7 above); *NPP v Inspector General of Police* (n 25 above), *Edusei v A-G* (n 24 above); *Republic v Independent Media Corporation of Ghana & Ors* [1996-97] SCGLR 258; *British Airways & Anor v Attorney-General* [1996-97] SCGLR 547; *Republic v Tommy Thompson Books Ltd & Ors* [1996-97] SCGLR 804; *Republic v Tommy Thompson Books Ltd (No 2) & Ors* [1996-1997] SCGLR 484; *The Republic v Mensa-Bonsu & Ors, ex-parte Attorney-General; Mensima & Ors v Attorney-General & Ors* [1996-97] SCGLR 676; *Adjei-Ampofo v A-G* (n 23 above) and generally SY Bimpong-Buta *The role of the Supreme Court in the development of constitutional law in Ghana* (2007), particularly chapter 7. For Botswana see for example, *Petrus v The State* (n 59 above); *Desai v The State* [1987] BLR 55; *Media Publishing (Pty) Ltd v Attorney-General* [2001] 2 BLR 485; *Kamanakao & Ors v Attorney-General & Anor* [2001] 2 BLR 654; *Rabana v Attorney-General* [2003] 1 BLR 330; *Masuku v The State* [2004] 2 BLR 239; *Charles v The State* [2005] 1 BLR 421 and generally Fombad (n 4) above.

such rights. It would however have been more helpful if the incorporation machinery had been used to make international law part of national law thereby placing an obligation on the judiciary to use them in the adjudication process.

There have been however, occasions when the courts have shied away from applying international treaties where it seems quite relevant to the issue in the case. In *Good*'s case, for example, the Botswana Court of Appeal refused to apply relevant international covenant on the ground of non-incorporation in a case where the applicant sought to challenge his deportation on the ground that it infringed his constitutional rights. In *Issa Iddi Abass & others v Accra Metropolitan Assembly and Another,*[92] the Ghana High Court rejected an argument based on the right to housing as set out in international human rights instruments.

The overall impression that comes out of the courts' reliance on unincorporated treaties in human rights adjudication is that the lack of constitutional/statutory legitimacy has not proved to be too much of an obstacle to the protection of human rights in the two countries. More robust and frequent reliance on these international instruments would have been preferable, but in the light of the constitutional constraints and political apathy towards incorporation of international treaties faced by the courts, the report cards of Ghana and Botswana look quite good.

6 Conclusion

Although the respective constitutions of the two countries do not contain specific provisions on the use of international law as an interpretive guide, the above discussion reveals that the courts have valiantly attempted, and to some satisfactory extent succeeded, in utilising international law as an interpretative tool in human rights litigation. However, it is clear that the use of international law is not core to most judgments but rather mentioned in *obiter dicta*.[93] This situation is explicable on the basis of the dualist approach to the incorporation of international law into national law adopted by the two countries. There is a clear need to dramatically increase the rate of incorporation of treaties into the national law of the two countries. It makes a mockery of the international obligations of the two countries that they ratify these international treaties but then leave them on the shelves of the respective implementing national authorities. Based on the basic principle of *pacta sunt servanda*, the courts should strive for an interpretation that is consistent with the legal commitments that the two countries made by ratifying international treaties. When this is done, pressure will be put on the implementing authorities to put the necessary incorporation process

---

92 n 30 above.

93 See Killander (n 6 above) 23.

in motion to incorporate the relevant treaties into national law thereby enhancing respect for international law.

Whilst the courts have demonstrated autonomy from both the legislature and the executive in their attitude towards non-incorporation of international law into national law, care should be taken to ensure that this is not stretched too far to upset the checks and balances regulating the relationship between the organs of state. In order to avoid this possible dislocation, the executive and legislature must be alive to their responsibilities and put into effect the required incorporation procedures to domesticate the relevant international treaties to enable them to acquired national legitimacy to facilitate their use to consolidate the protection of human rights in the two countries.

Finally, the frequent utilisation of case law from comparative jurisdictions in human rights litigation is to be welcomed. This is an acknowledgement of the 'cross-pollination of technology, and the realities of our ever shrinking world',[94] which demands a new paradigm shift towards the universalisation of laws and of the judicial rulings interpreting them. For cross-pollination to bear enduring fruits, it is incumbent on both bar and bench in the respective jurisdictions to raise the profile of international law by frequent citation in their briefs and judgments in order to advanced the course of international law in their jurisdiction in the face of an apparent political unwillingness on the part of the executive to domesticate such law.

---

94 Panganiban (n 84 above) 3.

4

The place of international law in human rights litigation in Tanzania

Chacha Bhoke Murungu*

Summary

This chapter examines the position of international law before courts and quasi-judicial bodies in Tanzania. It examines the status of international law in Tanzania and finds that Tanzania follows a dualist approach to international law. It presents ways of transforming international law into municipal law in Tanzania. It further examines how domestic courts have used international human rights law to interpret domestic human rights provisions in the Constitution. Further, factors influencing the use of international law by courts in Tanzania are highlighted, including the role played by judges and advocates. The chapter concludes that courts apply international law, albeit cautiously. It recommends a wider application of international law principles and foreign case law by courts in Tanzania.

1 Introduction

This chapter examines the application of international law principles and norms before courts and quasi-judicial bodies in Tanzania. It adds to the already existing Tanzanian scholarship on this topic.[1] Justice Mwalusanya, until his retirement one of the most proactive Tanzanian judges with regard to human rights cases, has highlighted the difficulties of invoking international human rights instruments and foreign case law

---

* LLB (Hons) (Dar-es Salaam); LLM (Pretoria); LLD Candidate in International Criminal Law (Pretoria); Advocate of the High Court of Tanzania and member of the Tanganyika Law Society and East Africa Law Society; cbmurungu@gmail.com.

1 See C Bhoke 'Application and compliance with international human rights standards in East Africa' in the Kenyan Section of the International Commission of Jurists *Reinforcing judicial and legal institutions: Kenyan and regional perspectives* (2007) 95-118; L Mwalusanya 'The Bill of Rights and the protection of human rights: Tanzania's court experience' in HK Bisimba and CM Peter (eds) *Justice and rule of law in Tanzania: Selected judgments and writings of justice James Mwalusanya* (2005) 624-645; K Kamanga 'International human rights law as reflected in Tanzania's treaty and court practice' in W Binchy and C Finnegan (2006) *Human rights, constitutionalism and the judiciary: Tanzanian and Irish perspectives* 53-70.

by asserting that the problem is Tanzania's adherence to the common law (dualist) system where international treaties are not part of the laws of the land.[2] Though this constraint exists, justice Mwalusanya has himself, through his judgments, shown that international law has a role to play in Tanzanian human rights jurisprudence.[3]

This chapter starts with the place of human rights and international law in the Tanzanian constitutional framework and thereafter turns to how courts have used international human rights law as an interpretative tool. As will be shown it is not uncommon to find both advocates and judges referring to the international conventions and decisions from regional human rights bodies, or foreign case law. How the new Commission for Human Rights and Good Governance has used international law in its quasi-judicial mandate is also considered before the chapter concludes with a discussion of factors influencing domestic application of international law principles in Tanzania

2 The place of international law and human rights norms in the constitutional framework of Tanzania

We must first answer whether Tanzania is a dualist or monist state in as far as international treaties are concerned.[4] The centre-piece in our discussion here is the Constitution of the United Republic of Tanzania, 1977 (the Constitution).[5] But, it is necessary to trace the history behind the constitutional provisions, particularly those on fundamental rights and freedoms. The examination involves both political and legal commitments in Tanzania in respect of international law principles.

Politically, immediately after the independence ceremonies on 9 December 1961, Julius Kambarage Nyerere, the then prime minister of Tanganyika (now Tanzania mainland), went to New York to address the United Nations General Assembly. His speech on 14 December 1961 outlined, among others, Tanzania's political commitment to international human rights norms, particularly the Universal Declaration of Human Rights (UDHR). Nyerere said: [6]

---

2 Mwalusanya (n 1 above) 635.

3 For a collection of landmark constitutional cases decided by Justice Mwalusanya, see Bisimba and Peter (n 1 above). Justice Mwalusanya's judgments were sometimes criticised by the Court of Appeal see eg *Mbushuu alias Dominic Mnyaroje and Kalai Sangula v Republic,* Court of Appeal of Tanzania at Dar es Salaam, Criminal Appeal 142 of 1994; [1995] LRC 216.

4 For more on monism, dualism and transformation theories in international law see J Dugard (2005) *International law: A South African perspective* 47-80; SK Kapoor *International law and human rights* (2007) 101-118; MN Shaw *International law* (2003) 120-172.

5 The Constitution of the United Republic of Tanzania of 1977, (as amended fourteen times until 2005), Chapter One, Part III titled 'Basic Rights and Duties' (covering arts 12-29).

6 See JK Nyerere 'Independence address to the United Nations' in JK Nyerere *Freedom and unity: A selection from writings and speeches 1952-1965* (1966) 146.

> [W]e shall try to use the Universal Declaration of Human Rights as a basis for both our external and our internal policies ... [T]he underlying theme of the Universal Declaration of Human Rights ... is the basic principle which we ourselves, in Tanganyika, and we believe other peoples in Africa and other parts of the world, have been struggling to implement ... In saying this, we have committed our country to a grand endeavour ... It will be in the light of this principle that we shall try at all times to determine our stand on every international issue which we shall be called upon to consider in this Assembly or elsewhere.

The human rights contained in the Constitution have their historical antecedents in the *Principles of Tanganyika African National Unity (TANU)*, and are reflected in the *Guide to the One-Party State Commission* of 1963.[7] The human rights set out in these documents later found their way into the Constitution through Act 15 of 1984 which introduced the Bill of Rights in the Constitution. The Bill of Rights only became justiciable on 1 March 1988, after a three year grace period given to the government.

Even before the introduction of the Bill of Rights, the Constitution in article 9(a) and (f) recognised the UDHR to the extent that it provided (and still provides) that:

> [T]he state authority and all its agencies are obliged to direct their policies and programmes towards ensuring - (a) that human dignity and other human rights are respected and cherished; ... (f) that human dignity is preserved and upheld in accordance with the spirit of the Universal Declaration of Human Rights ...[8]

Although the UDHR is not a binding treaty *per se*, it nevertheless plays a seminal role in the world of human rights. It is often cited as a statement or codification of customary international law on human rights, or as an authoritative interpretation of international human rights law.[9] Article 9(f) of the Constitution incorporates the UDHR into the Tanzanian Constitution, as recognised by the courts as discussed below. The UDHR is arguably part of customary international law and would thus be incorporated into Tanzanian law as customary international law forms part of national law in the common law tradition. However, the position of the UDHR as part of the Constitution is clearly stronger as customary international law as part of the common law can be altered by any Act of Parliament.

In Tanzania, the power to enter into treaties is entrusted completely to the executive branch of the government. The legislature plays no part in the treaty-making process. Consequently, if treaties were to become part of the law in Tanzania without legislative endorsement, wide law-making powers would be conferred on the executive. However, by Act 20 of 1992, the National Assembly was vested with power to 'deliberate upon and ratify all treaties and agreements to which the United Republic [of Tanzania] is a party and the provisions of which require ratification.'

---

7 See generally Nyerere (n 6 above) 261-265.

8 Part II '*Fundamental Objectives and Directive Principles of State Policy*' art 9(a) and (f) of the Constitution of the United Republic of Tanzania, 1977.

9 W Schabas *The abolition of the death penalty in international law* (2002) 23.

Article 63 of the Constitution also gives the National Assembly the power to 'enact legislation where implementation [of an international treaty] requires legislation'.[10] These provisions show that Tanzania is a dualist state and that international law treaties do not have force of law unless they are domesticated.

Essentially, the parliament must adopt enabling legislation to give effect to an international treaty. There are three principal methods that a legislature generally employs to transform treaties into municipal law.[11] Firstly, the provisions of a treaty may be embodied in the text of an Act of Parliament; secondly, the treaty may be included as a schedule to a statute; and thirdly, an enabling Act of Parliament may give the executive the power to bring a treaty into effect in municipal law by means of proclamation or notice in the *Government Gazette*. These three methods are also applicable in Tanzania. Legislation that transform international treaties into municipal law in Tanzania include the Diplomatic and Consular Immunities and Privileges Act,[12] the Treaty for the Establishment of the East African Community Act,[13] the Territorial Sea and Exclusive Economic Zone Act,[14] the International Development Association Act,[15] the Bretton Woods Agreements Act,[16] The Civil Aviation Act,[17] the Meteorology Act[18] and the World Meteorological Organisation Convention, the Tanzania-Zambia Railway Act,[19] the Articles of Union between the Republic of Tanganyika and the People's Republic of Zanzibar and the Union of Tanganyika and Zanzibar Act.[20]

In 2008, the Government of Tanzania enacted the Anti-Trafficking in Persons Act (Act 6 of 2008). This is a comprehensive legislation dealing will all aspects of trafficking in persons. The Act domesticates the Protocol to Prevent, Suppress and Punish Trafficking in Persons (Palermo Protocol). It addresses issues of sexual exploitation, prostitution, sexual slavery, servitude, pornography, forced labour, sex tourism and related matters.

In 2009, Tanzania enacted the Child Act (Act No 21 of 2009). The purpose of this law is to provide for reform and consolidation of laws relating to children, to provide for the rights of the child, to promote, protect and maintain the welfare of the child with a view to giving effect to international and regional conventions on the rights of the child. In

---

10 Article 63(3), (d) & (e) of the Constitution.
11 Dugard (n 4 above) 61.
12 CAP 356 R.E 2002.
13 CAP 411 R.E 2002.
14 CAP 238 R.E 2002.
15 CAP 350 R.E 2002.
16 CAP 363 R.E 2002.
17 CAP 80 R.E 2002.
18 CAP 157 R.E 2002.
19 CAP 143 R.E 2002.
20 Act 22 of 1964.

addition to such human rights treaties above, Tanzania has also enacted the HIV and AIDS (Prevention and Control Act), Act 28 of 2008. The law deals with prevention, treatment, care and support and control of HIV and AIDS.

At least from 2008 to date, one can rightly assert that Tanzania has moved from a restrictive or cautious human rights regime to the open policy human rights regime. The long term effect of this may be that judges and advocates will not hesitate to refer to international human rights treaties as ratified by the state and domesticated.

3 The approach of the courts to international human rights law

Generally, when the courts refer to foreign case law, they only do so for purposes of being guided and persuaded by such authorities, for such authorities do not bind the courts. Similarly, international human rights instruments, particularly those that Tanzania has ratified, and international law principles are applied as a guide to constitutional interpretation. International treaties are interpretative tools only if they are consistent with the Constitution. The binding law is the law enacted by parliament with the Constitution at the top and judicial precedents from the Court of Appeal and High Court of Tanzania.

The former Chief Justice of Tanzania, Francis Nyalali held in *Attorney-General v Lesinoi Ndeinai and Joseph Selayo Laizer and two Others*[21] that when basic human rights are at stake or the question of interpretation of a constitutional provision arises, regard should be had to foreign case law. He said:[22]

> On a matter of this nature it is always very helpful to consider what solutions to the problems other courts in other countries have found, since basically human beings are the same though they may live under different conditions.

That international law also had a role to play, even before the introduction of the Bill of Rights, was made clear by Justice Nyalali when he, based on the reference to the UDHR in article 9 of the Constitution, said:

> [A]lthough the failure by any person or state organ to observe any of the provisions of the Universal Declaration of Human Rights will not attract legal censure or invalidation by court, I have no doubt that the courts are required to be guided by it in applying and interpreting the enforceable provisions of the Constitution and all other laws.[23]

Thus when interpreting the constitutional right to property in *John Byombalirwa v Regional Commissioner, Kagera and Regional Police*

21 *Attorney-General v Lesinoi Ndeinai and Joseph Selayo Laizer and two Others* [1980] TLR 214.

22 At 222.

23 Paper presented at the University of Dar es Salaam Law Society, on the question of the Bill of Rights, quoted in *John Mwombeki Byombalirwa v Regional Commissioner and Regional Police Commander, Bukoba Another* [1986] TLR 73, 84.

Commander, Bukoba the High Court held that the provisions of UDHR should be consulted. The Court held:[24]

> If there is any doubt as to the obligation of the law enforcement agencies and other members of the executive branch of the Government in returning the seized goods to the suspects who have been cleared by the courts I wish to point to Art. 17(2) of the Universal Declaration of Human Rights of 1948 which provides that no one shall be arbitrarily deprived of his property.

The above case was decided right before the Bill of Rights had entered into force. In that case, the Court went further to note that the UDHR was included in the Constitution through article 9(f). It remarked that the authorities should perform their duties in accordance with the provisions of the UDHR, which include the duty not to arbitrarily deprive someone of his property.

That the UDHR is incorporated into the Constitution was confirmed by the High Court in its 2005 judgment in *Legal and Human Rights, Lawyers' Environment Action Team (LEAT) and National Organisation for Legal Assistance v the Attorney General.*[25] The High Court declared handouts known as *takrima* in connection with elections unconstitutional as the practice amounted to discrimination under article 13 of the Constitution and violated the right to political participation in article 21 of the Constitution. The High Court ordered the *takrima* provisions to be struck out of the National Elections Act. With regard to the UDHR the Court held:

> Tanzania is a party to various International Human Rights Instruments. The Universal Declaration of Human Rights (UDHR), which is the core of International Human Rights law, is incorporated in Article 9(f) of our Constitution. Article 7 of the UDHR provides for equality before the law and bars discrimination. Article 21 of UDHR provides for the right to participate in the government of one's country directly or freely chosen representative.

One of the leading human rights cases which discusses the role of international law is the 1993 judgment of the Court of Appeal in *Director of Public Prosecutions v Daudi Pete.*[26] While interpreting the constitutional right to bail the Court held that when interpreting the Bill of Rights, regard must be had to the African Charter on Human and Peoples' Rights (African Charter). In the words of the Court:

> This view is supported by the principles underlying The African Charter on Human and Peoples` Rights which was adopted by the Organisation of African Unity in 1981 and came into force on 21 October, 1986 after the necessary ratifications. Tanzania signed the Charter on 31 May, 1982 and ratified it on 18 February, 1984. Since our Bill of Rights and Duties was introduced into the Constitution under the Fifth Amendment in February, 1985, that is, slightly over three years after

24 *Byombalirwa* (n 23 above) 84.

25 See *Legal and Human Rights, Lawyers' Environment Action Team (LEAT) and National Organisation for Legal Assistance v The Attorney General,* High Court of Tanzania, at Dar es Salaam (Main Registry), Misc Civil Cause No 77 of 2005 (unreported) 39.

26 *Director of Public Prosecutions v Daudi Pete* [1993] TLR 22, 34-35.

> Tanzania signed the Charter, and about a year after ratification, account must be taken of that Charter in interpreting our Bill of rights and Duties.

The Court then considered the preamble to the African Charter and held that '[i]t seems evident in our view that the Bill of Rights and Duties embodied in our Constitution is consistent with the concepts underlying the African Charter on Human and People's Rights as stated in the Preamble to the Charter.'[27] The Court then declared denial of bail under section 148(5)(e) of the Criminal Procedure Act unconstitutional and struck it out of the statute book.

In the case of *Paschal Makombanya Rufutu v The Director of Public Prosecutions,* the High Court gave the following guidance which is in line with the approach in many other common law countries:[28]

> [I]f there is any ambiguity or uncertainty in our law, then the courts can look at the international instruments as an aid to clear up the ambiguity and uncertainty seeking always to bring it into harmony with the international conventions.

In *Munuo Ng'uni* the Court gave international human rights law a more prominent role than the one quoted above when it struck down a legislative provision with reference to international human rights law.[29] The facts of the case were that a judge had instructed the petitioner, an advocate by profession, to take a dock brief for an accused person as part of the free legal aid scheme. The advocate refused, stating that such legal services amounted to forced labour as prohibited by article 25(2) of the Constitution. He further argued that the fee payable was so inadequate as to constitute an infringement of the right to just remuneration under article 23(2) of the Constitution. The judge directed that the advocate be suspended from practising. The advocate challenged this directive contending also that the directive of the judge was contrary to the right to be heard as protected under article 13(6) of the Constitution, because he was not served with a show-cause notice. On petitioning the High Court, the advocate argued that the right to a hearing is a matter of natural justice and is guaranteed by article 13(6)(b) of the Constitution as well as the UDHR and the African Charter. He further argued that the provisions of the law that were relied upon by the judge to suspend him were *ultra vires* articles 23(2) and 25(2) of the Constitution as well as article 14(3) of the UDHR and article 7(1)(c) of the African Charter.

The Court stated that 'it seems to us that the petitioner actually intends to invoke article 23(1) of the Universal Declaration [of Human Rights], of which our Constitution's article 23(1) is a replica, and article 15 of the African Charter …'[30] and observed that article 15 of the African Charter

---

27 *Daudi Pete* (n 26 above) 35.

28 *Paschal Makombanya Rufutu v The Director of Public Prosecutions*, Miscellaneous Civil Cause No 3 of 1990 (unreported) 10-11. This case is reproduced in Bisimba and Peter (n 1 above) 356-378.

29 *NIN Munuo Ng'uni v Judge-in-Charge and the Attorney General* [1998] TLR 464.

30 *Munuo Ng'uni* (n 29 above) 479.

was in *pari materia* with article 23(2) of the Constitution. The Court further held that '[b]y article 1 of the Charter, Tanzania has undertaken to adopt legislative or other international instruments, ratified by Tanzania, which comprise similar articles.'[31] The Court then reiterated the practical significance of applying international human rights instruments and foreign judicial decisions. It said that: [32]

> We feel permitted to call in aid comparative case law from foreign courts and international Bills of Rights. That is precisely the path those eminent jurists who attended the judicial colloquium at Bangalore in India in 1988 have exhorted us to tread, in the famous statement they issued known as the Bangalore Principles. These principles have been confirmed, endorsed and re-affirmed in subsequent colloquia at Harare (1989), Banjul (1990), Abuja (1991), attended by some justices of our Court of Appeal. As correctly observed in the Bangalore Principles, there is at the present time plenty of judicial decisions and an impressive corpus of international and national jurisprudence in the commonwealth concerning the interpretation and application of human rights and freedoms, which is of practical value to judges and lawyers generally.

The Court found that section 13(2)(a) of the Basic Rights and Duties Enforcement Act went against the spirit of the UDHR and other human rights treaties to which Tanzania had subscribed, such as the ICCPR.[33] The Court concluded by stating that the UDHR (article 8) and the ICCPR (article 2(3)), provide that everyone has the right to an effective remedy by the competent national tribunals for violation of human rights.[34] The Court thus awarded damages to the petitioner.

Tanzanian courts have taken note of international human rights treaties in many cases. Some of these cases have confirmed that a right similar to the one recognised in the Constitution is also provided for in international human rights law.[35] In the case of *Chiku Lidah v Adamu Omari*,[36] which concerned the rights of the child born out of wedlock to his upkeep and maintenance by his putative father, the High Court stated in respect of the Convention on the Rights of the Child that:

> [T]he conclusion reached in this case is in line with ... UN international human rights norms as contained in the Convention of (sic) the Rights of the Child. A child born out of wedlock has the right to be maintained by his or her putative father.

The courts have also in some cases gone beyond just referring to international treaties and made use of case law from international courts in interpreting constitutional provisions. For example in the case of *Peter Ng'omango v Gerson MK Mwangwa and the Attorney-General*,[37] the High

31 *Munuo Ng'uni* (n 29 above) 485.
32 *Munuo Ng'uni* (n 29 above) 480.
33 *Munuo Ng'uni* (n 29 above) 487-488.
34 *Munuo Ng'uni* (n 29 above) 489.
35 On the right to legal representation see eg *Thomas Mjengi v Republic* [1992] TLR 157.
36 *Chiku Lidah v Adamu Omari* High Court of Tanzania, at Singida, Civil Appeal No 34 of 1991 (unreported) 8.
37 *Peter Ng'omango v Gerson MK Mwangwa and the Attorney-General* [1993] TLR 77.

Court interpreted the right to access to justice guaranteed by articles 13 of the Constitution in light of the case law of the European Court of Human Rights.

Another case where the High Court invoked and accepted decisions of regional human rights bodies is that of *Christopher Mtikila and Others v The Republic.*[38] In 1993 Mr Mtikila filed a petition in the High Court at Dodoma, seeking a declaration that the citizens of Tanzania have a right to contest for the posts of president, member of parliament and local government councillor without being forced to join any political party. He wanted independent candidates to vie for electoral posts. The High Court decided in his favour. The Court, while interpreting the 'claw-back clauses' in the Bill of Rights under the Constitution, stated that restriction which claw-back clauses impose with regard to the enjoyment and enforcement of basic rights must be accompanied by adequate safeguards and effective control against arbitrary interference. Accordingly, the Court observed that this view is also 'taken by the European Court of Human Rights.'[39] The Court further supported its position by referring to article 19(3) of the ICCPR.[40]

The government filed an appeal against that decision and Mr Mtikila cross-appealed against certain decisions made adverse to him. At the same time, the government tabled a bill in parliament to legislate in anticipation against that decision of the Court. The government later withdrew its appeal but the law was passed amending the Constitution in 1994 (Act 34 of 1994). Mr Mtikila sought declarations that the amendments of articles 39 and 67 of the Constitution were unconstitutional and that he had a constitutional right to contest for the post of the president or member of parliament as a private candidate. In their submission, advocates for Mr Mtikila submitted that the amendments violated articles 21(1) and 9(a) and (f) of the Constitution. They further submitted that, the amendments were a violation of international human rights treaties to which the United Republic of Tanzania is a state party, particularly articles 20(1) and (2) and 21(1) of the UDHR and articles 10(2) and 29 of the African Charter.[41] The state attorneys did not dispute that Tanzania 'was a signatory to the Universal Declaration of Human Rights and ratified the African Charter' but invoked article 29(2) of the UDHR placing limitations to the enjoyment of rights. Citing cases from South Africa as persuasive authorities, advocates for Mr Mtikila argued that the amendments were arbitrary in that they fell short of the proportionality test as enunciated in *S v*

---

38 *Christopher Mtikila and Others v The Republic* High Court of Tanzania at Dodoma, Criminal Appeal No 90 of 1990 (unreported).

39 *Mtikila* (n 38 above) 18.

40 *Mtikila* (n 38 above) 19.

41 *Christopher Mtikila and Others v The Republic* in the High Court of Tanzania, at Dar Es Salaam Main Registry, Miscellaneous Civil Cause No 10 of 2005, judgment of 5 May 2006 (unreported) 44.

Makwanyane[42] and *S v Bhuwana.*[43] The High Court agreed that these cases were 'persuasive authorities'.[44] The Court held that the amendments to article 21 of the Constitution under Act 34 of 1994 were unnecessary and unreasonable and did not meet the test of proportionality, and declared that amendments to articles 21(1), 39(1)(c) and 67(1)(b) were unconstitutional. The Court went on to hold that:[45]

> [W]e have no doubt that international conventions must be taken into account in interpreting, not only our constitution but also other laws, because Tanzania does not exist in isolation. It is part of a comity of nations. In fact, the whole of the Bill of Rights was adopted from those promulgated in the Universal Declaration of Human Rights. To come nearer to the case at hand, Articles 20 and 21 (as originally drafted before the Amendments) of the Constitution are replica of Articles 20(1) and (2) and 21 of the Declaration. The Covenant of [sic] Civil and Political Rights which followed the declaration and ratified by Tanzania in June 1976 provides in its Article 25 thus ...
>
> Article 2 of the Convention enshrines the right of an individual without any distinction of any kind as political or other opinion. Article 29(2) of the Universal Declaration of Human Rights, relied upon by Mr Mwaimu has the same effect as Article 30(1) of the Constitution of the United Republic of Tanzania ... And so, in our opinion, the impugned provisions are not saved even under Article 29 of the Universal Declaration of Human Rights. In the event, we agree with the learned Counsel for the petitioner that amendment to Articles 21(1), 39(1)(c) and 67(1)(b) of the Constitution also contravene the International Conventions ... We therefore proceed to declare the alleged amendments unconstitutional and contrary to the International Covenants to which Tanzania is a party.

The courts have also referred to 'soft law' provisions in some cases for example in *Republic v Mbushuu alias Dominic Mnyaroje and Another*[46] which dealt with the issue of the constitutionality of the death penalty. In the course of the discussion on the right to life and the prohibition against torture, the High Court interpreted the provisions of the Constitution in light of the provisions of international human rights instruments and the decisions from foreign countries and regional human rights bodies.[47] The Court not only made reference to treaties and case law but also to the Bangalore Principles, the Declaration of Stockholm (1977) which declared death penalty as inhuman, degrading and cruel form of punishment and the resolution adopted by the United Nations Human Rights Commission at its 1989 session which confirmed this finding. The Court held that the death penalty was unconstitutional since it was inhuman, degrading and cruel. The Court of Appeal did not dispute this

42 *S v Makwanyane* (1995) (3) SA 391 (CC).
43 *S v Bhulwana* (1996) (1) SA 388 (CC).
44 *Mtikila* (n 41 above) 40.
45 *Mtikila* (n 41 above) 45-47.
46 *Republic v Mbushuu alias Dominic Mnyaroje and Another* [1994] TLR 146.
47 See for example, *Soering v UK* [1989] EHRR 439; *Riley and Others v AG of Jamaica* [1982] 3 All ER 469; *Catholic Commission for Justice and Peace v AG and Others* [1993] (1) ZLR 242.

finding but held that the death penalty was constitutional because of the limitations clause in article 30 of the Constitution.[48]

Some of the cases above indicate that the courts have made reference to international human rights law even when not determinative for the outcome of a case. In *BAWATA v Registrar of Societies*,[49] the petitioners argued that the government's act of deregistering a National Women's Council known by its Swahili acronym of BAWATA (*Baraza la Wanawake Tanzania)* was unconstitutional because it violated articles 13(6)(a), 18 and 20 of the Constitution providing for the right to fair hearing, freedom of expression and association, and assembly respectively. They further argued violation of provisions in international treaties particularly the ICCPR, the African Charter and the Convention on Elimination of All forms of Discrimination against Women (CEDAW).

The Court ruled in favour of the petitioners in that, deregistration and suspension of BAWATA was unconstitutional for violating the provisions of the Constitution. Nevertheless, the Court stated in respect of international human rights instruments that:

> Before we conclude, we think we should make an observation on what Prof. Shivji raised touching on the Universal Declaration of Human Rights charter [sic]; the International Covenant on Civil and Political Rights (ICCPR); the African Charter on Human and People[s'] Rights (the African Charter) and the Convention on Elimination of all Forms of Discrimination against Women [CEDAW]. While we are in agreement with the principles pronounced therein, in view of what transpired and our findings, we are of the settled view that it is unnecessary to go into the alleged violations of those International and [sic] Human Rights Instruments.[50]

The Court should have gone further in considering the human rights instruments cited by the legal counsel. Had the Court done so, it would have contributed to the development of human rights law jurisprudence in the country. However, the outcome would not necessarily have been different.

4 The quasi-judicial mandate of the Commission for Human Rights and Good Governance

The Commission for Human Rights and Good Governance (the Commission) was established by law in 2001.[51] It is mandated to hear complaints on human rights violations under section 15 of the Act. Since its inception, the Commission has heard and given its recommendations

48 *Mbushuu* (n 3 above).

49 *Baraza la Wanawake Tanzania (BAWATA) and 5 Others v Registrar of Societies and 2 Others*, High Court of Tanzania at Dar es Salaam, Misc Civil Cause No 27 of 1997.

50 As above.

51 Commission for Human Rights and Good Governance Act (Act 7 of 2001), as amended by Act 16 of 2001.

on only one complaint.[52] This complaint involved the right to own property, particularly ownership to land and fair compensation for loss of land following forced eviction, and destruction of crops by state authorities and agents.

In its recommendations in *Nyamuma* case, the Commission in finding for the complainant referred to the South African case of *Government of the Republic of South Africa & Others v Irene Grootboom & Others,*[53] and invoked the provisions on equality before the law, the right to own property, the right to health and reasonable standards of living as protected by the Constitution and international human rights instruments. While counsel for the complainants heavily relied on the provisions of international human rights instruments,[54] the Commission only made a cursory mention of such treaties. The Commission recommended that the government pay compensation to the victims of the forced eviction. As the recommendations have not been complied with, the case is now before the Land Division of the High Court for purposes of enforcing the Commission's recommendations.

5 Factors influencing domestic application of international law principles in Tanzania

Some judges may be reluctant to accept arguments based on human rights treaties, even if ratified by Tanzania, because not all of them have been domesticated into municipal law. However, many judges now accept international law principles and norms, though cautiously and out of their own ingenuity, and not by express legal obligations.

The problems encountered in human rights litigation in Tanzania include: Lack of human rights literature; the dualist nature of Tanzania's treaty practice; claw back clauses in the Constitution; non-justiciability of some rights, particularly socio-economic rights; and passing of laws by parliament that undermine the decisions of courts.[55] Some magistrates, judges and advocates alike were not exposed to international law, particularly human rights principles and norms at the time of their university education. This is because in the past international law was not a compulsory course. Only recently has it become a core subject for law students in universities in Tanzania. However, international law as taught in Tanzania nowadays would not provide much room for students

52 See, *Ibrahim Korosso na Kituo Cha Sheria na Haki za Binadamu dhidi ya Thomas Loy Sabaya (Mkuu wa Wilaya ya Serengeti), Alexander Lyimo (Mkuu wa Polisi, Wilaya ya Serengeti) na Mwanasheria Mkuu wa Serikali, Katika Tume ya Haki za Binadamu na Utawala Bora*, Shauri Na.HBUB/S/1032/2002/2003/MARA.

53 *Government of RSA and others v Grootboom and others* (CCT11/00) [2000] ZACC 19, 2001 (1) SA 46 (4 October 2000); ILDC 285 (ZA 2000).

54 See, written submissions by complainants, particularly those prepared by Clement Mashamba, (on file with author).

55 Cf *Mtikila* (n 41 above). Cf also the response to the Court of Appeal judgment in *Ndyanabo v Attorney-General* (2002) AHRLR 243 (TzCA 2002).

of law to grasp the various core components of international law. Currently, public international law, humanitarian law, human rights law and refugee law are taught as one subject 'international law'. These subjects should have been separated and taught as independent though related subjects. It is difficult to convince that in a period of one year all three subjects are covered fully. The subjects have their inherent requirements. It is proposed that public international law should be taught as the fundamental course before one goes on to learn more about specific aspects of international law such as international criminal law, human rights law, refugee law, humanitarian law and environmental law.

6 Conclusion

This chapter has examined the position of international law before Tanzanian courts and the Commission for Human Rights and Good Governance. It has been shown that Tanzania follows a dualist approach in international law in that international law does not have the force of law unless domesticated or transformed into municipal law. On the other hand, courts apply international law principles to interpret domestic human rights provisions in the Constitution. However, courts have rarely gone into deeper analysis of international law principles. Judge Mwalusanya's judgments were an exception in this regard.

While domestication of international treaties by parliament provides the best prospects for their enforcement, it is recommended that courts in Tanzania should not hesitate to make use of international law principles as well as international human rights treaties in interpreting human rights provisions under the Constitution even if such instruments have not been domesticated. Courts have their inherent powers to decide on matters of public interest.

5

Domestication of international human rights law in Zambia

Michelo Hansungule*

Summary

Even though an independent sovereign nation since 1964, most of Zambia's legal system remains under the straight-jacket of the British legal system of which common law is the defining characteristic. International law faces stiff challenges infiltrating the defiant Zambian legal terrain. This is largely the result of colonial heritage rather than Zambia's deliberate choice. Courts have been reluctant to make use of international law with some notable exceptions.

1 Introduction

This chapter sets out the legal framework for the use of international law by courts in Zambia and also considers recent legislative reform that has taken into consideration international law.

2 Status of treaties in Zambia

2.1 The legal framework

Zambian law is made up of Acts of Parliament and subordinate legislation, English laws, judicial precedents (common law) and customary law.[1] The Constitution is the supreme law to which all other law must defer.[2]

Zambia's Constitution does not contain a clause stating the status of international law. Generally, this is governed by common law. Zambia is a typical dualist jurisdiction.[3] Treaties must either be enacted or transformed into national law before they form part of Zambian law.

---

* Professor of human rights law, Centre for Human Rights, Faculty of Law, University of Pretoria, South Africa; michelo.hansungule@up.ac.za.

1 See Zambia's Initial report pursuant to article 62 of the African Charter on Human and Peoples' Rights, Ministry of Justice, Lusaka (2006) para 67.

2 Constitution, 1991 (amended 1996), art 1(3).

3 R Layton 'When and how can domestic judges and lawyers use international law in dualist systems' http://training.itcilo.it/ils/CD_Use.../Dualist%20Systems_Layton.pdf (accessed 6 May 2010).

Reference to English law, in particular, as well as customary law clearly underscores the anti-international law setting the Zambian legal regime essentially is. The application of English common law, equity and statutes in force in England in 1911 raises questions about the country's independence.[4]

In the common law tradition, customary international law forms part of the law of the land. However, Zambian courts have not applied customary international law in deciding cases. One of the problems, of course, is that counsel do not argue their cases based on customary international law or international law at all. Consequently, judges are not ensnared to look to customary or positive international law as sources for their decisions. This is mostly due to the historical legacy of Zambia as a common law jurisdiction which looks towards common law rather than international law for precedents to use in cases before them.

It is common knowledge that the British legal system espouses the doctrine of dualism which sees international law as separate from and subordinate to municipal law. However, Britain has had several far-reaching changes, for instance, the domestication in 1998 of the European Convention on Human Rights.[5] This signalled Britain's tilt towards Europe and, therefore, embracing the principle of giving recognition to international human rights in domestic legal system. In contrast Zambia is largely content being a dualist legal system.

2.2 Human rights treaties

Zambia has participated actively in negotiating, adopting international human rights treaties and has ratified many of the human rights treaties of the United Nations and African Union. However, it is another story when it comes to giving those treaties which the country has accepted at the international level force of law in local jurisdiction.

Zambia ratified or acceded to several UN human rights treaties as far back as the 1980s. Zambia was among the first to ratify the African Charter on Human and Peoples' Rights after it was adopted by the OAU in June 1981. However, ratification of the treaties were not followed at home with appropriate enactments to give the treaties force of law. More than twenty years later, the treaties remain unrecognised in local law.

As indicated above, the law is that treaties concluded between Zambia and other countries or organisations have no status in Zambia *ipso facto*

4 This same question was raised in Malaysia another former British colony by the then Chief Justice in that country Justice Ahmed Fairuz Abdul Halim. His Lordship the Chief Justice questioned the need to resort to English common law despite Malaysia having been independent for 50 years and proposed to replace it with Islamic jurisprudence or Sharia law – see: 'Is common law still needed?' (http://www.Thestar.com.my) However, the Malaysia Bar Council responded by saying that the common law is part of Malaysian legal system and that there is no basis to replace it: 'Call to replace common law "baseless"' (http://www.thestar.com.my).

5 UK Human Rights Act, 1998.

until after they have been domesticated and legislated into law according to the constitution. International human rights treaties developed under the auspices of either the United Nations or the African Union routinely suffer this fate. The Zambian government has explained this on numerous occasions. During its engagement with the Human Rights Council, the government explained that:[6]

> Further, Zambia has ratified regional instruments for the protection and promotion of human rights and fundamental freedoms. It is worth noting that international instruments are not self-executing and require legislative implementation to be effective in Zambia as law. Thus, an individual cannot complain in a domestic court about a breach of Zambia's international human rights obligation unless the right has been incorporated into domestic law.

The non-incorporation of international human rights agreements has been a regular source of misgivings by international human rights treaty-bodies[7] as well as local academics[8] in Zambia insistent on seeing a proper harmonisation of laws between international law applicable to Zambia and the Zambian law especially the Constitution. UN human rights treaty monitoring bodies have lambasted Zambia for not taking steps towards full implementation of conventions the country has ratified. For example, the Committee on the Elimination of Racial Discrimination in its 'concerns and recommendations' following examination of Zambia's state report[9] called on Zambia to ensure the full implementation of the prohibition of racial discrimination by inviting the country to proceed with the incorporation into domestic law of the Convention. Similarly, the Human Rights Committee expressed concerns that 'steps still remain to be taken' to harmonise the Constitution with the International Covenant on Civil and Political Rights (ICCPR).[10] The Committee indicated, *inter alia,* that the non-discrimination clause in the Zambian Constitution limits the right to non-discrimination as recognised in the ICCPR.[11]

---

6 National Report submitted in accordance with paragraph 15(A) of the annex to Human Rights Council Resolution 5/1. Zambia. Human Rights Council. Working Group on the Universal Periodic Review, Second session, Geneva, 5-16 May 2008, A/HRC/WG.6/2/ZMB/1, 9 April 2008.

7 Zambia's Second Report introduced in the Human Rights Committee, 26 March 1996, Concluding Observations of the Human Rights Committee, Zambia, UN Doc CCPR/C/79/Add.62 (1996).

8 Statement made by Mrs Mushota, acting dean, School of Law, University of Zambia, quoted in the Report of the promotional mission to the Republic of Zambia, 14-18 April 2008, http://www.achpr.org/english/Mission_repots/Zambia/mission_Zambia.pdf.

9 Committee on the Elimination of Racial Discrimination, Sixty-seventh session, 2-19 August 2005, CERD/C/ZMB/CO/16, 27 March 2007.

10 Concluding Observations of the Human Rights Committee, Zambia, UN Doc CCPR/C/79/Add.62 (1996) para 7. The Committee against Torture has raised the same concerns. See Concluding Observations of the Committee against Torture (2008).

11 Concluding Observations of the Human Rights Committee (n 7 above) para 8.

There is a large chasm between treaty law that Zambia has freely and voluntarily ratified or acceded to on one hand and local law and legislation on the other. Often times, citizens have been left confused about the purpose of concluding treaties which are not going to afford them protection and other benefits promised in those instruments.

Though there is a case to be made with regards the fact that the Bill of Rights already contains provisions of international law which have been domesticated over the years, the point still remains that some of the provisions of the Zambian Bill of Rights do not give the same protection as international human rights law. An example regularly cited to demonstrate this is the non-discrimination clause in article 23 of the Constitution. UN treaty monitoring bodies, such as the Human Rights Committee and the Committee on the Elimination of Racial Discrimination, have regularly asked Zambia to amend or repeal and replace this clause to bring it in harmony with the applicable international standard. Article 23 contains extensive limitations clauses on personal law as well as clauses which exclude non-nationals from the ambit of protection.

3 Judicial discretion

Even though there is no specific statute mandating the judiciary to use its discretion to use undomesticated international law when presiding over disputes, courts have on some occasions done so. However, the majority of judges are still hesitant to resort to international law. From independence in 1964 there were several cases to do with flagrant violations of human rights of citizens that came to the courts for determination. However, international law was never used to fortify judgments based on constitutional violations.[12]

One of the earliest cases in Zambia with regards to the use of international human rights treaties is the 1992 case of *Longwe v Intercontinental Hotels Limited.*[13] Sara Longwe, a human rights and gender activist in Zambia, had gone to Lusaka's Intercontinental hotel with her partner. At the hotel, Sara's partner remained in the car in the garage while she went to the hotel to look for a friend. She was refused access by

---

[12] For cases where international human rights law could have played a role see eg *Miyanda v Attorney-General*, SCZ judgment 22 of 1983; *Nkaka Chisanga Puta v Attorney-General*, SCZ judgment 25 of 1983; *Patel v The Attorney-General* (1968) ZR 99; *Feliya Kachusu v The Attorney*-General (1967) ZR 145. More recently, the High Court in Livingstone, in a case involving mandatory HIV testing in the Zambian Airforce, made references to the practice as being contradictory to the country's regional and international obligations which forbid discrimination. It must be placed on record though that while the Court referred to international human rights treaties, it did not base its final decision on this but on the Constitution. See: http://southerafricanlitigationcentre.orgcases/item/Zambia-Discrimination_of_HIV_postive_former_employees_of_military

[13] *Sara Longwe v Intercontinental Hotels* 1992/HP/765; [1993] 4 LRC 221.

hotel security on the grounds that she was not accompanied by a male partner. Hotel policy dictated that it would disallow access to certain parts of the hotel to unaccompanied women. The restriction did not apply to unaccompanied men. In a bid to fight what she saw as discrimination based on gender and sex contrary to the non-discrimination clause in section 23 of the Zambian Constitution, Sara decided to petition the High Court. She argued that besides article 23 of the Constitution, the conduct of the hotel constituted discrimination from which she is protected under the Convention on the Elimination of all Forms of Discrimination against Women (CEDAW) and the African Charter on Human and Peoples' Rights. The respondent (Intercontinental Hotels Limited) averred that the petitioner had no right to cite conventions which Zambia had not yet domesticated in local law and which the Court, therefore, had no jurisdiction to apply. However, the Court was alive to its discretion to apply the undomesticated conventions which the country had ratified. In his seminal ruling, Musumali J held:

> It is my considered view that ratification of such documents by a nation state without reservations is a clear testimony of the willingness of the State to be bound by the provisions of such a document. Since there is willingness, if an issue comes before court by which would not be covered by local legislation but would be covered by such international document, I would take judicial notice of that treaty or Convention in my resolution of the dispute.

The case was decided in favour of the petitioner. In his seminal decision, the judge held that:

> In deciding an issue not covered by domestic legislation, a court could take judicial notice of international treaties and conventions, like the African Charter on Human and Peoples' Rights and the Convention on the Elimination of All Forms of Discrimination against Women, when they had been ratified without reservation by a state, indicating its willingness to be bound by their provisions ...

In other words, the judge used the case to point to the important concept of 'judicial notice' which he said could be invoked as a tool in instances where the issue to be decided is not already covered by domestic legislation. In the particular case, however, discrimination that the judge was called upon to rule on was already covered specifically under article 23 of the Constitution. However, it cannot be denied that international instruments had persuasive value and helped in the ultimate decision of the Court.

Based on the common law principle of *stare decisis,* however, High Court decisions, important as they are, nevertheless do not create binding law, save for inferior courts and only in circumstances where there is no contrary ruling by another High Court or Supreme Court. Unfortunately, the High Court in Zambia was seized by a similar application a few years after the *Sara Longwe* case. In *Elizabeth Mwanza v Holiday Inn Hotel,*[14] the

---

14 *Elizabeth Mwanza v Holiday Inn Hotel*, 1997/HP/2054 (unreported).

petitioner had tried to enter another hotel in Lusaka, the Holiday Inn, when she was blocked by hotel security. Just like in the *Sara Longwe* case, hotel security cited policy which restricted unaccompanied women from accessing certain parts of the hotel. In this case, however, the judge decided there was nothing wrong with the restrictive hotel policy. In his ruling, Chitengi J found there was no violation of the prohibition from discrimination as alleged by the petitioner and found the restriction on unaccompanied women to be reasonable based on the same public policy which Sara Longwe had used in seeking remedies from the Court. Because the two cases were both decided by the High Court, the rulings did not bind other courts.

In another case, politician Edith Nawakwi, successfully petitioned against the decision of the Chief Passport Officer not allowing her to include her children on her passport without consent of their biological father with whom she no longer had contact. The consent of the other parent was demanded of female guardians only while male guardians did not have to produce consent of the mothers of their children when applying to add them to their passports. The judge in quashing the Passport Officer's decision as discriminatory cited the country's ratification of CEDAW. Based on this case, the Immigration Department has since struck out the offensive regulation.[15]

The Supreme Court, the apex court in the country, by and large remained aloof to international law until the 1995 case of *Sata v Post Newspapers Ltd and Another*.[16] Briefly, this was a case in which the applicant, a long-serving senior politician who held various positions in different governments since the country's independence, petitioned the High Court alleging that he had been defamed by the *Post* newspaper. An editorial had stated that the plaintiff's 'political prostitution' prompted the former president to fire him.

In addition to allegedly defamatory statements, the newspaper published a cartoon depicting a large snake with a human head pinned down by a prone on which was inscribed '1.6 billion'. The plaintiff's nickname was 'King Cobra'. The statement of claim included a prayer for perpetual injunction to restrain the defendants from repeating the alleged libels. The defendants pleaded that the editorial had constituted fair comment on matters of public interest. Based on this, the defendants argued that article 20 of the Constitution which guaranteed freedom of expression and the right to information provided that no law shall make provision which derogated from the freedom of the press. Further, the defendants argued that section 7 of the Defamation Act which the plaintiff had relied on permitted a margin of misstatement of facts on the

---

15 *Edith Nawakwi v Attorney-General* (1991) HP/1724, http://www.saflii.org/zm/cases/ZMHC/1991.

16 *Sata v Post Newspapers Ltd and Another* [1995] ZMHC 1 (13 February 1995); http://www.saflii.org/zm/cases/ZMHC/1995.

defence of fair comment. In other words, they argued that defence of fair comment allowed the one who pleads it not to be hundred percent sure of the facts that are the subject of comment.

In his judgment Chief Justice Ngulube, sitting as High Court Judge, made several references to international instruments as sources of law. Being the first time a member of the Supreme Court and, therefore, with power to bind inferior courts and create precedent, this case signified a major turning point in the use of international law by judges' discretion in Zambia. After referring to the First and Fourteenth Amendments to the US Constitution, Chief Justice Ngulube opened his references to international law with this line:

> It should be noted that there are international human rights instruments with similar provisions. For instance, an English court would take heed of art 10 of the Convention for the Protection of Human Rights and Fundamental Freedoms … (the European Convention) …

The Chief Justice then quoted relevant parts of article 10 of the European Convention which guarantees freedom of expression. After that, he cited article 19 of the ICCPR. He then went on to cite the African Charter in the following terms:

> In the case of Zambia and other African countries, there are also the more modest provisions of article 9 of the African Charter on Human and Peoples' Rights which declare the right of every individual to receive information and to express and disseminate his opinions 'within the law'.

So, besides making copious references to United States jurisprudence, the country's most senior jurist easily sought the help of international law in the resolution of the dispute between a powerful politician and an equally powerful newspaper. However, his observation of the African Charter as providing for what he described as 'more modest provisions of article 9 …', suggests that the Judge only had access to the Charter and may not have taken into account the decisions of the African Commission on claw back clauses ironically including those on Zambia in which the Commission decided that claw back clauses should not be interpreted in a manner that narrowed the scope of the Charter to protect rights.[17]

In *Christine Mulundika and 7 Others v The People*,[18] a constitutional reference from the magistrate court where the applicants, had been charged with unlawful assembly, the same Chief Justice, reading majority judgment of the Supreme Court, again traversed far and wide in

---

[17] *Rencontre Africaine pour la Defense des Droits de I'Homme v Zambia* (2000) AHRLR 321 (ACHPR 1996); *Amnesty International v Zambia* (2000) AHRLR 325 (ACHPR 1999). In both the two communications, Zambia unsuccessfully tried to invoke both the limitations in the Charter and its own law as escape clauses. In the latter case, the Commission stated (at para 42) that it 'is of the view that the claw-back clauses must not be interpreted against the principles of the Charter. Recourse to these should not be used as a means of credence to violations of the express provisions of the Charter …'.

[18] *Christine Mulundika and 7 Others v The People* SCJ 25 of 1995; SCZ Appeal 95 of 1995.

seeking for good practices to use in respect of freedom of assembly. The Chief Justice referred to the *Handyside* case in the European Court of Human Rights.[19] The Supreme Court found the Public Order Act Cap 104, a colonial piece of statute which required prior permission from authorities before convening assemblies unconstitutional. The reliance on case law from the European Court can be seen in the context of the drafters of the Bill of Rights being heavily influenced by the European Convention as well as practices in Commonwealth jurisdictions subject to common law.

In *Standard Bank Zambia Limited v Peter Zulu and 10 others*,[20] the applicants claimed that they had been being denied wages and gratuities. They argued that they had therefore been subjected to forced labour contrary to article 14(2) of the Constitution. The Court, in defining 'forced labour' enshrined in the Constitution as indicated, referred ILO Convention 29, which Zambia had ratified.

In a more recent decision, *Roy Clarke v The Attorney-General*,[21] which involved an attempted deportation of the applicant from Zambia to the United Kingdom, the High Court made copious references to international human rights instruments. The applicant, a British national resident in Zambia for over forty years, published a satire in one of the national newspapers in which he mocked politicians, including the president, calling them monkeys and other names of animals. The minister of home affairs under whose docket immigration and deportation falls immediately made it known he would not tolerate insults from a foreigner abusing his welcome to the country. This was followed by definitive steps to deport the applicant resulting in him lodging an emergency application to restrain the government from doing so. In his ruling, Musonda J easily upheld the application holding, *inter alia*, that the applicant only exercised his freedom of expression enshrined in the Constitution and in international law for which if he was Zambian, he would not have been punished. Consequently, the deportation order issued against him was quashed.

As shown above the judiciary has been quite slow in responding to international law applicable to Zambia in deciding cases before them. There is, in particular, a trend indicating that only certain judges are willing to make use of international law. As indicated, the former Chief Justice was quite open to the use of international law but this is now dying in the Supreme Court with his departure.[22]

---

19 *Handyside v UK* (1976) Series A No 24.

20 *Standard Chartered Bank Zambia Limited v Peter Zulu and 118 others*, SCZ 59 1996.

21 *Roy Clarke v The Attorney General*, HP/003/2004; see also the judgment of the Supreme Court, *Attorney-General v Clarke* (2008) AHRLR 259 (ZaSC 2008).

22 At a workshop on the application of human rights standards convened by this author on behalf of the Raoul Wallenberg Institute (RWI) of Human Rights and Humanitarian Law for all judges of High and Supreme Court held at Livingstone in Zambia in 1996, Chief Justice Ngulube strongly defended the judiciary against accusations that it

4 Future role of international law in the country

Leaving aside the judiciary there have been increased signs of the government embracing international law. In 1973, the one-party state Constitution had at least one important clause which it borrowed from international law. Article 24 extended protection to the 'youth', which term includes children, from exploitation and other employment-related hazards. This provision reflected ILO conventions which Zambia was party to. Government has also consistently reviewed the Industrial Relations Act governing labour and industrial relations in the country to align it with international labour conventions Zambia has ratified over time.[23]

Notwithstanding the concerns about the limitation clauses attached to the freedom from discrimination, the 1991 Constitution expanded the scope of the non-discrimination clause in article 23 by adding 'sex' among the factors for which citizens are protected from discrimination. Until then, sex-based discrimination was not one of them. Secondly, article 20 of the 1991 Constitution which guarantees freedom of expression was amended to add 'press freedom', in line with article 19 of the ICCPR.

Currently, Zambia is reviewing its Constitution through the National Constitutional Conference (NCC).[24] An important source of reference material at the disposal of the conference is international instruments Zambia has ratified or acceded to. Although there are difficulties especially from the government side in embracing international standards, in particular socio-economic rights, there is a sense in which it can be said that the country is moving towards harmonisation of international and local standards.

Similarly, policies such as the National Gender Policy adopted by the government in 1998 reflect a clear desire to incorporate international standards in the local political domain. CEDAW was central in the National Gender Policy's definition of discrimination against women. Civil society was instrumental in originating the Gender Policy and therefore, in reminding government to model the policy on CEDAW.

Civil society, in particular women's organisations, has also been instrumental in advocating for stronger women's rights. While article 23 of the Constitution prohibits the enactment of discriminatory laws, and therefore protects women's rights, it permits laws which discriminate

---

ignored international law. The Chief Justice even thought there was no need for the topic to be on the agenda because courts were already applying international human rights standards in their judgments something which, as this paper shows, was an exaggeration.

23 The Industrial and Labour Relations Act, Chapter 269 of the Laws of Zambia; Trade Union Country Report – Zambia, http://www.library.fes.de/pdf.bures.sambia/50015.pdf.

24 National Constitutional Conference (Act 19 of 2007), http://www.parliament.gov.zm/index.php?opinion-com.

against women to the extent that it has subordinated the principle of non-discrimination to a series of exceptions based on the personal laws of the individuals concerned. This leaves open the possibility to enact legislation or apply existing penal laws and tribal customs and traditions which discriminate against women. Zambian-based women's organisations have submitted proposals to the government through the constitutional review process and these submissions ensured the inclusion of some of the proposals in the draft 'Mungomba Constitution.'[25] Additionally, the women's organisations have submitted the same proposals in the form of the 'Women's Bill of Rights'.[26] The proposals are intended to strengthen protection of women using the Bill of Rights as a tool. In the end, of course, the women's bill is not going to be included in the Constitution as a separate bill but is likely to be integrated into the new Constitution's Bill of Rights. An important source of law for the proposals to the constitutional review exercises has been CEDAW and the Protocol to the African Charter on Women's Rights in Africa.

Another area in which the executive has enshrined international standards lately is children's rights. This is a difficult area because Zambia still applies the antiquated British law on family. However, Zambia has taken the first small steps, within the NCC, to harmonise children's rights in local legislation, including the Constitution, with the internationally recognised human rights of the child as set out in the UN Convention on the Rights of the Child and the African Charter on the Rights and Welfare of the Child. It is hoped that the end result of the constitutional review will lead to strong commitment to the international rights of the child.

The recognition of children's rights has received impetus from the judiciary. Following a High Court decision outlawing the practice of meting corporal punishment on children,[27] the government revised the Penal Code and relevant legislation[28] to enshrine the principle in line

---

25 http://www.crc.org.zm/download/The Draft Constitution.pdf; see also http://www.ncczambia.org.

26 SH Longwe & R Clarke 'The long struggle to stop Zambian hotels discriminating against women: The implications for the women's movement in Zambia' (2008) (on file with author).

27 *Banda v The People* (2002) AHRLR 260 (ZaHC 1999).

28 Following the *Banda* case, government took legislative steps to implement the judgment through a series of amendments to the relevant penal legislation as follows: Criminal Procedure Code (Amendment) Act 9 of 2003, Penal Code (Amendment) Act 10 of 2003, Education (Amendment) Act 11 of 2003, Prisons (Amendment) Act 16 of 2004, www.parliament.gov.zim/index/php?opinion-com. All these amendments were meant to expunge the penalty of corporal punishment in line with the judgment. However, it would appear the legislature ignored corporal punishment in the Local Courts Act, Cap 29 of the Laws of Zambia. Sections 15 to 18 of this Act provide for the penalty of corporal punishment for anyone found to have acted or omitted to act contrary to African customary law as determined by a local court within its jurisdiction. If this is

with international trend to outlaw the application of corporal punishment and declare the sentence a violation of human rights. Therefore, corporal punishment is illegal under the penal and criminal procedure codes, illegal in schools, and illegal in prisons. However, it is not yet illegal in society under African customary law which means by failing to amend the Local Courts Act, government seems to be saying that it can still be applied in institutions like family as part of enforcing customary law. This leaves a serious loophole that urgently needs to be filled.

As illustrated above, while government may not positively incorporate a particular treaty into domestic law, some of the international standards are already found in local law or in the process of being incorporated. The country's direction in as far as finding a harmony between international and domestic law is therefore not totally disappointing.

5 Conclusion

Zambia is a practicing dualist. English law is still strong in Zambia as it is in most common law jurisdictions. It is said that 'old ideas die hard'. Old ideas on law, rights and justice introduced by colonialism still haunt the country. This has deprived citizens of benefits due to them under international law. It also means that the state, which negotiates, adopts and ratifies these instruments which give citizens additional rights, does not do so in good faith. The sacred international law principle of *pacta sunt servanda* is easily breached by the state when at home. However, all is not lost. As shown above, courts have to some extent used their discretion to make reference to international law when adjudicating cases. We have also seen positive signs from the government itself rescinding its earlier strong position against international law and bowing to civil society demands for a government based on law, including international law.

the case, corporal punishment, though outlawed by the High Court and subsequently legislation, is still in force with regards offences under the Local Courts Act.

6

The application of international law in the Ugandan judicial system

Busingye Kabumba*

Summary

This chapter examines the approach that courts in Uganda have taken with regard to the application on international law. Judges have on many occasions not been comfortable engaging with questions of international law that have arisen in domestic cases. In these instances, they have chosen to substantially avoid engaging with the international law aspects of the disputes by deciding the cases on municipal law grounds where possible. However, sometimes the failure to invoke applicable international legal norms has been a deliberate strategy on the part of advocates who might either have felt that arguments based on international law may not be availing, or were themselves not adequately conversant with the relevant norms. At other times, courts have used international law as an aid to interpretation of domestic law, particularly in the context of constitutional litigation. The courts' use of international law constitutes a recognition that the Constitution of Uganda (1995), and the Bill of Rights in particular, was inspired by and based upon the international human rights law regime. Judges have therefore felt comfortable having regard to the jurisprudence of international and regional human rights tribunals to shed light on the scope of constitutional provisions that mirror those in various conventions on human rights.

---

* LLB (1st Class Hons) (MU), Dip LP (LDC), BCL (Oxford), LLM (Harvard). Lecturer on law, Makerere University, Uganda. E-mail: bkabumba@law.mak.ac.ug. I would like to thank the Centre for Human Rights, University of Pretoria as well as the Amsterdam Centre for International Law, University of Amsterdam, for facilitating my attendance at the Conference on International Law and Human Rights Litigation in Africa, held in Lagos, Nigeria, where I first presented this paper. The comments on the paper that I received from the various participants at this conference are also gratefully acknowledged. Special thanks also go to the anonymous reviewer of this paper whose very helpful insights and comments have greatly improved the quality of this final version of the paper. Last but by no means, the diligent effort and untiring patience of Magnus Killander of the Centre of Human Rights, University of Pretoria, throughout the process of commissioning and production of this paper are appreciated. All errors or omissions in the text are of course my sole responsibility.

1 Introduction

Uganda is a common law country having been a former British colony.[1] The highest court in the land is the Supreme Court, followed by the Court of Appeal and the High Court.[2] It is a dualist country, and international law therefore does not operate automatically but requires a process of domestication and incorporation into the national legal system. This chapter examines the application of international law in the above courts of record.[3] The legal framework for the application of international law in Ugandan courts is first examined, followed by a study of how courts have actually dealt with the interaction of international and national law.

2 Legal framework for the application of international law in Uganda

Judges in Uganda are enjoined to administer law in accordance with the Judicature Act (Cap 13), section 14(2) of which gives the framework for the exercise of the courts' powers:

> Subject to the Constitution and this Act, the jurisdiction of the High Court shall be exercised – (a) in conformity with the written law, including any law in force immediately before the commencement of this Act; (b) subject to any written law and insofar as the written law does not extend or apply, in conformity with – (i) the common law and doctrines of equity; (ii) any established and current custom or usage; and (iii) the powers vested in, and the procedure and practice observed by, the High Court immediately before the commencement of this Act insofar as any such jurisdiction is consistent with the provisions of this Act; and (c) where no express law or rule is applicable to any matter in issue before the High Court, in conformity with the principles of justice, equity and good conscience.

It is apparent that international law is not explicitly recognised as a source of law under the above provision, and that, to be applied in Ugandan courts, a treaty must be ratified in accordance with the Ratification of Treaties Act (Cap 204) and then domesticated by an Act of the Ugandan parliament.[4]

---

1 The country achieved her independence from Britain on 9 October 1962.

2 The Court of Appeal also serves as court of first instance with regard to constitutional matters, appeals from which lie to the Supreme Court. The Court of Appeal is referred to as the Constitutional Court when it adjudicates in this capacity.

3 The judicial system includes lower courts such as magistrates courts, as well as specialised tribunals and courts that while having the powers of the High Court, operate in substantially diverse spheres. These include: The Tax Appeals Tribunal, the Industrial Court, the Non-Performing Assets Recovery Trust (NPART) Tribunal, the General and Field Courts Martial (for military matters) and the Uganda Human Rights Commission.

4 See for instance the Arbitration and Conciliation Act (Cap 4), the Atomic Energy Act (Cap 143), the Bretton Woods Agreements Act (Cap 169), Diplomatic Privileges Act (Cap 201), the East African Development Bank Act (Cap 52), the East and Southern African Management Institute Act (Cap 126), the Eastern and Southern African Trade

Section 2(b) of the Ratification of Treaties Act gives parliament the power to ratify treaties by way of resolution of that body where the treaty in question relates to armistice, neutrality or peace; or with regard to a treaty in respect of which the Attorney-General has certified in writing that its implementation would require an amendment of the Constitution. All other treaties can be ratified by Cabinet in accordance with section 2(a) of the Act, provided that they are laid before parliament 'as soon as possible' in accordance with section 4 of the Act.

It should also be noted that the Constitution is the supreme law of the land and has binding force on all authorities and persons throughout Uganda.[5] Under article 2(2), where any other law is inconsistent with any of the provisions of the Constitution, the Constitution shall prevail and that other law or custom shall be null and void to the extent of the inconsistency. To the extent that international law is incorporated into the national legal order as written law, it is subordinated, as a matter of Ugandan law, to the provisions of the Uganda Constitution.[6]

Regard may also be had to article 119(5) of the Constitution which provides that no agreement, contract, treaty, convention or document by whatever name called to which the government is a party or in respect of which government has an interest, shall be concluded without the legal advice from the Attorney-General. The Constitutional Court has noted, in the context of a contract signed between a government parastatal and a private entity, that failure to comply with this provision has the effect of rendering a contract null and void in terms of article 2(2) of the Constitution.[7] It would appear that, as a matter of national law, this would be the same position in the case of an international agreement concluded without the advice of the Attorney-General as required under article 119(5).

---

and Development Bank Act (Cap 53), the Foreign Judgments (Reciprocal Enforcement) Act (Cap 9), the Geneva Conventions Act (Cap 363), the International Development Association Act (Cap 189), the International Finance Corporation Act (Cap 190), and the Reciprocal Enforcement of Judgments Act (Cap 21). See also *East African Development Bank v Ziwa Horticultural Exporters Limited* (High Court Misc Application No 1048 of 2000, arising from Companies Cause No 11 of 2000), http://www.ulii.org/ug/cases/UGCommC/2000/8.html (last accessed November 15, 2009), wherein Okumu-Wengi J made passing reference to the fact that the Arbitration and Conciliation Act (Cap 4) domesticated the Convention on the Recognition and Enforcement of Foreign Arbitral Awards (1958), at 5.

5 Art 2(1).

6 Of course, the position under international law is that expressed under art 27 of the Vienna Convention on the Law of Treaties (1969) to the effect that a state cannot invoke the provisions of its internal law as justification for its failure to perform a treaty.

7 See *Nsimbe Holdings Ltd v The Attorney General & Anor,* Constitutional Petition No 2 of 2006, [2007] UGCC 4 (6 November 2007), http://www.kituochakatiba.co.ug/nsimbe%20holdings.pdf (last accessed April 24, 2010), at 11-14.

Further, the Constitution under article 123(1) vests the president or a person authorised by him with the power to make treaties, conventions, agreements or other arrangements between Uganda and any other country or between Uganda and any other international organisation or body, in respect of any matter. Parliament is given the duty under article 123(2) to make laws to govern the ratification of treaties, conventions, agreements or other arrangements made by the president under article 123(1).[8]

In addition, article 286 provides that where any treaty, agreement or convention with any country or international organisation was made or affirmed by Uganda or the government on or after 1962 and was still in force immediately before the coming into force of the Constitution,[9] or where Uganda or the government was otherwise a party immediately before the coming into force of the Constitution to any such treaty, agreement or convention,[10] then such treaty, agreement or convention shall not be affected by the coming into force of the Constitution, and Uganda or the government, as the case may be, shall continue to be a party to it.

Finally, it is also important to have regard to the provisions of principle 28(i)(b) of the National Objectives and Directive Principles of State Policy, an introductory section in the 1995 Constitution of Uganda. This principle is to the effect that the foreign policy of Uganda shall be based on, among other things, respect for international law and treaty obligations.[11] There thus appears to be a positive constitutional requirement upon the executive arm of government to conduct the nation's foreign affairs in a manner that respects international law. It should be noted however that the provisions of principle 28(1)(b) are not in and of themselves a basis for the application of international law in Uganda, but rather provide a domestic legal basis holding the executive

---

8 The law made under this provision is the Ratification of Treaties Act (Cap 204) and the regulations made there under.

9 Art 286(a).

10 Art 286(b).

11 Although the justiciability of such introductory statements in constitutions has been questioned, there is a growing body of jurisprudence to the effect that such sections have a measure of enforceability. See for instance: *Société United Docks v Government of Mauritius* [1985] LRC (Const) 801 (Mauritius Supreme Court and Privy Council); *Minerva Mills & Ors v Union of India* (1981) (1) SCR 206 (Indian Supreme Court); and *NTN Pty Ltd & NBN Ltd v The State* [1988] LRC (Const) 333 at 352 (per Barnett J, Papua New Guinea Supreme Court). In the Ugandan context, early validation of the importance of their importance came in the form of a statement by Justice Egonda-Ntende in *Tinyefuza v Attorney General* Constitutional Petition 1 of 1996 (unreported) to the effect that these principles '... ought to be our first canon of construction of this constitution' and that they provided '... an immediate break or departure with past rules of constitutional construction.', at 18. In any case, the matter has been definitively settled by the introduction of a new art 8A in the Constitution under clause (1) of which the country is to be governed based on 'principles of national interest and common good enshrined in the national objectives and directive principles of state policy.'

accountable in the municipal sphere for infractions of international law. Admittedly, in the course of such enquiry the court would have to enquire into the relevant 'international law and treaty obligations' alleged to have been disrespected, but it would do so only in such manner as it would for instance enquire into the content of French law if the constitutional duty upon the executive were to respect that law in the conduct of Uganda's foreign policy.

Having set out the legal framework for the application of international law in Ugandan courts, we now proceed to examine how the courts have actually approached the question of the interaction between international law and the national legal order.

3 International law in Ugandan courts

As shown below, a number of approaches have been taken by the courts when faced with questions concerning the application of international law to disputes or other matters that have arisen before them.

3.1 Judicial avoidance of questions of international law

One approach adopted by judges has been to simply avoid engaging with questions of international law which has taken the form of deciding cases on the narrowest possible grounds as long as they are perceived to be sufficient to dispose of the case at hand.

In *Soon Yeon Kong Kim and Another v Attorney General,*[12] a reference to the Constitutional Court arising from the criminal trial of two Korean nationals before a magistrate for several offences under the Penal Code Act, the question was whether, under article 28 of the Constitution (right to a fair trial), an accused person was entitled to disclosure of copies of statements made to police by persons who would or might be called to testify as prosecution witnesses as well as of copies of documentary exhibits that would be offered in evidence by the prosecution before being called upon to plead the charges.

In advocating for an affirmative answer to the question, counsel for the applicants argued, among other things, that the wording used in the provision was deliberately similar to the wording of most international instruments and constitutions of foreign countries relating to human rights. He cited in particular article 14 of the International Covenant on Civil and Political Rights and article 6 of the European Convention on Human Rights, both of which he said were in *pari materia* with article 28.[13] He further submitted that the judicial considerations of the articles of international instruments or constitutions of foreign countries that

---

12 *Soon Yeon Kong Kim and Another v Attorney General* Constitutional Reference No 6 of 2007, [2008] UGCC 2 (7 March 2008). http://www.ulii.org/ug/cases/UGCC/2008/2.html (accessed 15 November 2009).

13 *Soon Yeon Kong Kim* (n 12 above) 3.

were in *pari materia* with the provision of the Ugandan Constitution under consideration were persuasive authorities to the Court.[14]

For her part, the Senior State Attorney who represented the respondent did not specifically reply to these arguments although she referred to the rule of constitutional interpretation to the effect that where the words in question were clear and unambiguous, the Court had to give effect to their primary, plain, ordinary and natural meaning unless that would lead to absurdity or to conflict with some other provisions of the Constitution thus seeming to imply that it was unnecessary to have recourse to extraneous legal authorities.[15]

Although the Court ruled in favour of the applicants, it did not refer to the arguments based on reference to international law, choosing to rely instead on judicial authorities from Kenya and South Africa.[16]

In *Uganda Association of Women Lawyers and Others v Attorney General,*[17] the plaintiffs sought a declaration that certain provisions of the Divorce Act (Cap 249) contravened constitutional guarantees to equality and non-discrimination. Twinomujuni JA observed, in reference to arguments of counsel for the plaintiffs, that since no issue had been framed as to whether contravention of an international human rights convention amounted to a contravention of the Constitution, he would make no consideration or holding on the matter.[18]

In the above cases, it was open to the judges to use the opportunity availed by the case to offer guidance regarding the application of the relevant international legal norms. However, the judges were more comfortable operating within the realm of pure municipal law, a trend perhaps attributable to the fact they may have felt themselves unqualified to opine on questions of international law.

3.2 Advocates' case strategies

On other occasions the failure to deal squarely with questions of the application of international law has been a result of a deliberate choice by counsel to restrict their assertions to domestic law as opposed to judicial reluctance to engage with the relevant international law issues.

For instance, in *Law and Advocacy for Women in Uganda (LAWU) v Attorney General,*[19] a petition that sought a finding that certain sections of

---

14 As above.

15 *Soon Yeon Kong Kim* (n 12 above) 4.

16 *Soon Yeon Kong Kim* (n 12 above) 8-9.

17 *Uganda Association of Women Lawyers and Others v Attorney General* Constitutional Petition 2 of 2003, [2004] UGCC 1 (10 March 2004) http://www.kituochakatiba.co.ug/law%20&advocacy%204%20women(2)(Judgment%20of%20the%20court).pdf (accessed 15 November 2009).

18 *Uganda Association of Women Lawyers* (n 17 above) 24-25.

19 *Law and Advocacy for Women in Uganda (LAWU) v Attorney General* Constitutional Petitions Nos. 13 /05 /& 05 /06 [2007] UGCC 1 (5 April 2007) http://www.ulii.org/ug/cases/UGCC/2007/1.html (accessed 15 November 2009).

the Penal Code Act (Cap 120) and the Succession Act (Cap 162) contravened constitutional guarantees to, among others, equality and non-discrimination, violation of international law was initially framed as issue for the Court to determine. Thus, the very first declaration sought was that:

> [S]ection 154 of the Penal Code Act and the relevant provisions of the succession Act ... violate Articles 20, 21,(1), 21 (2), 21 (3), 24, 31 (1), 33(6) and 44(a) of the Constitution of Uganda, 1995 and *infringe fundamental human rights enshrined in International Conventions that Uganda is signatory to.* [Emphasis added][20]

However, when the parties appeared before the Registrar of the Constitutional Court for a scheduling conference (as required by the Court rules) the reference to violations of rights contained in international conventions was dropped leaving no room for the Court to address the issue.[21]

Similarly, in *Attorney General v Paul K Ssemogerere and Anor*,[22] the petition sought, among other things, a declaration that the Referendum (Political Systems) Act 2000 was unconstitutional,

> in that it violates the obligations of Uganda to respect the Fundamental Rights to free speech, free and fair elections, freedom of association and freedom of assembly *embodied in various International Human Rights Conventions to which Uganda is a party or with which Uganda is otherwise obligated to comply* and in the premises the Act is in contravention of Articles 20, 52 (h) and 286 of the Constitution and Clause XXVIII of the National Objectives and Directive Principles of State Policy of the Constitution. [Emphasis added][23]

There was thus a clear issue for the determination of the Court, that is to say, whether there is a distinct obligation to respect, as a matter of national law, its obligations under international law. However, as in the *LAWU* case (above), at the hearing of the petition before the Constitutional Court (more than three years after its filing), this issue was not among those framed for determination, and was in the event never pronounced upon either by the Constitutional Court or by the Supreme Court in its appellate jurisdiction.[24]

Therefore, lawyers must share the blame for the times that arguments could or ought to have been made on the basis of the country's international legal obligations. It is difficult to account for these 'disappearing' international law issues. Evidently counsel in both cases were cognisant of the applicable international legal norms, otherwise they would not have framed issues touching thereon in the first place. The explanation must therefore be that somewhere in between the filing

---

20 *LAWU* (n 19 above) 3.

21 *LAWU* (n 19 above) 6.

22 *Attorney General v Paul K Ssemogerere and Anor* Constitutional Appeal 3 of 2004, [2004] UGSC 35 (2 September 2004) http://www.ulii.org/ug/cases/UGSC/2004/35.html (accessed 15 November 2009).

23 *Ssemogerere* (n 22 above) 3.

24 *Ssemogerere* (n 22 above) 4.

of the petitions and the hearing of the cases, counsel made conscious and deliberate decisions not to assert claims based on applicable international law. If this is the case, their choice must have been informed either by their lack of confidence in the courts to appreciate and engage with claims based on international law, or by lack of confidence in their own ability to properly articulate these particular issues. Unfortunately, neither of these possibilities bodes well for the development of a coherent body of jurisprudence on the application of international law in Uganda.

3.3 International law as a guide to constitutional interpretation

The above notwithstanding, one major application of international law by Ugandan judges has been as a guide to interpretation of the 1995 Constitution, following an approach that has been adopted by a number of other commonwealth jurisdictions.[25]

Perhaps the earliest stipulation of such a role for international law was the dictum of Egonda-Ntende J in *Tinyefuza v Attorney General*[26] wherein he stipulated that:

> In matters of interpretation where the words of the Constitution or other law are ambiguous or unclear or are capable of several meanings a benchmark has been established to enable us make a choice. And the choice ought to lead to a just, free and democratic society ... In doing so we may have to use aids in construction that reflect an objective search for the correct construction. *These may include international instruments to which this court has acceded and thus elected to be judged in the community of nations.*[27] [Emphasis added]

The Supreme Court used international law in the case of *Charles Onyango Obbo and Anor v Attorney General.*[28] In finding that section 50 of

---

25 See for instance: *Shehla Zia & Others v WAPDA* [1996] 1 CHRLD 83 at 85 (Pakistan); *Chu Kheng Lim v Minister of Immigration, Local Government and Ethnic Affairs* (1992) 176 CLR 1 (Australia); *R v Secretary of State for the Home Department, Ex Parte Brind* [1991] 1 AC 696 (United Kingdom); *Re Public Service Employee Relations Act (Alberta)* [1987] 1 SCR 313 at 349-350 (Canada); *R v Goodwin* (No 2) [1993] 2 NZLR 390 (New Zealand Court of Appeal); *R v Sin Yau-ming* (1991) 1 HKPLR 88, at 107 (Hong Kong Court of Appeal); *Vishaka v State of Rajasthan* AIR 1997 SC 3011, at 3015 (India Supreme Court); *Attorney-General of Botswana v Unity Dow* [1991] LRC (Const) 574 (High Court of Botswana), [1992] LRC (Const) 623 (Court of Appeal of Botswana); *State v Ncube* 1990 (4) SA 151 (Supreme Court of Zimbabwe); *In re Corporal Punishment* 1991 (3) SA 76 (Supreme Court of Namibia); *Rattigan v Chief Immigration Officer of Zimbabwe* (1994) 103 ILR 224, [1994] 1 LRC 343, 1995(2) SA 182 (Supreme Court of Zimbabwe); *Matadeen v Pointu* [1999] 1 AC 98 (Judicial Committee of the Privy Council on appeal from the Supreme Court of Mauritius); *Kartinyeri v Commonwealth* (1998) 152 ALR 540, at 598 (Kirby J of the High Court of Australia); *Tavita v Minister of Immigration* [1994] 2 NZLR 257, at 266 (Cooke P of the New Zealand Court of Appeal); and *Athukorale v Attorney General of Sri Lanka* (1997) 2 BHRC 610 (Supreme Court of Sri Lanka).

26 *Tinyefuza* (n 11 above).

27 *Tinyefuza* (n 11 above) 18.

28 *Charles Onyango Obbo and Anor v Attorney General*, Constitutional Appeal No 2 of 2002, ILDC 166; [2004] UGSC 1, 11 February 2004 http://www.ulii.org/ug/cases/UGSC/2004/1.html (accessed 15 November 2009).

the Penal Code Act (which made publication of false news a criminal offence) contravened article 29 of the 1995 Constitution (freedom of expression) the Court had recourse to various international instruments to interpret the Constitution.

Mulenga JSC for instance observed that the European Convention for the Protection of Human Rights and Fundamental Freedoms (ECHR) protected the right to freedom of expression under article 10 and went ahead to cite the European Court of Human Rights (ECtHR) decision in the *Lingens* case[29] to the effect that freedom of expression constituted one of the essential foundations of a democratic society and one of the basic conditions for its progress and for each individual's self-fulfilment.[30] Odoki CJ similarly relied on article 10 of the ECHR as well as on article 19 of the International Covenant on Civil and Political Rights (ICCPR) to make the point that although the Uganda Constitution did not define what constituted freedom of expression, it was generally accepted that it entailed the freedom to hold opinions and to seek, receive and impart information and ideas of all kinds, either orally, in writing, in print, in the form of art, or through other chosen media, without inference by public authority and regardless of frontiers. He went on to quote the European Court's judgment in *Handyside v The United Kingdom*[31] as authority for the assertion that freedom of expression was inherent in the concept of a democratic and pluralistic society.[32] Tsekooko JSC for his part took the view that by incorporating into the Constitution human rights provisions set out in 'various international instruments', the framers of the Constitution had consciously opted for an objective test in determining what was restrictions on fundamental rights were 'acceptable and demonstrably justifiable in a free and democratic society' as required under article 43(2).[33]

A similar use of international law was made in *Muwanga Kivumbi v Attorney General*[34] a constitutional petition that sought a declaration that section 32(2) of the Police Act (giving the power to police to prohibit the convening of an assembly or the formation of a procession in any public place) contravened, among others, the constitutional rights to freedom of expression and assembly. In upholding the petition, Byamugisha JA (who delivered the lead judgment) noted that while the state had attempted to justify the extensive police powers by referring to section 13 of the United Kingdom Public Order Act of 1986 (which gave to the police similar powers to prohibit a procession if they had reasonable

---

29 *Lingens v Austria* (1986) 8 EHRR 407.

30 *Lingens* (n 29 above) 9.

31 *Handyside v The United Kingdom* (1976) 1 EHRR 737 para 49.

32 *Onyango Obbo* (n 28 above) 22-23.

33 *Onyango Obbo* (n 28 above) 33.

34 *Muwanga Kivumbi v Attorney General* Constitutional Petition No 9 of 2005, [2008] UGCC 4 (27 May 2008), http://www.ulii.org/ug/cases/UGCC/2008/4.html (accessed 15 November 2009).

ground to believe that it would result in public disorder) the position in that country had changed with the enactment of the Human Rights Act of 1998 which domesticated the ECHR. The judge noted that article 29 of the Uganda Constitution was modelled on the ECHR and that it protected, with regard to political protest, the rights to peaceful assembly, freedom of expression, freedom of thought, conscience and religion as well as the right to respect for family and private life.[35]

Similarly, in *Col (Rtd) Dr Kiiza Besigye v Yoweri Museveni Kaguta and the Electoral Commission*,[36] a presidential election petition, Odoki CJ took the view that article 1(4) of the Constitution ('The people shall express their will and consent to be governed through regular free and fair elections of their representatives or through referenda') incorporated the principles enshrined in articles 21 of the Universal Declaration of Human Rights (UDHR) and article 25 of the ICCPR (that all citizens have the right to take part in the government of their country directly or through freely chosen representatives) such that the breadth of the right to participation had to be considered with reference to those international instruments.[37]

In the same vein, in *Shabahuria Matia v Uganda*,[38] a criminal revision on reference from a lower court, in which the question before the High Court was whether there had been an abuse of court process in respect of an accused person who had been on remand on a murder charge for close to four years because of failure of the state to commit him to the High Court for trial. Justice Egonda-Ntende observed that it was useful to examine the considerations that had been developed in other common law jurisdictions and international tribunals in respect of whose founding treaties or conventions Uganda had acceded to.[39] The judge went on to cite the United Nations Human Rights Committee (HRC) decision in *Lubuto v Zambia*[40] in support of the proposition that consideration had to be taken of the period between laying of the charge and the completion of proceedings against the accused and noted that in the instant case the three year and nine month period the accused had been on remand constituted inordinate delay amounting to an abuse of court process.[41]

---

35 *Kivumbi* (n 34 above) 11.

36 *Col (Rtd) Dr Kiiza Besigye v Yoweri Museveni Kaguta and the Electoral Commission* Election Petition 1 of 2001 (Supreme Court) (unreported).

37 *Besigye* (n 36 above) 40. Cited with approval by Justice Arach-Amoko in *Nambooze Betty Bakireke v Bakaluba Peter Mukasa and Another* (Election Petition No. 14 of 2006) [2007] UGHC 6 (19 January 2007) http://www.ulii.org/ug/cases/UGHC/2007/6.html (accessed 15 November 2009) 5-6.

38 *Shabahuria Matia v Uganda* Criminal Revisional Cause No MSK 00 CR 0005 of 1999 [1999] UGHC 1 (30 May 1999) http://www.ulii.org/ug/cases/UGHC/1999/1.html (accessed November 15, 2009).

39 *Shabahuria Matia* (n 38 above) para 29.

40 *Lubuto v Zambia*, communication 390 of 1990, UN Doc CCPR/C/55/D/390/1990/Rev. 1 (1995).

41 *Shabahuria Matia* (n 38 above) para 38.

However, perhaps the most extensive reference to international law as an interpretative aid was by the Supreme Court in the important case of *Attorney General v Susan Kigula & 417 Ors,*[42] that challenged the constitutionality of the death penalty in Uganda. Although it is not apparent that any issue was framed regarding the state's international obligations, the majority of the Court, as well as the sole dissenting judge, used references to international law to support their alternating views of the relationship between constitutional provisions on the death penalty and on the right to life and freedom from torture.

The majority noted that the fact that the UDHR, the African Charter on Human and Peoples' Rights (ACHPR) as well as the ICCPR provided for the right to life and the right to freedom from torture it could not be said that by these provisions these international instruments had thereby abolished the death penalty.[43]

The Court further observed that the inclusion of the word 'arbitrarily' in article 6(1) of the ICCPR and in article 4 of the ACHPR was a recognition that under certain circumstances a person could be lawfully deprived of their life, and further that article 6(2) of the ICCPR recognised the reality that certain countries retained the death penalty while article 6(4) of the same Covenant provided safeguards for the imposition of such sentences. To buttress the point, the Court cited the decision by the UN Human Rights Committee in *Chitat Ng v Canada*[44] which found that extradition of a fugitive to a country that enforced the death sentence in accordance with the requirements of the Covenant could not be regarded as a violation of the obligations of the extraditing country under the ICCPR.[45]

The Court similarly had regard to the Convention Against Torture and Other Cruel, Inhuman or Degrading Treatment or Punishment (CAT) and noted that article 1 thereof left no doubt that the Convention did not apply to a lawful death sentence.[46]

Further, in considering the question whether hanging as a method of execution was constitutional, the Court considered paragraph 9 of the United Nations Resolution on Safeguards Guaranteeing the Rights of Those Facing the Death Penalty to the effect where capital punishment occurred, it had to be carried out so as to inflict the minimum possible suffering.[47]

Having noted the relevant international law position, and after observing that the Ugandan Constitutional provisions guaranteeing the

---

42 *Attorney General v Susan Kigula & 417 Ors* Constitutional Appeal No 03 OF 2006, ILDC 1260; [2009] UGSC 6, 21 January 2009 http://www.ulii.org/ug/cases/UGSC/2009/6.html (accessed 15 November 2009).

43 *Kigula* (n 42 above) 9-11.

44 *Ng v Canada*, communication 469/1991.

45 *Kigula* (n 42 above) 10-14.

46 *Kigula* (n 42 above) 12.

47 *Kigula* (n 42 above) 13.

right to life and freedom of torture were in *pari materia* with the corresponding provisions in the ICCPR, the Court went ahead to observe that: [48]

> The above instruments are some of those that lay out the framework governing the imposition of capital punishment. States are urged to strive to achieve the goal of the abolition of capital punishment by guaranteeing an unqualified right to life. But it is also recognized that for various reasons some countries still consider it desirable to have capital punishment on their statute books. *The retention of capital punishment by itself is not illegal or unlawful or a violation of international law. It is in that context that we now proceed to discuss the constitutional provisions regarding capital punishment in Uganda.* [Emphasis added]

Although it might appear at first blush as though the Court were consciously considering the question as to whether Uganda's retention of the death penalty violated its international legal obligations, a holistic reading of the judgment reveals that this extensive discussion was merely a backdrop to the substantive discussion on the meaning and application of the provisions of the Uganda Constitution to the matter before the Court.

A similar use of international law was made by the sole dissenting judge, Egonda-Ntende Ag JSC, who took a different view on the question as to whether the death penalty specifically provided for in article 22(1) of the Constitution had to be read in conformity with article 24 (freedom from torture) and article 44 (non-derogability of the right to freedom from torture). The learned judge found authority for the proposition that all three articles had to be read together in a decision of the European Court in *Soering v United Kingdom*[49] wherein the Court had noted that the Convention had to be read as a whole and that article 3 (freedom from torture) had to be construed in harmony with the provisions of article 2 (right to life).[50] Like the majority, he placed reliance on the HRC decision in *Chitat Ng v Canada*,[51] although to different effect. He highlighted the fact that the Committee in that case had actually noted that while article 6(2) of the Covenant allowed the imposition of the death penalty under certain limited circumstances, any method of execution had to be designed in such a way as to avoid conflict with article 7, and that specifically, it had to be carried out in such a way as to cause the least possible physical and mental suffering.[52] He went on to make this revealing statement:[53]

> Article 2(1) of the European Convention on Human Rights is in *pari materia* with article 22(1) of our Constitution. So is article 3 with article 24 of our Constitution.

---

48 *Kigula* (n 42 above) 14.

49 Application No 14038/88 delivered on 7 July 1989. The judge also referred to the ECtHR decision in *Ireland v United Kingdom* (application No 531 of 1971) regarding the meaning of inhuman treatment under article 3 of the ECHR.

50 *Kigula* (n 42 above) 49-51.

51 n 44 above.

52 *Kigula* (n 42 above) 50-51.

53 *Kigula* (n 42 above) 51.

> The approach by the European Court to read the said provisions in harmony is in line with the established approach to constitutional interpretation here in Uganda. Reading the provisions together is essential in order to grasp the full meaning of the provisions bearing upon the same subject. *The reasoning of the European Court is very persuasive. The European Convention on Human Rights is the forerunner of the bill of rights found in many independence constitutions, and post independence constitutions.* The jurisprudence of the European Court is therefore quite persuasive. [Emphasis added]

Later when discussing the HRC's decision in *Ng v Canada*, the judge noted:[54]

> It is clear that the Committee treated articles 6 and 7 of the International Covenant as not in conflict as noted by the majority judgment. It is also very clear that the Committee read and interpreted both articles in harmony, without separating them, or ignoring one provision in preference to the other, an aspect of the decision ignored by the majority judgment. The approach of the Committee is very persuasive as it is clearly consistent with our rule of harmony in constitutional interpretation as espoused by this Court in *Paul Ssemogerere v Attorney General*, Constitutional Appeal No.1 of 2002.

Reading the above enumeration, the judge may as well have been referring to a judgment of a Constitutional Court in another jurisdiction regarding the interpretation of a similar constitutional provision.

Finally, regard may also be had to the case of *Victor Juliet Mukasa & Yvonne Oyo v The Attorney General,*[55] which was an unprecedented judgment in the area of rights of lesbians, gays, bisexual, transgender and intersex (LGBTI) persons in Uganda. The case arose from an incident in 2005 when the two applicants, two lesbians living in a Kampala suburb, were subjected to various indignities by the police and local council officials. Their home was forcefully entered and ransacked, some of their property confiscated, and the second applicant undressed in the presence of male officers in a bid to ascertain whether she was really a woman. The presiding judge, Justice Arach Amoko found that the applicants' rights to privacy and to freedom from torture, inhuman and degrading treatment, under articles 27 and 24 of the Ugandan Constitution respectively, had been violated and awarded them damages.

What is important here is the fact that, in finding that there had been a violation of the right to freedom from torture, Justice Arach Amoko made reference to article 1 of the Universal Declaration of Human Rights on the equality of all human beings in dignity and rights. The judge also referred to article 3 of the Convention on the Elimination of All Forms of Discrimination against Women (CEDAW) on the entitlement of women to the equal enjoyment and protection of all human rights.[56]

---

54 *Kigula* (n 42 above) 52.

55 *Victor Juliet Mukasa & Yvonne Oyo v The Attorney General* High Court Miscellaneous Cause 247 of 2006; (2008) AHRLR 248 (UgHC 2008).

56 *Mukasa* (n 55 above) para 42. For a commentary on this case, see B Kabumba 'The Mukasa judgment and gay rights in Uganda' (2009) 15(1) *East African Journal of Peace and Human Rights* 218-224.

The picture that emerges is one of constant regard to international law as an aid to constitutional interpretation, with courts providing various justifications for such reliance. While Justice Egonda-Ntende's early dicta in *Tinyefuza v Attorney General*[57] and *Shabahuria Matia v Uganda*[58] seemed to suggest that reliance in this regard could only properly be had to those treaties to which Uganda had acceded since they represented the standards by which the country had 'elected to be judged in the community of nations', subsequent cases appear to have departed from this strict approach. The dominant view, and one later adopted by Justice Egonda-Ntende himself in *Attorney General v Susan Kigula & 417 Ors,*[59] appears to be that the Bill of Rights had been modelled upon various international conventions, including the European Convention on Human Rights (which Uganda is not a party to), and that it was only logical to have regard to the jurisprudence of international tribunals interpreting provisions similar to those of the Uganda Constitution.

However it is important to note in this regard the decisions of international tribunals are treated as merely persuasive and not as binding upon the court. In this sense, they are at par with decisions of foreign courts and tribunals touching on similar subject matter. In effect, when used as aids to constitutional interpretation there is no distinction between 'international' law and 'comparative' law – both being employed as external, albeit persuasive, law.

3.4 The place of international law in the Ugandan legal order

Apart from the use of international law as a guide to constitutional interpretation, courts have also on occasion seriously reflected upon the interaction between international law and municipal law and, in particular, the proper place of international law in the domestic legal framework.

However the views they have expressed on this question have been diverse and, on occasion, rather radical. We therefore propose in this section to critically assess these views in light of the constitutional provisions and statutory law in Uganda on the application of international law in the domestic sphere.

3.4.1 The duty to interpret domestic law in a manner consistent with undomesticated international agreements

We may take as a starting point of reference the dictum by Egonda-Ntende Ag JSC in *Attorney General v Susan Kigula & 417 Ors,*[60] wherein in

---

57 *Tinyefuza* (n 11 above).
58 *Shabahuria Matia* (n 38 above).
59 *Kigula* (n 42 above).
60 *Kigula* (n 42 above).

considering the implications of Uganda accession to the ICCPR he opined as follows:

> It is worthwhile noting that Uganda acceded to the International Covenant on Civil and Political rights on 21st September 1995 and to the First Optional Protocol on 14th February 1996. At the very least the decisions of the Human Rights Committee are therefore very persuasive in our jurisdiction. *We ignore the same at peril of infringing our obligations under that treaty and international law. We ought to interpret our law so as not to be in conflict with the international obligations that Uganda assumed when it acceded to the International Covenant on Civil and Political Rights.* [Emphasis added][61]

Justice Egonda-Ntende's statement above highlights the crucial distinction between the use of international law in the persuasive sense as an aid to constitutional interpretation and a serious consideration of the consequences of international legal obligations upon domestic adjudication. While he establishes the former as the basic minimum where international legal obligations are entailed, he further postulates what appears as a commonsense approach whereby the judiciary strives to adopt an interpretation of domestic law that as far as possible conforms to international legal obligations already assumed. The latter approach would serve to ensure that the executive arm, whose function it is under the Constitution to conduct Uganda's foreign relations, is not embarrassed in that function by domestic decisions that disregard obligations assumed under international agreements.

At the same time, implicit in the statement is a recognition that unless international agreements are incorporated into domestic law by Act of Parliament, the courts can only take cognisance of the obligations contained therein and try to avoid interpretations of the domestic law that would conflict with undertakings on the international plane.

Justice Egonda-Ntende's guidance is a useful and uncontroversial postulation of the delicate balance that must be struck between maintaining the integrity of domestic law and respecting obligations assumed under international agreements that have yet to be domesticated.

3.4.2 International agreements as part of the Constitution?

A more radical statement of the position of international treaties in Ugandan law has been postulated by Twinomujuni JA in *Uganda Law Society & Anor v The Attorney General.*[62] This case concerned the indictment, trial and execution of two soldiers in March 2002 for murder. The petitioners sought declarations that the entire process was unconstitutional as contravening the rights to a fair trial and to life.

---

61 *Kigula* (n 42 above) 52.

62 *Uganda Law Society & Anor v The Attorney General* Constitutional Petitions No 2 & 8 of 2002, [2009] UGCC 1 (5 February 2009) http://www.ulii.org/ug/cases/UGCC/2009/1.html (accessed 15 November 2009).

While no issue was framed regarding violations of international law, Justice Twinomujuni JA, in delivering the lead judgment of the Constitutional Court, observed as follows:[63]

> It is said that there is no right of appeal as such unless that right has been specifically created by the relevant statute. This means that where a Statute grants a jurisdiction to a court, then unless the Statute states that a person aggrieved by a decision of such a court can appeal, then there is no right of appeal. This further means that there is no automatic right of appeal. This is frequently asserted in our courts as if we forget that the African Charter on Human and Peoples Rights [Banjul Charter] which was adopted on 27th June, 1981 by the OAU and which came into force on 21st October, 1986 *is part and parcel of our Constitution.* This is so by virtue of (Article 286 – international agreements, treaties and conventions remain valid upon coming into force of the Constitution) … [Emphasis added]

Twinomujuni JA's assertion to the effect that the Banjul Charter is 'part and parcel of our Constitution' is surprising insofar as it seems to suggest that, by virtue of article 286 of the Constitution, treaties which entered into force before the coming into force of the 1995 Constitution are automatically incorporated into the Constitution. In fact, article 286 was only meant as a saving provision, to avoid a construction that the treaties were invalidated by the promulgation of the new constitutional order. In the language of article 286, such treaties were not to be 'affected by the coming into force of this Constitution' and Uganda would continue to be a party to them. The effect of this *dicta* would be to elevate what would at best be an Act of Parliament (if domesticated), and subject to the provisions of article 2 of the Constitution (the supremacy clause), to the status of a part of the Constitution, whose provisions would then be understood as having primacy over any other inconsistent law.

This anomaly was pointed out Kavuma JA who noted that: [64]

> I agree that by virtue of (Article 286) of the Constitution, the African Charter on Human and Peoples' Rights (the Banjul Charter) remains part of our law and Uganda as a country and its Government continue to be a party to it. …
> I find myself unable to state with absolute certainty that by virtue of that article the African Charter on Human and Peoples' Rights automatically became a part of our Constitution although it remains part of the law of the land.

This appears to be a more accurate statement of the position under article 286, and was an important clarification coming as it did in the same case.

3.4.3 International agreements as sources of rights not expressly stipulated under the Constitution

The two learned Justices of Appeal in the *Uganda Law Society* case (above) however had another divergence of opinion that is important to consider, regarding the effect of the African Charter.

---

63 *Uganda Law Society* (n 62 above) 19.

64 *Uganda Law Society* (n 62 above) 34.

Twinomujuni JA took the view that the Charter could be used, not just as an aid in the interpretation of the Constitution, but as an authoritative source of rights not expressly provided for under the Constitution. Having noted that article 7 of the African Charter provided for a right of appeal as an aspect of the right to due process, he then related this to article 45 of the Constitution and was of the opinion that this provision was authority for reading a right of appeal into the Constitution. In his words:[65]

> I stated earlier in this judgment that article 45 … of our Constitution clearly states that Chapter IV of the Constitution is not exhaustive of fundamental human rights and freedoms available to the people of Uganda. An automatic right of appeal where one's fundamental rights and freedoms have been violated is one good example. In the instant case the accused persons in the Kotido trial were entitled to a right to life guaranteed under article 22(1) of the Constitution. *The right of appeal was therefore automatic. A denial of that right was clearly unconstitutional.* [Emphasis added]

For his part, Kavuma JA did not think that article 45 could be interpreted as allowing the 'reading in' of the right to appeal in particular. In his view, the solution lay in article 286 of the Constitution by virtue of which the African Charter and other treaties entered into before the coming into force of the Constitution remained 'part of the law of the land':[66]

> [T]he accused persons had a right of appeal, the Banjul Charter playing the role of being the equivalent to an operationalizational (sic) law to Article 28 of the constitution ...
>
> In my view, a right of appeal *should be specifically conferred by statute*. This, as just indicated above, is where the (Banjul Charter) comes in handy to provide the necessary bridge between the UPDF Act and Article 28 which calls for confirmation of the death sentence by the Highest Appellant Court. This removes an apparently serious lacuna in our law. [Emphasis added]

The irony of course is, the African Charter has not in fact been domesticated by an Act of the Ugandan parliament and cannot therefore be regarded as part of the 'law of the land' as Kavuma JA consistently refers to it. As such, if it is indeed the case, as he notes, that a right of appeal 'should be specifically conferred by statute' then the true legal position must be that there was no right of appeal in the instant case as there was no 'statute' in force providing for it.

However, the broader doctrinal divergence between the two justices remains important. Which of the two approaches better reflects the position under Ugandan law: the Twinomujuni JA position to the effect that article 45 of the Constitution allows for reading into the Constitution rights provided for under treaties Uganda has signed; or the stricter and, arguably, more positivist Kavuma JA stance that requires a treaty to first

---

65 *Uganda Law Society* (n 62 above) 20.

66 *Uganda Law Society* (n 62 above) 34.

be domesticated by an Act of Parliament before it can be said to confer rights and obligations?

Having regard to the generous and purposive wording of article 45, as well as the manifest intention of the framers which appears to have been a desire to expand rather than restrict the scope and breadth of rights protected under the Constitution, it would appear that Twinomujuni's approach is better reflective of the legal position. It appears that the framers of the Constitution left open the question as to what would be the legitimate sources of the 'silent' rights contemplated under article 45. It is pertinent for the purposes of this analysis to set out this provision in its entirety:

> The rights, duties, declarations and guarantees relating to the fundamental and other human rights and freedoms specifically mentioned in this Chapter shall not be regarded as excluding others not specifically mentioned.

It is difficult to imagine a broader or more generously worded provision. However it is noteworthy that the provision is restricted to 'fundamental and other human rights', such that the Twinomujuni approach would not apply to for instance purely commercial rights or other interests not related to human rights.

The question that arises however is – if it is to be accepted that treaties can be a source of rights not expressly mentioned in the Bill of Rights, which treaties can be accepted as being competent for this purpose? Must Uganda have signed, ratified and domesticated the treaty? Is it even necessary that Uganda have some nexus to the treaty by way of having been involved in the negotiations leading up to it, or can, for instance, the courts look to an agreement entered into in East Asia suffice for article 45 purposes? It is noteworthy that in the instant case Twinomujuni JA seemed satisfied that Uganda was a party to the African Charter and even though it is not clear that he ascertained that the Charter had been ratified.[67]

The question of which treaties can be incorporated through article 45 is best considered using the lenses of constitutional law and the rules on constitutional interpretation. One of the most cardinal of these rules is what is referred to as the 'harmonisation' principle, which requires that the Constitution be read as a whole and in such a manner that its provisions reinforce each other. As stated by the United States Supreme Court in *State of South Dakota v State of North Carolina*,[68] which formulation has been cited with approval in a number of Ugandan constitutional cases:[69]

---

67 Uganda ratified the Charter on 10 May 1986.

68 *State of South Dakota v State of North Carolina* 192 US 286 1904 448 at 465.

69 See for instance *Paul K Ssemogerere and 2 Others v Attorney General* Constitutional Appeal 1 of 2002, per Mulenga JSC at 4-5 of his judgment; cited with approval in *Paul Kafeero & Herman Kazibwe v The Electoral Commission & The Attorney General*, Constitutional Petition 22 of 2006, http://www.kituochakatiba.co.ug/Paul%20Kafeero%20&

> It is an elementary rule of constitutional construction that no one provision of the Constitution is to be segregated from the others and to be considered alone, but that all the provisions bearing upon a particular subject are to be brought into view and to be interpreted as to effectuate the great purpose of the instrument.

In view of this principle, and in further view of article 123 (providing a role for parliament with regard to treaties entered into by the president or his representative); article 20(1) (fundamental rights and freedoms of the individual are inherent and not granted by the state) as well as article 126(1) (judicial power is derived from the people and must be exercised in conformity with the law and with the values, norms and aspirations of the people); it would appear that, as a minimum, judges using the Twinomujuni approach should refer to treaties signed and ratified in accordance with the Ratification of Treaties Act.

This approach would increase the legitimacy and acceptability of the norms thus adopted, by addressing the democratic deficiency that would arise from a process that circumvented parliament, and at the same time would give effect to the manifest intention of the framers in wording article 45 in the way they did. In the same vein, it would not be necessary that the treaty in question be actually domesticated by an Act of Parliament, as required by section 14(2) of the Judicature Act, as this would seem to be an unjustifiable fetter on the operation of article 45.

The above notwithstanding, it should be emphasised that the article 45 mechanism by which international law norms can be incorporated into the constitutional fabric of the land is restricted to the special situation of 'fundamental and other human rights' and should not be widened to include such cases as, for instance, pure commercial disputes.

However it is also true that often the line between human rights and other rights and obligations may be blurred as illustrated in the case of *Nantume Shamira v Kampala City Council & 2 Ors.*[70] This was an action brought by the plaintiff (who was at the time of filing, a minor) against, among others, two other minors for fraudulent acquisition of the tenancy of two shops in Kampala. In finding for the plaintiff, Choudry J felt compelled to address the peculiar circumstances of the case which involved minors and their capacity to contract and to sue or be sued:

> In my view the minor's contractual obligations and their rights under the Human Rights Legislation can only be resolved if the test applied is that of choice or right to express his or her view as stated in Article 12 of the Convention on the Rights of the Child (1989) which states that: 'Parties shall assure to the child who is capable of forming his or her own view the right to express that view freely in all matters affecting the child, the views of the child being given due weight in accordance with the age and maturity of the child.' If the child lacked the capacity to choose or

---

%20anor%20vs%20A.G._%20Const%20Pet%2022_06.pdf (accessed 25 April 2010), per Kitumba JA, at 10.

70 *Nantume Shamira v Kampala City Council & 2 Ors* High Court Civil Suit No. 33 of 2007, [2009] UGCommC 8 (30 March 2009) http://www.ulii.org/ug/cases/UGCommC/2009/8.html (accessed 15 November 2009).

> give a view, he or she cannot be a party to an agreement and suit agreement would be void (sic).[71]

It is apparent that the learned judge used the language of 'human rights' and then proceeded to use this as a basis to apply the Convention of the Rights of the Child (CRC) in what appears to have been a clear cut commercial dispute that fell to be resolved by black letter principles of contract law. Although the Judge did not refer to article 45, this particular case illustrates the uncertainty that can ensue if the Twinomujuni approach is not restricted to cases that squarely implicate human rights.

The preceding analysis highlights the fact that on the whole the Ugandan bench is not quite appraised with the proper application of international law in Uganda. Fortunately, the courts' jurisprudence has so far proved to be more enhancing than restrictive of human rights. However, since the integrity of judicial system based on the doctrine of precedent requires a coherent and rational application of legal principles in a way that promotes certainty and predictability, it is imperative that subsequent cases reflect the constitutional and legal framework governing the relationship between international law and domestic law.

3.5 Judges as advocates of international law

The preceding discussion has shown that judges in Uganda, when they do choose to address themselves to international law questions, seem to have a special affinity towards this body of law. This affection has in some instances seen judges actually emerge as champions or 'advocates' of international law in some sense, insofar as they have exhorted the parliament to domesticate certain international conventions to which Uganda is a party, or reprimanded the executive when they have attempted to shirk international obligations already entered into.

For instance, *Re Muwanguzi Perez (An Infant) & In Re: An Application For Guardianship By Steven William Denney & Anor*[72] involved a married couple from the United States that sought an order for legal guardianship of a Ugandan minor. Although Egonda-Ntende J granted the order sought, he pointed out that the most appropriate order in the circumstances would have been an adoption order. At the same time, however, he recognised that despite the best intentions of the applicants and their evident suitability to adopt the child, as well as the fact that the surviving parent of the minor favoured adoption to guarantee him a better life than she could provide, the applicants could not qualify for the order, given that they had not resided in Uganda for three years or fostered the child

---

71 *Nantume Shamira* (n 70 above) 5.

72 *Re Muwanguzi Perez (An Infant) & In Re: An Application For Guardianship By Steven William Denney & Anor* HCT-00-FD-FC-0170-2008, [2008] UGHC 78; [2008] 62 (26 November 2008), available at http://www.ulii.org/ug/cases/UGHC/2008/144.html (accessed 15 November 2009).

for 36 months as required by the law. The judge went ahead to make this interesting observation:

> *[T]his country has not signed on to the Convention on Protection of Children and Co-operation in respect of Inter-Country Adoption which entered into force on the 1st May 1995.* This convention establishes, inter alia, safe mechanisms and avenues of cooperation between states in respect of inter-country adoptions that allow for state agencies to cooperate and ensure that there is protection for children that are the subject of the inter- country adoptions. *As Uganda has not acceded to this convention, there is no mechanism available for our agencies involved with children services to cooperate with agencies of the states that form the major destinations for our children in need of a home. The time is overdue for the executive and parliament to reconsider our law on adoption to bring it in line with the said convention, while at the same time, acceding to the convention.*[73] [Emphasis added]

The Supreme Court made a similar plea in *Bank of Uganda v Banco Arabe Espanol,*[74] a case that concerned the Central Bank's liability, as guarantor, to repay US $ 1 000 000 that the Uganda government had borrowed from a Spanish bank. The Central Bank sought to deny liability to pay on the grounds that the loan agreement had been frustrated by the Uganda government policy of liberalising coffee and foreign currency trading and that the agreement was not enforceable against the Bank as it had not been executed under seal. In dismissing both grounds, and affirming the Bank's duty to repay the loan, Kanyeihamba JSC (who delivered the lead judgment) noted that: [75]

> *The facts and circumstances of this case have always been simple, clear and admitted. Uganda, a sovereign state and its central bank, freely and willingly sent their emissaries to Spain looking for a loan which they got from the respondent, a respectable banking institution, and they accepted the terms and conditions of that loan which the Government received* ... In pursuit of technical points and questionable arguments and authorities, the borrower and the guarantor hired the services of advocates to delay the repayments on sheer technicalities. It is now more than ten years and after some seven volumes of records of proceedings and submissions in this court, and in courts below that this case has been finally disposed of in favour of the respondent ... *There have been cases in the past and presumably there will be more such cases in the future, in which it is right and proper to plead and argue vigorously for the sovereignty of the state of Uganda and in its defence and its institutions against all sorts of claims. In my opinion, this was not one of them.* [Emphasis added]

The Supreme Court in this regard appears to have taken a stance decisively in favour of good conduct by Uganda as a member of the community of nations. The Court's observations are especially interesting insofar as they recognise that the conduct of international relations might involve situations where the state has to protect its interests against the claims of other members of that community. The Court seems to advise the executive to choose its 'battles' carefully. It

---

73 *Muwanguzi Perez* (n 72 above) paras. 14-16.

74 *Bank of Uganda v Banco Arabe Espanol* Supreme Court Civil Appeal No. 8 of 1998 [1998] UGSC 1 (1 January 1998) http://www.ulii.org/ug/cases/UGSC/1998/1.html (accessed 15 November 2009).

75 *Bank of Uganda* (n 74 above) 11-12.

would further appear that the Court holds out to the executive the promise of 'cooperation' in deserving cases, when, presumably, the sovereignty of the state, the security of its people or the integrity of its institutions are at stake.

A similar stance is observed in the remarks by Mpagi-Bahigeine JA in *Uganda Association of Women Lawyers and Others v Attorney General,*[76] wherein she noted that:[77]

> It is ... important to note and appreciate that the 1995 Constitution is the most liberal document in the area of women's rights than any other Constitution South of the Sahara. This was noted at the Judicial Colloquium on the Application of International Human Rights Law at the Domestic Level, held on 9-11 September 2003 in Arusha-Tanzania. It is fully in consonance with the International and Regional Instruments relating to gender issues. (The Convention on the Elimination of All forms of Discrimination Against Women (CEDAW) which is the women's Bill of Rights and the Maputo Protocol on the Rights of Women in Africa [2003]). Be that as it may, its implementation has not matched its spirit. *There is urgent need for Parliament to enact the operational laws and scrape all the inconsistent laws so that the right to equality ceases to be an illusion but translates into real substantial equality based on the reality of a woman's life, but where Parliament procrastinates, the courts of law being the bulwark of equity would not hesitate to fill the void when called upon to do so or whenever the occasion arises.* [Emphasis added]

While the learned Justice could be taken as primarily advocating for the operationalisation of the Constitution and not necessarily CEDAW or the Maputo Protocol, it is clear that she considered that the fact that the Constitution incorporated the provisions of the 'women's bill of rights' increased its legitimacy and informed her call for parliament to give effect to its provisions through the enactment of consistent laws and the repeal of inconsistent ones.

It is thus evident that some Ugandan judges appreciate the advantages to be gained from the interaction of domestic and international law. They seem in particular to recognise that domestic law has a lot to gain from this interaction, insofar as international legal standards may be the best vehicle for achieving justice in the adjudication of domestic disputes. It goes without saying that this attitude bodes well for the future development of a coherent jurisprudence on the application of international law in Uganda.

3.6 The silence regarding the applicability of customary international law

While, as evidenced above, there has been a reasonable amount of discussion of the application of international law in Uganda, it is apparent that the greater part, if not all, of this discussion has centered on

---

76 *Uganda Association of Women Lawyers and Others v Attorney General* Constitutional Petition No. 2 of 2003, [2004] UGCC 1 (10 March 2004) http://www.kituochakatiba.co.ug/law%20&advocacy%204%20women(2)(Judgment%20of%20the%20court).pdf (accessed 15 November 2009).

77 *Uganda Association of Women Lawyers* (n 76 above) 45.

international conventions and the decisions of international tribunals considering their provisions, and there has been no discussion regarding the place of customary international law in the Ugandan legal order.

This may be due in part to the fact that while the Constitution variously mentions international conventions, it appears to be silent regarding customary international law. While the Constitution is similarly silent regarding the place of decisions of international tribunals, the common law training of Ugandan judges ensures that they are comfortable using as persuasive authority not only decisions from other jurisdictions but also those of international courts and tribunals as seen above. The closest the Constitution comes to recognizing customary international law as a source of legal obligations is in principle 28(i)(b) which, as noted earlier, enjoins the state to base its foreign policy on respect for 'international law' as well as treaty obligations and which appears to be a recognition of the clear distinction between treaty obligations specifically entered into and 'general' international law, including customary international law.[78]

The temptation in the face of this silence is to comment as Stephen Toope once did in the Canadian context: '[w]e know for certain that we do *not* know whether customary international law forms part of the law of Canada'.[79] While we would not go as far as this in light of the language of principle 28(i)(b) there is a real lack of clarity as to how customary international law can properly be applied in Uganda. It appears clear that Uganda's reception of English common law and adoption of certain statutes has involved the incorporation into the country's legal system of a number of principles grounded in customary international law.[80] However it remains unclear what role, if any, the courts have as regards that customary international law that is not reflected in Acts of Parliament or in the common law as at the date of its reception in Uganda.[81] This is an area where the guidance of the courts is much needed.

---

78 However, see the discussion above regarding the nature of the enquiry into international law under this principle.

79 SJ Toope, 'The uses of metaphor: International law and the Supreme Court of Canada' (2001) 80 *Canadian Bar Review* 534 at 536, cited in S Beaulac 'Customary law in domestic courts: Imbroglio, Lord Denning, stare decisis' in CPM Waters (ed) *British and Canadian perspectives on international law* (2006) 379-392 at 386.

80 Such statutes may include the Visiting Forces Act (Cap 308), Extradition Act (Cap 117), the Trading with the Enemy Act (Cap 364), the Control of Alien Refugees Act (Cap 62), the Diplomatic Privileges Act (Cap 201), the Diplomatic Property and Consular Conventions Act (Cap 202), the Foreign Seamen Deserters Act (Cap 300)

81 English law was received in the Uganda Protectorate (as it then was) on 11 August 1902 by virtue of the British Order-in-Council, of the same date establishing Jurisdiction in the Uganda Protectorate, London, vol 95, 1901-02, 636-696.

4 Conclusion and recommendations

This paper has shown that while judges in Uganda have not been entirely comfortable dealing with questions of international law that arise before them, there are signs that the courts are increasingly willing to engage with the question of the interaction between international law and the national legal system.

It is crucial that this nascent awareness of, and engagement with, international law by Ugandan judges be actively nurtured and groomed. One way to do this could be through the recently established Judicial Studies Institute, an initiative by the judiciary aimed at enhancing the capacity of judicial officers. International law and its relation to Ugandan law should be introduced as one of the subjects taught at this Institute as a way of equipping the judiciary with the knowledge necessary to adequately deal with these complex issues when they do arise before them.

Moreover, this process can be facilitated by a bar that is similarly abreast of the potential uses to which international law can be employed in asserting claims before domestic courts. As such, a deliberate process needs to be put in place to develop a bar that is cognisant of the principles of public international law and how they relate to the domestic system. A first step in this process could be the upgrading of international law as a subject in the nation's law schools, from its elective status to a compulsory course, while permitting students a choice regarding whether or not to take up more specialised course offerings such as international criminal law, international economic law and others. In addition, international law should be integrated into the curriculum of the bar course at the Law Development Centre (LDC), which qualification is a prerequisite for one to practice law in Uganda. This would be a good way to ensure that all advocates are aware of international law and its interaction with the Ugandan legal order.

The above steps are especially important given the introduction of a War Crimes division of the Uganda High Court, which will be tasked with trying members of the Lord's Resistance Army (as an alternative to their hand over to the International Criminal Court), and which is already having difficulty identifying Ugandan lawyers with knowledge of international criminal law to serve as prosecutors, defence counsel and to fulfil other roles in the Court.

To cater for those attorneys already in practice, and in view of the fact that judges are usually appointed from the ranks of senior advocates who might not have had exposure to international law at the time they were in law school,[82] it is also important to include training in international law

[82] Under art 143(1)(e) of the Constitution of Uganda, a person is only eligible for appointment as a judge of the High Court if they have practised as an advocate for not less than ten years.

as part of the Continuous Legal Education (CLE) offered to lawyers by the Uganda Law Society.

At the same time, it is noteworthy that there is a dearth of local scholarship in international law. Apart from the occasional newspaper commentary or journal article, no local text exists on international law; this notwithstanding the fact that a number of current law teachers have done dissertations on the subject that could be published for wider dissemination. Those students who do choose to offer international law will therefore be presented with texts by authors such as Harris and Brownlie, which, while authoritative, do not sufficiently engage with questions such as the relevance of international law for developing countries in general and African countries in particular.[83]

There is an evident need for Ugandan scholars to undertake research into the trends of judicial application of international law in Uganda as well as wider questions of the relevance of international law to the country's development and other needs. In this regard, as the saying goes, the harvest is plentiful, but the (Ugandan) labourers are few.

83 Many international law courses offered in Ugandan law schools do not, for instance, discuss critiques to mainstream international law doctrine, such as what has been termed as Third World Approaches to International Law (TWAIL) or feminist approaches to international law.

7

International law and human rights litigation in Côte d'Ivoire and Benin

Armand Tanoh[*] & Horace Adjolohoun[**]

Summary

Some African countries have made significant progress to make human rights litigation a reality while others are still finding their way. This is illustrated by the two countries examined in this article, Côte d'Ivoire and Benin. Benin is taking human rights litigation seriously as seen by the establishment of a Constitutional Court with a specific mandate to decide on cases of alleged human rights violations. The task of the Constitutional Court of Benin has been made easier with the incorporation of the African Charter on Human and Peoples' Rights in the Constitution of 1990. However, the Constitutional Court has its limitations as it does not order compensation or reparation to the victims of human rights violations. In Côte d'Ivoire, complainants still have to rely on the ordinary courts which have not proven to be efficient in the enforcement of human rights. There is therefore a need to establish a specialised court with a specific human rights mandate.

1 Introduction

African Francophone states share the same basic structure in terms of judicial organisation with some differences depending on the evolution of their political history since independence. The objective of this chapter is to analyse human rights litigation, with particular focus on the role of international law, in two Francophone West African countries, Côte d'Ivoire and Benin. As will be shown below Côte d'Ivoire has not yet opened up to extensive use of human rights litigation while Benin is often portrayed as having made significant progress in this regard.

Côte d'Ivoire and Benin both adopted multiparty democratic systems in 1990. But the similarities in the history of the two countries end with this. From independence Benin was marked by a large number of military coups whereas the situation in Côte d'Ivoire was stable for more

---

* Doctoral candidate, Centre for Human Rights, Faculty of Law, University of Pretoria, South Africa; armand.tanoh@up.ac.za.

** Research fellow, Centre for Human Rights, Faculty of Law, University of Pretoria, South Africa (based in Benin); sathorace@yahoo.fr.

than 30 years under the presidency of Felix Houphouët-Boigny.[1] Today Benin is the more stable country, commended for its democratic system while Côte d'Ivoire is still on its way to regain political stability after a military coup in 1999 and a civil war which started in 2002.

As all African French speaking countries in Africa, Côte d'Ivoire and Benin have adopted a monist system in relation to treaties. An international treaty which has been ratified and published has thus, at least in theory, a higher normative status than national legislation.[2]

2 Côte d'Ivoire

2.1 The constitutional framework

Côte d'Ivoire gained its independence in 1960. The independence Constitution was replaced by a new constitution in 2000 following the military coup. One of the features of the independence constitution was the absence of an adequate bill of rights. Only three articles out of 76 mentioned broadly a few civil and political rights.[3] As many other constitutions in Africa, the independence Constitution also made reference to the Universal Declaration of Human Rights. The wording 'judicial power' was not used in the 1960 Constitution. This reflected the reality that the judiciary was not independent because of the omnipresence of the first president of Côte d'Ivoire, 'the father of the nation'.

Many stakeholders were involved in the drafting of the 2000 Constitution, as opposed to the independence constitution which was drafted without popular involvement. One of the major differences between the Constitution of 1960 and the Constitution of 2000 is the replacement of 'judicial authority' by 'judicial power'. By so doing, the drafters of the Constitution wanted to entrench once and for all the independence of the judiciary in Côte d'Ivoire. The Council of State (*Conseil d'Etat)* is the final appeal court in administrative matters while the Court of Cassation decides appeal with regard to civil and criminal matters. The Constitutional Council has a mandate to deal with constitutional matters, interpretation of laws, and conformity of the laws to the Constitution.

The new constitution of Côte d'Ivoire included for the first time civil and political rights as well as socio economic rights. The Bill of Rights is contained in the first chapter which contains 22 articles. In addition to the rights enshrined in the Bill of Rights the Constitution makes reference in the Preamble to the 'people's adherence' to the Universal Declaration

---

1 President of Côte d'Ivoire from 1960 to 1993.

2 Cf Constitution of Benin art 147 and Constitution of Côte d'Ivoire art 87. See also chapter 1 of this book.

3 Articles 3, 5 and 6 of the Constitution of 1960.

of Human Rights and to the African Charter on Human and Peoples' Rights.

2.2 The approach of the judiciary with regard to human rights litigation

The Ivorian legal system is governed by what is called *unité de juridiction.* This means that in principle any matter should be referred to the same court of first instance.[4] First instance courts have different sections. For example, if the court has to deal with civil matters, the judges specialised in civil matters should hear the case. However this is seldom applied in practice due to lack of human resources.

Litigation in Côte d'Ivoire on all matters is governed by the Code of Civil, Criminal and Administrative procedure.[5] Basically, the Code provides that anyone could seize a magistrate's court in respect of the matter of their concern in order to get reparation or sanction for the offence committed. The courts could be seized for matters mentioned in the Code which includes matters related to human rights violations. However, despite the large number of human rights violations in Côte d'Ivoire, aggravated by the political crisis the country is witnessing since 2002, very few cases alleging human rights violations have been dealt with by domestic courts.

The Constitutional Council of Côte d'Ivoire was first established in 1994.[6] The new Constitution of 2000 sets out the mandate and composition of the Council.[7] According to article 94, the Constitutional Council determines the eligibility of candidates to presidential and legislative elections and the whole certification of the electoral process, interpretation of the Constitution, the constitutionality of laws and the conformity of international treaties to the Constitution. Since its establishment, the Constitutional Council rendered 38 decisions, 36 on electoral disputes and two on constitutionality.[8] Many of these decisions have been categorised by the Council itself as decisions pertaining to civil and political rights. In fact, these decisions are related to the electoral contest after the elections organised in 1995 and 2000. Many candidates

---

4 This rule has few notable exceptions. In case of serious crimes, the *Cour d'assises* is competent. In addition, another procedure is followed for crimes committed by the president and the members of the cabinet. The court competent to hear any case related to these personalities is the *Haute cour de justice* which has not been established though provided for by art 108 of the Constitution.

5 Loi 72-833 du 21 decembre 1972 portant code de procedure civile, commerciale et administrative.

6 See Loi 94-438 of 16 August 1994. Before the creation the Constitutional Council, the Supreme Court had a Constitutional Chamber in charge of dealing with constitutional issues.

7 Arts 88-100.

8 As of 2009.

who did not agree on the outcomes of the presidential and legislative elections lodged complaints with the Constitutional Council.[9]

2.3 The lack of appropriate judicial bodies in Côte d'Ivoire that have the specific mandate to deal with human rights violations

Litigating human rights at the domestic level requires the creation of appropriate judicial bodies capable of dealing with human rights violations. With the notable exception of Benin which established a Constitutional Court able to deal with human rights violations (discussed below), Francophone African countries do not have specialised human rights courts. Given the rule of unity of courts there is no specialised body in what can be called the normal judicial system. In other words, in order to bring about serious human rights litigation, one should not rely on the ordinary system which has proven its limits for such a long time.[10]

The limited mandate and lack of access to the Constitutional Council prevents it from becoming a genuine protector of human rights. The Constitutional Council of Côte d'Ivoire offers very limited options for human rights litigation. Article 88 of the Constitution provides that the Council shall judge the constitutionality of laws. However, the option of referring a case to the Constitutional Council is not open to most litigators. Access to the Constitutional Council is limited to personalities such as the President of the Republic and the President of the National Assembly and members of parliament.[11] The African Commission on Human and Peoples' Rights noted when deciding a complaint about discriminatory provisions in the Constitution of Côte d'Ivoire that 'the complainant does not have the possibility of resorting to any judicial means to remedy the alleged violation as the mechanism provided for by article 124 of the Constitution is not available to him.'[12]

The quasi absence of cases pertaining to human rights violations before the Ivorian courts[13] and the inexistence of a specialised body having this

---

9 See decisions of the Constitutional Council: CIV/1995/A01 Cote d'Ivoire/Conseil Constitutionnel/27-10/1995/Décision n E 0005-95/extraits; CIV/1995/A02 Cote d'Ivoire/Conseil constitutionnel/ Décision n E 023-95/extraits; CIV/1995/A 03 Cote d''Ivoire/Conseil constitutionnel/extraits; CIV/1995/A04 Cote d'Ivoire/Conseil constitutionnel/29-12-1995/extraits, CIV/1995/A 05 Cote d'Ivoire/Conseil constitutionnel/29-12-95/Décision n E 031-95 http://www.accpuf.org/images/pdf/cm/cotedivoire/051-jc-principe_ega.pdf (accessed on 25 July 2009).

10 The courts have mandate to protect human rights. However, the lack of litigation based on human rights violations means that other avenues should be explored such as the establishment of courts with specialised human rights competence as in Benin.

11 Exceptionally human rights associations could challenge the constitutionality of a specific law before its promulgation if the said law is believed to infringe "civil liberties"(article 77 of the Ivorian Constitution). In practice, this provision has been rarely used since the Constitution entered into force in 2000.

12 *Mouvement Ivorien des Droits Humains (MIDH) v Côte d'Ivoire* (2008) AHRLR 75 (ACHPR 2008) para 49.

13 The quasi absence of human rights litigation before domestic courts has many origins. These include lack of judicial activism in most French speaking countries, the absence

mandate explain the absence of human rights cases. The new Constitution of Côte d'Ivoire proclaims the attachment of the republic to all relevant human rights instruments such as the Universal Declaration of Human Rights and the African Charter on Human and Peoples' Rights.[14] There should be coherence between the rights proclaimed and the mechanisms to ensure that those rights are not violated or they are remedied in case of violation. The provision regarding the seizure of the Constitutional Council mentioned above frames and limits the possibilities of a litigant and does not respond adequately to the demand for fruitful human rights litigation.

There is a need to establish a judicial body competent to entertain matters pertaining to human rights violations. It will therefore be important to broaden the mandate of the Constitutional Council in order to include the competence of dealing with human rights issues. This could enhance the protection and the promotion of human rights in the Ivorian context that was marked these last years by numerous human rights violations.

The Ivorian National Human Rights Commission was established by Decision 2005-08 of 15 July 2005.[15] The Commission started functioning in January 2008 and has recently issued its first report documenting human rights violations. The establishment of the Human Rights Commission is a valuable step towards human rights promotion and protection in the country.[16] The Commission has the power to receive complaints based on human rights violations and to conduct investigations. However, like most other human rights commissions, the Ivorian Commission is a quasi judicial body which does not adopt binding, enforceable decisions.[17] The Commission is weak and there is thus still a need for the establishment of a judicial body able to properly deal with human rights violations.

2.4 The role of international human rights law

In the overwhelming majority of cases that have been decided by courts and tribunals in Côte d'Ivoire, judges referred to the Constitution and statutory law alleged to have been violated.[18] In other words, judicial

of human rights law litigation in the curriculum of the magistrate school and the reliance of lawyers on domestic law (laws adopted by the parliament).

14 See the Preamble of the Constitution.

15 In French, *Commission Nationales des Droits de l'Homme de Côte d'Ivoire* (CNDHCI).

16 There is however many limitations in the mandate of the National Human Rights Commission. According to article 3 of the Decree creating the Human Rights Commission, the Commission may receive complaints of individuals or groups regarding human rights violation. The Commission may also conduct investigations but the matter has to be referred to the courts at the end of the process. The Commission compiles all its findings and issues a report.

17 Art 3(2).

18 This is a based on a survey made by the authors at the *Centre National de Documentation Juridique de Côte d'Ivoire* while preparing this article.

practice is one of municipal law based adjudication with poor if no reference to international law and foreign or international case law.

Judges may claim not to be bound by international law or do not understand its role in relation to domestic law.[19] Training of judges and litigators is thus needed to ensure increased use of international law. Judges are not exposed enough to international treaties and international law in general to the extent that they consider international law as foreign law by which they are not bound. The National School of Administration, in charge of judicial training, does not emphasise the importance of international law in its curriculum. Training efforts should not target only judges but also on lawyers who rarely refer to international instruments in their submissions.

There is a lack of initiatives to popularise basic human rights instruments such as the African Charter on Human and Peoples' Rights and the Universal Declaration of Human Rights. These instruments are only discussed during commemoration and celebration. Publicity around human rights treaties would not on its own guarantee the use of international human rights instruments in courts. However, the more the people is informed of the existence of these instruments, the greater the possibility that they will be invoked in courts. As a monist country, international treaties are once ratified directly incorporated in the domestic order and become law of the land. Reference to these instruments should therefore be similar to reliance on other laws adopted by parliament.

3 Benin

3.1 The constitutional framework of Benin

The 1990 Constitution of Benin is commended for many reasons. First, because it was the product of a national conference known as the starting point for democracy in Benin. Secondly, the Constitution is commended because of the inclusion of the African Charter on Human and Peoples' Rights as part of the Constitution.[20] In addition, the Constitution established a Constitutional Court to deal with human rights complaints.

---

[19] It seems that some of those judges who do not apply international law are fully aware of it, but their refusal to apply it is based on the fact that they do not understand the extent of it and the preeminence of international law over domestic laws under the Constitution.

[20] See in this regard A Rotman 'Benin Constitutional Court: a model of guaranteeing human rights' http://www.law.harvard.edu/students/orgs/hrj/iss17/rotman.shtml (accessed on 14 July 2009). See also article 7 of the Constitution of Benin.

3.2 The approach of the judiciary with regard to human rights litigation

The democratic era in Benin which started after the national conference held in February 1990 brought significant changes in Benin as far as human rights litigation is concerned. Benin has the same organisation as far as the judiciary is concerned as Côte d'Ivoire. The ordinary courts can be seized for interpretation and application of international treaties provided that the state has signed and ratified the said treaty, though in practice this has rarely happened. Indeed, any court may hear a human right case and rely on international human rights law in adjudication. However, the Constitutional Court has become the avenue of choice for human rights complaints.

The Constitutional Court of Benin is provided for in the 1990 Constitution.[21] It has a much broader mandate than the Constitutional Council of Côte d'Ivoire.[22] Since its inception in June 1993, the Constitutional Court[23] received and dealt with a significant number of cases related to human rights violations.[24] In Benin the reluctance of municipal judges to apply international human rights law is overcome by the provisions of the African Charter on Human and Peoples' Rights having been made part of the Constitution.[25] Therefore by referring directly to the provisions of the African Charter on Human and Peoples' Rights, the Constitutional Court is seen to apply domestic law.[26]

---

21 Arts 114-124.

22 The Benin Constitutional Court is the highest jurisdiction in constitutional matters, judge of the constitutionality of the law, guarantor of the fundamental rights and public freedoms, and regulatory body of state organs and for the activity of public authorities. See art 114 of the Constitution.

23 The Court has a comprehensively informative website at http://www.cour-constitutionnelle-benin.org/courconsbj.html.

24 Reliable counts (studies and online counter of the Court's website) number over 800 decisions on human rights as of August 2007 pertaining to some 30 categories of human rights. See H Adjolohoun 'The right to reparation under the African Charter on Human and Peoples' Rights as applied by the Constitutional Court of Benin' https://www.up.ac.za/dspace/bitstream/.../1/adjolohoun.pdf (accessed on 23 July 2009).

25 Art 7 of the Constitution provides: 'The rights and the duties proclaimed and guaranteed by the African Charter on Human and Peoples' Rights adopted in 1981 by the OAU and ratified by Benin on 20 January 1986 are part of this Constitution and the Beninese law'.

26 In a monist country like Benin the inclusion of the provisions of the African Charter on Human and Peoples' Rights in the Constitution was not strictly necessary because the ratification of the Charter already made the latter part of the law of Benin. Therefore, this inclusion should be interpreted as the reaffirmation of the commitment of the Beninese people to promote and respect human rights principles. It is important to stress, however, that the recourse to technicalities such as non publication of treaties, lack of domestication and implementation statutes might explain the insistence of drafters to use express constitutional insertion thus making African Charter articles constitutional provisions.

3.3 Analysis of the cases filed before the Constitutional Court of Benin

An overview of the cases filed before the Constitutional Court shows that they involve mostly individuals and state agents. Cases involving only individuals are rare.[27] In deciding, the Court follows the general principles related to a fair trial by hearing all the stakeholders before reaching a decision. One problem is when a human rights violation has been found in a given case. From its operation in 1993 to 2002, the Constitutional Court merely declared that there has been a violation. It did not provide for a determined remedy such as compensation. From 2002 the Court inaugurated an era of a 'right to reparation'.

The Court has considered various human rights issues such as: the right to trial within a reasonable time,[28] torture and inhuman and degrading treatment,[29] right to property,[30] freedom of association,[31] and the right to a safe environment.[32] In its decisions the Constitutional Court generally quotes articles of the African Charter on Human and Peoples' Rights and the Constitution and declares whether or not a violation has occurred.[33]

3.4 Strengths in the Beninese human rights litigation system

Benin has adopted a framework conducive to human rights and international law litigation by allowing individuals direct access to the Constitutional Court for human rights violations.[34] Article 122 of the Constitution allows citizens to approach the Constitutional Court directly. In this respect, it can be submitted that Benin has a progressive and advanced system as far as human rights litigation is concerned. From the number of cases that the Constitutional Court has had to deal with, it could be noticed that people are fully aware of the mandate of the Constitutional Court and use it accordingly. The direct access to the Constitutional Court for all citizens is a very strong point in the Beninese

---

27 However see eg *Okpeitcha v Okpeitcha* (2002) AHRLR 33 (BnCC 2001) where the Court held that Mr Okpeitcha had 'ceased without grounds to ensure the upkeep and education of his children'. The Court held that Mr Okpeitcha had thus violated art 29(1) of the African Charter which provides that every individual has the duty to 'preserve the harmonious development of the family'.

28 See DCC 97-006 of 18 February 1997 where the Courts declares a procedure was unduly prolonged, See also decision DCC 97-011 of 6 March 1997, decision DCC 98-059 of 2 and 4 June 1998.

29 DCC 98 of 23 December 1998.

30 DCC 97-056 of 8 October 1997.

31 DCC 33-94 of 24 November 1994.

32 DCC 02-065 of 5 June 2002.

33 This could be noticed in all the decisions of the Constitutional Court of Benin.

34 A Diarra 'La protection des droits et libertés en Afrique Noire Francophone depuis 1990' http://www.afrilex.u-bordeaux4.fr/sites/afrilex/IMG/pdf/2doc8diarra.pdf (accessed on 22 July 2009). Benin is among the few countries where individuals can directly seize the Constitutional Court to allege violations of their fundamental rights.

system which guarantees the effectiveness of the system put in place by the Constitution.

3.5 Weaknesses in the Beninese human rights litigation architecture

Though Benin can be said to have a very advanced system as far as human rights litigation is concerned some weaknesses can be pointed out. The Constitutional Court limits itself to the finding of a violation and does not order any reparation or compensation to be given to the victim of the violation.[35] This poses the problem of the effectiveness of the Constitutional Court in addressing human rights violations. In the absence of the pronouncement of any compensation or reparation the problem remains.

In some cases the Constitutional Court's judgment opened the possibility of getting reparation for the violation committed.[36] In the *Fanou* case,[37] the petitioner was beaten up after an unresolved issue of dismissal. The Court found that the treatment amounted to inhuman and degrading treatment without pronouncing what amount of compensation the complainant was entitled to. In another case, the Court found that the right of Mrs Favi had been violated. Eventually the complainant was able to get reparation after a decision of a tribunal of first instance.[38]

The fear of the Court not to become a tribunal of first and final instance should not override the rights of citizens to have a court with all attributions and powers. For this reason it is important to enact a law or to develop a framework that will precise clearly the matters the Court is able to deal with and what shall be attributed to lower courts. This initiative can either come from the Court itself or from parliament. In other countries the judiciary has on many occasions taken steps in order to reinforce human rights in their respective countries.[39] The Court should therefore be the one taking steps to enforce and promote human rights. This attitude which can be seen as judicial activism should be adopted by the Constitutional Court in order to fill the gap and avoid the petitioner to face the challenge of going back to other courts in order to receive reparation.

---

35 Adjolohoun (n 24 above).

36 As above.

37 DCC-02-52 of 31 May 2002.

38 DCC-058 of 4 June 2002. See Adjolohoun (n 24 above).

39 See for example *Fose v Minister of Safety and Security*, 1997 (3) SA 786 (CC), where the Constitutional Court of South Africa contented that '[I]t is left to courts to decide what would be the appropriate relief in a particular case. Appropriate relief will be in essence relief that is required to enforce the Constitution. Depending on the circumstances in each particular case the relief may be a declaration of rights, an interdict, a mandamus or such other relief as may be required to ensure that the rights enshrined in the Constitution are protected and enforced. If it is necessary to do so, the courts may have even to fashion new remedies to secure the protection and enforcement of all these important rights'.

3.6 The use of international law by courts

Although the Constitutional Court of Benin holds a unique human rights mandate, its practice is quite unprincipled especially with regards to the African Charter.[40] The Constitutional Court judges often invoke the Charter in its decisions but then conclude that only the Constitution was violated.[41] Some cases mention a violation of both the Charter and the Constitution.[42] There is an overlap between the rights recognised in the Bill of Rights of the Constitution and in the African Charter and to invoke the latter is often unnecessary in relation to the outcome of the case as the Bill of Rights of the Constitution provides for the same right.[43] The application of article 29 of the African Charter as the only ground for a claim for maintenance in *Okpeitcha v Okpeitcha*[44] is clearly innovative but the claim could perhaps more effectively have been brought to an ordinary court under national legislation which would have provided for an enforceable order.

International treaties are not only referred to by the Constitutional Court, but also on occasion by other courts. The case of *Yaovi Azonhito and Others v Public Prosecutor*[45] illustrates the need for lawyers to properly formulate their international law arguments so as to convince the Court. To challenge the imposition of the death penalty on her client by the Assizes Court, counsel for appellant invoked the 'violation of human rights – right to life'. She argued that:

> Article 6 of the ICCPR *abolished* capital punishment by providing that "Every human being has the inherent right to life. This right shall be protected by law. No one shall be arbitrarily deprived of his life'. (Emphasis added)

In its decision, the Supreme Court of Benin (Criminal Chamber) held:

> No human rights violation occurred where the death penalty was imposed by a legally constituted and competent tribunal, in virtue of provisions of article 381 of the Criminal Code and during proceedings where essential guarantees of the good administration of justice were upheld.

In the view of the Court, by providing that no one shall be arbitrarily deprived of one's' life, 'the ICCPR thereby concedes the very possibility of such deprivation as long as imposed by a competent court and in virtue of law'.[46] It must be noted that the Court made no reference to the

40 See Adjolohoun (n 24 above) 24-34.

41 See for example DCC 03–071 of 16 April 2003 (violation of right to equal treatment in access to public service) and DCC 03-083 of 28 May 2003 (cruel treatment personally inflicted to the victim by the General Director of the National Police).

42 See for example DCC 05-050 of 16 June 2005 and DCC 05-114 of 20 September 2005.

43 The Constitutional Court of Benin has never cited any other international instrument than the African Charter.

44 n 27 above.

45 *Yaovi Azonhito and Others v Public Prosecutor* Supreme Court of Benin, Criminal Chamber, Case number 034/CJ-P 29 September 2000, ILDC 1028 (BJ 2000).

46 Cf ICCPR art 6(2).

inviolability and sacred value of life guaranteed by the Constitution with no legal or formal exception.[47] The same is provided under the African Charter,[48] which is part of the Constitution and is law in Benin.[49] Judges gave a literal interpretative approach to the ICCPR, giving no attention to worldwide efforts towards abolition, including adoption of the Second Optional Protocol to the ICCPR and the work of United Nations human rights treaty bodies. Particularly, there was no reference to Benin's status as a *de facto* abolitionist of the death penalty as no death sentence had been carried out in Benin for 12 years at the time of the judgment. The judges further ignored the provision under the Covenant that nothing should prevent or delay abolition.[50] As an arm of state, the duty lies upon judges to urge and prompt major changes in legislation for a better protection of rights. In any event, the way lawyers argue is important. The case could arguably have had another outcome had counsel prayed the Court to commute the penalty to life imprisonment for instance. She could have argued that it is the duty of judges to send a signal to Benin authorities that preventing or delaying abolition is a violation of international commitments.

In some instances, judges have applied international law principles with no mention of the relevant treaty. For example, courts have held that an estate share that excluded females is 'contrary to the law in force',[51] without making any reference to provisions of the UN Convention on the Elimination of All Discrimination against Women (CEDAW). Even if the outcome is worth praising, the extremely vague 'law in force' formula leaves litigants in the dark as to the law applied by the Court. In the same vein, judges invariably decide on so various grounds as the 'prime interest of the child' or 'security and welfare of the child' with no mention to a particular law such as the Convention on the Rights of the Child.[52] The administrative judge equally finds violations of 'fundamental rights of the individual', 'defence rights', and 'equality before the law', none of these pronouncements relying on a relevant treaty.[53]

47 Art 15.

48 Art 4.

49 Art 7 of the Constitution.

50 Art 6(6).

51 Late *Hounkanrin Ahouansou* case, Decision No 106/2001 of 14 December 2001 (Appeal Court of Cotonou, 1st Traditional Chamber).

52 See eg Decisions 102 of 24 October 2001 (Appeal Court of Cotonou), 077 of 4 July 2001 (Appeal Court of Cotonou), 007 of 21 January 1998 (Appeal Court of Cotonou) and 182 of 18 November 1997 (Appeal Court of Cotonou).

53 See eg Decision 48/CA of 17 June 1999 (Appeal Court of Cotonou).

4 Conclusion

Côte d'Ivoire still has in place the system inherited from the French without any significant improvement whereas Benin adapted its laws to the evolution of its democracy. The Constitutional Court of Benin despite the criticism is a sign of hope in the West Africa region. However to become a real beacon of justice, the Court should go beyond mere statements finding violations of rights and order reparation in favour of the victims. In this way the moral satisfaction given by the Court will be merged with the financial or administrative relief that may be necessary in some instances.

Côte d'Ivoire is in need of a judicial body specifically in charge of protecting and enforcing human rights. This body could be the Constitutional Council which may be transformed in a Constitutional Court competent to deal with human rights violations. With the recent history of Côte d'Ivoire where thousands of people died as victims of the war and of all types of abuse, the establishment of the Court will be the testimony that Ivorians are definitely committed to human rights protection and promotion. The National Human Rights Commission is a good step but not sufficient to ensure the effectiveness of human rights.

PART III

THEMES

8

Equality has no mother but sisters: The preference for comparative law over international law in the equality jurisprudence in Namibia

Dunia P Zongwe*

Summary

This chapter explains why in controversial equality cases Namibian higher courts prefer comparative law over international law. For that purpose, the chapter discusses the holdings of the Namibian Supreme Court on the issue of sexual orientation in the case of *Chairperson of the Immigration Selection Board v Frank and Another*. It concludes that legitimacy is the most plausible explanation for the judicial preference for comparative law over international law in Namibia. The central argument is that higher courts prefer comparative law in controversial equality cases because the values attributed to the international community cannot sustain judgments where they contradict local values, especially in cases involving unpopular minorities. The legitimacy argument also indicates which legal position in a foreign legal system is closest to guiding court decisions in a given controversial equality case. It is the most credible account of why, despite its connection to international law by a constitutional umbilical cord, the interpretive practice of Namibian higher courts prefers the legal position in sister states over international law in controversial equality cases.

1 Introduction

The Namibian Supreme Court[1] and High Court, considered among the

---

* JSD candidate (Cornell); LLM (Cornell); LLB, B Juris (Univ Namibia); dzongwe@yahoo.com. I thank Cynthia G Bowman, Rutendo Hlatshwayo, Magnus Killander, Joanna Mansfield, Andre Nollkaemper and Olakemi Salau for their constructive comments and suggestions. All the remaining shortcomings are mine.

1 Examples can be found in the following cases: *Kauesa v Minister of Home Affairs* 1995 NR 175 (SC); *Ex parte Attorney-General: In re Corporal Punishment* 1991 NR 189; and *Ex parte Attorney General: In re Constitutional Relationship between the Attorney-General and the Prosecutor-General* 1998 NR 282; *Minister of Defence v Mwandinghi* 1993 NR 63 (SC); and *Myburg v Commercial Bank of Namibia* 2000 NR 255 (SC).

most effective and independent in Southern Africa,[2] have handed down many decisions on constitutional law and human rights that read like works of comparative constitutional law. In seminal equality cases, these courts have attached more weight to comparative constitutional law than to international human rights law. The judicial preference for comparative law over international law, which may seem on the face of it a normal court practice, is on closer scrutiny a constitutional anomaly. While the Constitution, the supreme law in Namibia,[3] does not forbid the courts from resorting to comparative law, it expressly instructs the courts to consider international law as part of Namibian law.[4] The latter constitutional provision is crucial because it means that international law, as part of Namibian law, is binding on the courts whereas comparative law is merely of persuasive authority. Thus a fundamental question is whether the judicial preference for comparative law over international law is in some instances a violation of the Namibian Constitution.

In 2001, the Supreme Court of Namibia held in *Chairperson of the Immigration Selection Board v Frank and Another*[5] that the Namibian Constitution does not enumerate sexual orientation as one of the prohibited grounds of discrimination.[6] The Court reasoned that, like Zimbabwe, the people in Namibia do not recognise same-sex relationships. In that case, the Court espoused an interpretive approach that the United Nations Human Rights Committee (HRC) rejected in a

---

2 P VonDoepp 'Executive-judicial relations in African democracies', presented at the Cornell Institute for African Development seminar on *Two decades of democratization in Africa: Current challenges and prospects for good governance* (1 May 2008). In a comparative study of the judiciary in Zambia, Malawi and Namibia for his upcoming book, Professor VonDoepp stated that, while relations sometimes witnessed conflicts, challenges and worrisome developments, Namibia's leaders largely avoided manifest or subtle efforts to control and manipulate the courts. P VonDoepp 'Politics and judicial decision-making in Namibia: Separated or connected realms?' in N Horn & A Bösl (eds) *The independence of the judiciary in Namibia* (2008) 177-205 (in a statistical analysis of nearly 250 High Court and Supreme Court cases, the author came to the conclusion that the Namibian judiciary has performed admirably well in terms of independence from the other branches of government).

3 Constitution of the Republic of Namibia Act 1 of 1990 art 1(6) (Namibian Constitution).

4 Namibian Constitution art 144.

5 *Chairperson of the Immigration Selection Board v Frank and Another* 2001 NR 107 (SC), (*Frank*). For quotation purposes, this chapter directly cites to the original judgments. Original judgments can be found at the official website of the High Court and Supreme Court of Namibia, http://www.superiorcourts.org.na/. The citation of the original judgment of the *Frank* case is: *The Chairperson of the Immigration Selection Board v Erna Elizabeth Frank and Elizabeth Khaxas*, Case No: SA 8/99 (Sup Ct).

6 *Frank* (n 5 above) para 124: 'A Court requiring a "homosexual relationship" to be read into the provisions of the Constitution and or the Immigration Act would itself amount to a breach of the tenet of construction that a constitution must be interpreted "purposively".'

subsequent Namibian equality case.[7] In the process, the Supreme Court of Namibia preferred comparative law (Zimbabwe) over international law.

The purpose of this chapter is to explain why in controversial equality cases Namibian higher courts prefer comparative law over international law. To achieve that purpose, the chapter discusses the holdings of the Namibian Supreme Court on the issue of sexual orientation in the *Frank* case. The chapter addresses the following questions. First, why in controversial equality cases do the Namibian higher courts prefer comparative law over international law? Second, why is comparison preferable to internationalisation? Third, what, if anything, does the term 'preference' mean and entail in this context?

2 Controversial equality cases in Namibia

2.1 Theoretical framework

This chapter is premised upon the proposition that particular situations, rather than universalised norms, determine the manner in which equality is understood. Stated differently, the proposition means that there is no equality in the abstract but often, if not always, equality in context. Three strands of cultural relativism, rooted in legal postmodernism and legal realism, inform this proposition. The first strand disputes the grand narrative that is the human rights discourse and exposes the contradiction between the unifying ambitions in the international human rights discourse and the plurifying local realities. The second strand stresses, in the words of renowned American judge Oliver Wendell Holmes, that general propositions of law do not solve concrete cases.[8] The third strand of cultural relativism recycles the argument that human wrongs are the source of human rights[9] and proposes that inequalities in a particular society, rather than the oft-declared equality in an imagined international community, are the appropriate foundation of a sound reading of equality clauses in national constitutions.

---

7 *Müller and Engelhard v Namibia*, communication 919/2000, CCPR/C/74/D/919/2000 (26 March 2002). The citation of the Supreme Court judgment is *Michael Andreas Müller v The President of the Republic of Namibia and The Minister of Home Affairs*, case No SA 2/98 (Sup Ct) (*Müller*). Although Müller was not a case on sexual orientation it was a case that tackled the issue of equality and its construction.

8 *Lochner v New York* 198 US 45, 76 (1905) (Holmes J dissenting).

9 See CH Heyns 'A "struggle approach" to human rights' in CH Heyns and K Stefiszyn (eds) *Human rights, peace and justice in Africa: A reader* (2006) 15 (arguing that it is easier to identify injustice than justice and to work out a way through from human wrongs to human rights); R Alexy 'A defence of Radbruch's formula' in D Dyzenhaus (ed) *Recrafting the rule of law; The limits of legal order* (1999) (arguing that law loses its legal validity when its contradiction with justice reaches an 'intolerable level'); EN Cahn *A sense of injustice* (1949) (arguing that demands for equality, dignity and fair adjudication are rooted in a sense of injustice).

2.2 The concept of equality

Equality is one of the philosophical foundations of human rights.[10] It is an essential part of the international normative regime for human rights. It is intimately connected and fundamental to the concept of justice.[11] The concept of equality is as wide and deep as the Atlantic Ocean on the Namibian coast: It connotes different things in political, social and legal theories.[12] This chapter only speaks to equality in various legal theories. The classical formulation of the right to equality in the context of international law is article 7 of the Universal Declaration of Human Rights (UDHR),[13] which stipulates that: 'All are equal before the law and are entitled without any discrimination to equal protection of the law.'

There is no such thing as a single component of the legal concept of equality. Instead, there is a cluster of components, including 'equality before the law', 'equal protection' and 'non-discrimination'. 'Equality before the law' operates at two different levels, the level of the enforcement of rules (formal equality) and the level of the contents of the rules (substantive equality).[14] Non-discrimination is closely linked to equality but it is best viewed as a means to achieve equality.[15] Wojciech Sadurski contrasts 'equality *before* the law' with another useful concept of equality, 'equality *in* law', which stresses two essential features of equality: Non-negotiability and fundamental ambiguity.

The non-negotiability principle of legal equality means that equality *in* law is usually unwilling to accept any trade-offs between equality and other values.[16] The ambiguity of the ideal of equality differs from 'mere' ambiguity because

> individuals can, and frequently do, disagree in good faith about its application, and may propose mutually antithetical specific prescriptions, without this being affected by any judgments of degree related to the values used in the process of argument.[17]

The fundamental ambiguity of equality emerges in a variety of guises. Attempts to define equality have floundered, like the tautological definition of equality in a recent Southern African gender instrument.[18]

---

10 JJ Shestack 'The philosophical foundations of human rights' (1998) 20 *Human Rights Quarterly* 210 (explaining that equality is one of the philosophical foundations of human rights).

11 E Rakowski *Equal justice* (1991) 1.

12 See W Sadurski *Equality and legitimacy* (2008).

13 Universal Declaration of Human Rights, UNGA Res 217A (III), 10 December 1948.

14 Sadurski (n 12 above) 95.

15 J Cooper 'Applying equality and non-discrimination rights through the Human Rights Act' in G Moon (ed) *Race discrimination: Development and using a new legal framework* (2000) 39-64 42.

16 Cooper (n 15 above) 98.

17 Cooper (n 15 above) 100.

18 Southern African Development Community (SADC) Protocol on Gender and Development, SADC/MJ/2/2008/3, August 2008, art 1(2) sv 'equality',: '"equality" means *state of being equal* in terms of enjoyment of rights, treatment, quantity or value, access to opportunities, and outcomes, including resources.' Emphasis added.

The 'equal protection' component of legal equality is found in several human rights instruments, for instance the African Charter on Human and Peoples' Rights (African Charter), Africa's regional human rights treaty: 'Every individual shall be entitled to equal protection of the law.'[19] In *Social Economic Rights Action Centre (SERAC) v Nigeria*, the African Commission on Human and Peoples' Rights (African Commission) stated that the African Charter creates four types of obligations of states,[20] namely the duty to respect, protect, promote and fulfill. Like Thomas Pogge argued,[21] these obligations impose a collective responsibility on government and fellow citizens to structure the social system so that all its participants have secure access to the objects of their human rights.

2.3 Equality in the Namibian legal system

2.3.1 Equality in Namibian history

The preamble of the Namibian Constitution recounts some of the major historical events that informed the drafting of the Constitution. Like South Africa, Namibia's past is marked by the 'deep scars' of apartheid.[22] Under the C Mandate of the League of Nations, which entrusted South Africa with the administration of South West Africa/Namibia on behalf of the British Crown,[23] South Africa was allowed to extend its judicial system over South West Africa/Namibia, which it did until Namibia's independence.[24] Inexorably, the extension of South Africa's legal system to Namibia was co-extensive with the introduction of apartheid laws and policies in Namibia in 1948.[25]

The apartheid policy meant in the first place that Blacks had to be separated from people of another colour in constitutional, political, social

19 African Charter on Human and Peoples' Rights 1520 UNTS 363, 27 June 1981, entered into force 21 October 1986, art 3(2). Namibia ratified the African Charter on 30 July 1992.

20 *Social and Economic Rights Centre Action Centre (SERAC) and Another v Nigeria* (2001) AHRLR 60 (ACHPR 2001) para 44.

21 TW Pogge 'How should human rights be conceived?'(1995) 3 *Jahrbuch für Recht und Ethik* 103.

22 *Brink v Kitshoff NO* 1996 4 SA 197 (CC) para 40.

23 After the defeat of Germany at the end of World War I, the League of Nations placed Namibia under a trusteeship whereby South Africa was to administer South West Africa/Namibia on behalf of the British Crown. After the United Nations (UN) succeeded the League of Nations, South Africa refused to allow the UN to replace South Africa's earlier mandate with a trusteeship in terms of which the UN had to monitor closely the administration of South West Africa/Namibia. From thenceforth, South Africa's administration became an illegal occupation of South West Africa/Namibia.

24 S Schulz 'Legal interpretation and the Namibian Constitution (A paradigm shift: Through reason towards justice)' in M Hinz *et al* (eds) *The Constitution at work: 10 years of Namibian nationhood* (2002) 192.

25 In 1948, the then ruling party in South Africa, the National Party (NP), introduced apartheid and its concomitant segregationist and discriminatory legislation.

and other respects; and in the second place that Blacks were ethnically divided into different nations.[26] The idea gradually developed of establishing each nation in its own 'homeland'.[27] Until the country's independence from South Africa on 21 March 1990, inequality had persisted for a long time.

2.3.2 Equality in the Namibian Constitution

It is against this historical backdrop that the Namibian Constitution declares that:[28]

> We, the people of Namibia, have finally emerged victorious in our struggle against colonialism, racism and apartheid; ... are determined to adopt a Constitution which expresses for ourselves and our children our resolve to cherish and to protect the gains of our long struggle;

The very first article of the Constitution proclaims that Namibia is a 'sovereign, secular, democratic and unitary state founded upon the principles of democracy, the rule of law and *justice for all.*'[29]

The Constitution, which is the supreme law in Namibia,[30] enshrines the right to equality. Article 10 of the Namibian Constitution provides that:

> (1) All persons shall be equal before the law.
>
> (2) No persons may be discriminated against on the grounds of sex, race, color, ethnic origin, religion, creed or social or economic status.

Article 10 was born out of constitutional principles that the United Nations Security Council incorporated into one of its resolutions in 1989,[31] one year before Namibia's independence.[32] Drawn up in 1982 by a group of Western countries,[33] designated as the 'Western Contact Group', those principles created the framework for Namibia's Constitution. Among other provisions, the 1982 constitutional principles provided for the right to equality, the independence of the judiciary, and a bill of rights consistent with the Universal Declaration of Human

---

26 HP Viljoen 'The constitutional law of separate development' trans in C van der Walt *South African constitutional law* (1988) 307, 309. The Promotion of Black Self-Government Act 46 of 1959, which created eight national units along ethnic lines.

27 Viljoen (n 26 above).

28 Namibian Constitution Preamble.

29 Namibian Constitution art 1(1). Emphasis added.

30 Namibian Constitution art 1(6): 'This Constitution shall be the Supreme Law of Namibia'.

31 SC Res 632, UN Doc S/Res/632 (16 February 1989).

32 This statement should not be taken to mean that Namibians did not possess any notions of justice, equality, human dignity, discrimination or injustice, before the adoption of the 1982 constitutional principles by the United Security Council in 1989 and the coming into force of the Namibian Constitution in 1990.

33 Canada, France, West Germany, the United Kingdom and the United States.

Rights.[34] On 21 November 1989, the Namibian Constituent Assembly unanimously resolved to adopt the 1982 constitutional principles as the framework of the Namibian Constitution.

Article 10, like all the fundamental human rights and freedoms in the Bill of Rights,[35] is enforceable and binds the executive, the legislature, and the judiciary and all government organs and its agencies and, where applicable, all natural and legal persons in Namibia.[36] An aggrieved person who claims that her right to equality has been infringed on or threatened is entitled to approach a competent court to enforce or protect her right to equality, and may approach the Ombudsman to provide her with such legal assistance or advice that she requires.[37] In addition, the right to equality is free-standing,[38] entrenched[39] and non-derogable;[40] it can only be limited by affirmative action legislation.[41]

2.4 Equality in the Namibian courts

Former Chief Justice Strydom said that the culture of non-discrimination in Namibia is 'not yet out of its infancy.'[42] In view of the importance of equality and non-discrimination in international and Namibian law, it is therefore imperative that Namibian courts interpret the right to equality in a manner that is justifiable both in terms of Namibian constitutional law and international law. It is just as important that Namibian courts adopt an interpretation of the right to equality that is sound both conceptually and philosophically. The onus is on Chief Justice Peter Shivute and High Court Judge President Petrus T Damaseb to spearhead the accomplishment of this enormous jurisprudential task.

---

34 The 1982 constitutional principles first appeared in The Secretary General, *Report of the Secretary-General, delivered to the Security Council,* UN Doc S/15287 (1982)..

35 Namibian Constitution ch 3.

36 Namibian Constitution art 5.

37 Namibian Constitution art 25(2).

38 International Covenant on Civil and Political Rights (ICCPR) art 26; Cooper (n 15 above) 44.

39 Namibian Constitution art 131.

40 Namibian Constitution art 23(3): 'Nothing contained in this article shall permit a derogation from or suspension of the fundamental rights or freedoms referred to in articles … 10 [equality] …'.

41 Namibian Constitution art 23(2): 'Nothing contained in article 10 hereof shall prevent Parliament from enacting legislation providing directly or indirectly for the advancement of persons within Namibia who have been socially, economically or educationally disadvantaged by past discriminatory laws or practices, or for the implementation of policies and programs aimed at redressing social, economic or educational imbalances in the Namibian society arising out of past discriminatory laws or practices, or for achieving a balanced structuring of the public service, the police force, the defense force, and the prison service'.

42 *Müller* (n 7 above) 11.

In Namibia, as in countries the world over, equality is in its conceptualisation and practice problematic and highly controversial.[43] Despite elaborate provisions in the law, prescriptions of equality tend to shrink in practice.[44] One of the great challenges to a sound understanding of the right to equality in Namibia concerns claims that the right to equality has been infringed on a ground not expressly enumerated in the Constitution. For example, pregnancy, disability, sexual orientation, national origin, and HIV/AIDS status are not expressly enumerated in the Namibian Constitution as prohibited grounds of discrimination. The challenge of non-enumerated grounds seems unsurmontable as the Supreme Court in *Müller* declared that the list of the prohibited grounds of discrimination is not open-ended,[45] mirroring as it does historical forms of discrimination.[46] Currie and de Waal say that it is not even always obvious whether one can so construe a particular basis of discrimination as falling under one of the enumerated and prohibited grounds.[47] It follows that any position or court decision in favour of or against discrimination on those grounds is inevitably controversial.

This chapter defines a 'controversial equality case' as a case in which the equality rights, interests and claims of unpopular minorities conflict with those of a larger political group or the majority of Namibians. 'Unpopular minorities' are minority groups whose identity, beliefs, practices, and claims conflict with those of a larger political group or the majority of Namibians. In the Namibian context, unpopular minorities include gays and lesbians, commercial sex workers (ie prostitutes),[48] foreigners,[49] migrant workers, refugees, the Caprivi secessionists,[50] accused persons, people living with HIV/AIDS, and people associated with the apartheid regime. In other words, unpopular minorities are minorities who cannot protect their rights adequately through the

---

43 See EK Cassidy 'Article 10 of the Namibian Constitution: A look at the first ten years of interpretation of the rights to equality and non-discrimination and predictions for the future' in M Hinz *et al* (n 24 above) 168, 184; the dissenting opinion of International Court of Justice (ICJ) Judge Tanaka in *South West Africa* 1966 ICJ Reports 6; I Currie & J De Waal *The Bill of Rights Handbook* (2005) 230.

44 OM Arnardottir *Equality and non-discrimination under the European Convention on Human Rights* (2003) 18.

45 *Müller* (n 7 above) 16.

46 *Müller* (n 7 above).

47 Currie & de Waal (n 43 above) 259.

48 Executive summary of Legal Assistance Centre 'Whose body is it?' in *Commercial sex work and the law in Namibia* (2002) (stating that 70% of the general population in Namibia feel that commercial sex work should be illegal for both clients and sex workers).

49 'Regionalizing xenophobia?' http://www.queensu.ca/samp/sampresources/samppublications/policyseries/policy30.htm (accessed on 19 April 2010).

50 In August 1999, a group of armed men in Caprivi attempted to break the northern Caprivi region away from the rest of Namibia. Those men and any person associated with or supporting the attempted secession of Caprivi are generally disliked by the vast majority of Namibians.

democratic process, the 'social outcasts', marginalised people, 'the worst and the weakest amongst us.'[51]

Two features in the definition of controversial equality cases are salient. First, by understanding 'controversial equality cases' as 'claims of unpopular minorities', the chapter foregrounds that the preeminent basis of human rights in the African context is not the rights declared in multilateral forums but the claims, the daily struggles,[52] and the resistance[53] of individuals. 'Unpopular minorities' suggests that certain social groups are political minorities. These groups have not organised themselves politically to defend their rights, interests and claims through the legislative process, in part due to their unpopularity, that is their conflicts with larger political groups. Certain non-governmental organisations (NGOs), like the Legal Assistance Centre (LAC) and the National Society for Human Rights (NSHR), fight to protect the rights of political minorities, among other vulnerable social groups in Namibia. The intervention of these NGOs does not belie the vulnerability of political minorities or the difficulties they face in organising politically; on the contrary, the intervention is evidence of such vulnerability.

The characterisation of unpopular minorities as political minorities is pertinent because, as a matter of public policy, decision-makers and judges in Namibia have to assess the implications of deciding against constituencies that cannot readily secure favourable legislation for themselves. Former South African Chief Justice Chaskalson was certainly right to hold that if the views of the majority were decisive there would be no need for constitutional adjudication and the protection of rights could be left to parliament, which has a mandate from and is answerable to the public.[54] If that were to happen, constitutional dispensation would revert back to the parliamentary sovereignty that reigned in the apartheid days[55] – a situation that would violate the constitutional supremacy heralded by the Namibian Constitution.[56]

The label 'unpopular minorities' encompasses an extremely heterogeneous whole and includes groups of people engaged in activities that are legally criminal. Even if the chapter draws attention to asymmetries in the relatively weaker position of these political minorities, it does in no way argue that one group (eg gays and lesbians) is necessarily comparable to another (eg accused persons) in any respect other than their position in the legislative process. Nor does the chapter argue that people found guilty of serious crimes, as is the case with the

---

51 *S v Makwanyane and Another* 1995 3 SA 391 (CC) 88. (*Makwanyane*).

52 Heyns (n 9 above) 15.

53 IG Shivji *The concept of human rights in Africa* (1989) 3: 'it is through a critique of the ideology of domination that the elements for the reconstruction of the ideology of resistance and struggle are crystallized.'

54 *Makwanyane* case (n 51 above).

55 As above.

56 Namibian Constitution art 1(6).

Caprivi secessionists, should be absolved thereof. Rather, the recommendation is that laws be interpreted so as to preserve the most fundamental rights of individuals in these groups, regard being had to their smaller voice in the making of those laws.[57]

2.5 Examples of controversial equality cases

The High Court and Supreme Court of Namibia have adjudicated a number of controversial equality cases. In *Müller v President of the Republic of Namibia,* a white German male, Mr Müller, who had immigrated to Namibia after independence in 1990 wanted to change his surname to that of his Namibian wife, Ms Engelhard. The Namibian Aliens Act exempted women from complying with certain formalities when changing their name upon marriage but required men to meet those formalities in the same circumstances. Müller argued that this differentiation between married women and married men was discriminatory on the basis of sex. The Supreme Court rejected Müller's claim. It reasoned that the differentiation was intended to create legal security and certainty of identity and as such it was rationally connected to the object of the Namibian legislator to serve the interests of the state and the public at large.[58] Such differentiation had, according to the Court, hardly any effect on the Namibian community and was in essence artificial.[59]

In *Kauesa v Ministry of Home Affairs*[60] a police officer, who in a televised panel discussion on the topic of affirmative action had accused the white command structure of the police of corruption, challenged a regulation that forbade members of the police from publicly commenting unfavourably on the administration of the police force or any government department. The Court upheld his claim. The High Court elaborated on the relationship between the right to equality and affirmative action. However, the Supreme Court declared the issue *obiter* and did not address it, and as a consequence the High Court's holding – on the relationship between equality and affirmative action – is no longer binding.[61]

Frank v Chairperson of the Immigration Selection Board is the leading case on alleged discrimination on a ground not enumerated by the

---

[57] In this respect, it is noteworthy that the tendency of the European Court of Justice has been to expand the protective scope of the right to equality, going as far as finding racial discrimination in a case where there was no identifiable victim: *Centrum voor gelijkheid van kansen en voor racismebestrijding v Firma Feryn* (C-54/07), judgment of the Court (Second Chamber), 10 July 2008. See also A Eriksson 'European Court of Justice: Broadening the scope of European nondiscrimination law' (2009) 7 *International Journal of Constitutional Law* 731 746.

[58] *Müller* (n 7 above) 24.

[59] As above.

[60] *Kauesa* (n 1 above).

[61] Cassidy (n 43 above) 179.

Constitution. In that case, two lesbian women, a German citizen who had resided in Namibia since 1990 and a Namibian citizen, challenged the denial of a permanent residence permit to the German citizen, Elizabeth Frank. Even if the Supreme Court ruled in favour of Frank on the issue of the permanent residence permit, it decided against Frank on the issue of the recognition of same-sex relationships in Namibia, as explained below.

Though the above cases may be statistically an unrepresentative sample, they are nonetheless legally significant as they are the leading controversial equality cases in Namibia. The next section of this chapter studies at length the *Frank* case given its prominence in the Namibian equality jurisprudence.

3 *Frank v Chairperson of the Immigration Selection Board*

3.1 Facts

Two women, a white German citizen (Erna Elizabeth Frank) and a black Namibian citizen (Elizabeth Khaxas), had a lesbian relationship. Frank had resided in Namibia and had been working at the University of Namibia since Namibia's independence in 1990. She applied to the Immigration Selection Board for a permanent residence permit in 1995. In support of her application for a permanent residence permit, Frank stated that she was in a long-term relationship with a Namibian woman. The Board denied Frank's application for a permanent residence permit, explaining that the women's 'long-term relationship was not one recognised in a court of law and was therefore not able to assist the application.'[62]

Frank and her partner challenged the decision of the Board to deny Frank's application. The High Court of Namibia ruled in favour of the two women and held that administrative justice required the Board to give reasons for its denial to grant permanent residence permit. The Court further stated that the reasons relied upon by the Board demonstrated that the Board was 'motivated by several factors which should not have been taken into account while some relevant factors were not taken into account at all.'[63]

The Court found that the Board was wrong in its treatment of the two women's longstanding lesbian relationship partly because of the equality provision of the Namibian Constitution. The Court recognised the existence of the common law concept of a 'universal partnership' where parties agree to put in common all their present and future property, and which can be entered into expressly or tacitly where a man and woman live together as husband and wife but have not been married by a

62 As recited in the judgment of the Supreme Court: See *Frank* (n 5 above) 43.

63 *Frank* (n 5 above) 55.

marriage officer. The Court reasoned that, if a man and a woman can tacitly conclude such a partnership, the long-term relationship between the women in this case, in so far as it is a universal relationship, is recognised by law because of the equality provision in the Constitution. It upheld the women's challenge and directed the Board to issue the permit on the ground of administrative justice.

The government (ie Chairperson of the Immigration Selection Board) appealed to the Supreme Court of Namibia against the decision of the High Court.

3.2 Legal questions and decision

Frank raised one major constitutional issue in the Supreme Court of Namibia: The right to equality (or the right not to be discriminated against). The most directly relevant provision of the Constitution is article 10 (the equality and non-discrimination clause). The Supreme Court in *Frank* outlined the analytical framework for equality and non-discrimination cases as follows:[64]

> Article 10(1) of the Constitution: The questioned legislation would be unconstitutional if it allows for the differentiation between people or categories of people and that differentiation is not based on a rational connection to a legitimate purpose [Mwellie[65]]
> Article 10(2): The steps to be taken in regard to this sub-article are to determine –
> Whether there exists a differentiation between people or categories of people;
> Whether such differentiation is based on one of the enumerated grounds set out in the sub-article;
> Whether such differentiation amounts to discrimination against such people or categories of people; and
> Once it is determined that the differentiation amounts to discrimination, it is unconstitutional unless it is covered by [the provision on affirmative action].

After a lengthy and thorough examination of the equality clause in the Constitution and other applicable laws, the Supreme Court concluded that the provisions of the Namibian Constitution and the Immigration Act did not discriminate against Frank and her partner. It held that a court judgment requiring a 'homosexual relationship' to be read into the provisions of the Constitution and the Immigration Act would itself amount to a breach of the tenet of construction that a constitution must be interpreted 'purposively'.[66] It observed in passing that whether or not an amendment shall be made to the challenged provision of the Immigration Act to add the words 'partner in a permanent same-sex life partnership' was a matter best left to the Namibian parliament.[67]

The conclusion that a certain differentiation between people or categories of people is not rationally connected to a legitimate purpose,

---

64 *Frank* (n 5 above) 121.

65 This part of the framework was developed in *Mwellie v Ministry of Works, Transport and Communication and Another* 1995 (9) BCLR 1118 (NmH).

66 *Frank* (n 5 above) 124.

67 *Frank* (n 5 above) 125.

or that it amounts to discrimination, is eminently an interpretive act by judges of the Namibian Constitution, involving both value judgments[68] and constitutional preferences. In *Frank*, the Namibia Supreme Court preferred the way the Zimbabwean Supreme Court interpreted the right to equality over alternative interpretations in other legal systems and legal instruments, and by certain international forums, as explained below. While the decision in *Frank* is justified by the constitutional interpretive tradition in Namibia, that interpretive tradition is less justifiable both conceptually and philosophically.

4 The attractions of comparative and international law

4.1 The attractions of international law

The principal attraction of international law for a Namibian judge is that she will fulfil her oath to defend and uphold the Namibian Constitution and the laws of Namibia,[69] which encompass international law. Article 144 of the Namibian Constitution incorporates public international law into Namibian law:

> Unless otherwise provided by this Constitution or Act of Parliament, the general rules of public international law and international agreements binding upon Namibia under this Constitution shall form part of the law of Namibia.

Article 144 of the Namibian Constitution makes international law and all the human rights treaties ratified by Namibia applicable in the Namibia directly:[70] Their application does not require any enacting laws. Article 144 is the umbilical cord that links the Namibian legal system to international law. However, the question that article 144 does not elucidate relates to the relative status of international law within the Namibian legal system. What is the position when a provision in the Constitution or an act of parliament in Namibia violates the stipulations of international law or the 'civilized international community of which Namibia is a part'? The phrase '[u]nless otherwise provided by this Constitution or Act of Parliament' in article 144 suggests that the 'general rules of public international law and international agreements binding upon Namibia' are subject to the Namibian Constitution and national legislation. The application of article 144 may probably lead to a violation of international law because the law of treaties lays down that a

---

68 *Ex parte: Attorney General In Re: Corporal Punishment by Organs of State* (n 1 above) 2: 'the decision which this Court will have to make in the present case is based on a value judgement, which cannot be primarily determined by legal rules and precedents, as helpful as they may be, but must take full cognisance of the social conditions, experiences and perceptions of the people of this country.'

69 See Namibian Constitution schedule 1.

70 See N Horn 'International human rights norms and standards: The development of Namibian case and statutory law' in N Horn & A Bösl (eds) *Human rights and the rule of law in Namibia* (2008) 141-164.

state may not invoke its national law as a justification for its failure to perform an international treaty that it has ratified voluntarily.[71] Similarly, Namibia may not brandish article 144 to justify why, in the case of a conflict between national law and international law, the former prevails. It necessarily follows that, notwithstanding the text of article 144, international law supersedes national legislation indisputably.[72]

However, despite the constitutional requirements, references to international law in Namibian courts do not enjoy as much preference as comparative foreign case law. To be sure, in *Frank,* the Court only referred to international law once when it quoted a book by Ramcharan on the international bill of rights.[73]

4.2 The attractions of comparative law

It is undeniable that international law is a distinct and separate body of law. But, from the vantage point of its sources, international law shares certain mechanical linkages with comparative law. The 'general principles of law recognized by civilized nations' are, by virtue of article 38(1)(c) of the ICJ Statute, one of the sources of public international law.[74] As de Cruz infers, the interpretation of these general principles of law 'can only be rooted in the comparative law method.'[75] Decisions of foreign courts dealing with bills of rights are in any event one of the sources of international human rights law.[76] Consequently, comparative law, to the extent that it is a method used to ascertain 'general principles of law recognized by civilized nations', is logically one of the tools to interpret Namibian law.

Regarding the attractions of comparative law, virtually all the standard texts on comparative law recite the same purposes and utility:[77]

> (1) to enhance education and appreciation of foreign legal systems;
> (2) to serve as an aid to law reform and legislation;
> (3) to serve as a tool of construction when confronting gaps in legislation or case law;
> (4) to provide knowledge of others' rules which will help in growing cross-jurisdiction practice; and

---

71 Vienna Convention on the Law of Treaties art 27.

72 *Müller* (n 7 above) 23 (holding that, although counsel for the appellant relied on the Convention on the Elimination of All Forms of Discrimination Against Women (CEDAW) that the Namibian parliament ratified in 1992, such conventions were subject to the Namibian Constitution and could not change the situation).

73 *Frank* (n 5 above) 122.

74 J Dugard *International law: A South African perspective* (2005) 38.

75 P de Cruz *Comparative law in a changing world* (2007) 9.

76 C Botha *Statutory interpretation: An introduction for students* (1998) 42; N Jayawickrama *The judicial application of human rights law: National, regional and international jurisprudence* (2002) 169: 'Human rights case law is forthcoming in increasing measure from countries such as India, Canada, South Africa and Sri Lanka'.

77 MM Feeley 'Comparative criminal law for criminologists: Comparing for what purpose?' in D Nelken (ed) *Comparing legal cultures* (1997) 94; see also de Cruz (n 75 above) 18; K Zweigert & H Kötz *Introduction to comparative law* (1998) 16.

(5) to facilitate unification and harmonization of the law.

Comparative law is an *école de vérité* and can offer a much richer range of model solutions than a legal science devoted to single nations, if only because the different systems of the world can offer a greater variety of solutions than could be thought up in a lifetime by even the most imaginative jurist who was corralled in his own system.[78] It is unnecessary to reinvent the wheel of justice over and over again. Much may be gained by looking at how other countries apply corresponding principles or address common problems. In Namibia, legal comparison is frequently applied in case law[79] and in the creation of legislation. For instance, the Insolvency Act[80] was based on Australian, French and Israeli legislation;[81] and the Companies Act[82] [83] and the Bills of Exchange Act[84] were substantially based on English commercial law.

Another crucial point – which many Western writers tend to overlook or ignore altogether in the case of former colonies – is the fact that Namibian law was 'received' from South Africa,[85] which in turn was based on Roman-Dutch law and English common law. Therefore, like South Africa, Zimbabwe, Lesotho, Botswana and Swaziland, Namibia is a hybrid or mixed legal system,[86] standing midway between Roman-Dutch law and English common law, and perforated at many points by indigenous law. This mixed legal heritage signifies that since certain foreign laws – Roman law, Roman-Dutch law, English law and South African law – are useful for a historical understanding of Namibian law, it follows by necessary implication that the study and teaching of comparative law is illuminating for the understanding of Namibian legal history.[87]

---

78 Zweigert & Kötz (n 77 above) 15; HC Gutteridge *Comparative law: An introduction to the comparative law method of legal studies* (1971) 35-36. *Makwanyane* case (n 51 above) 37 *held*, that comparative human rights jurisprudence will be of great importance while an indigenous jurisprudence is developed).

79 See eg *Feldman (Pty) Ltd v Mall* 1945 AD 733 and *Government of the Republic of South Africa v Ngubane* 1972 2 SA 601 (A) (*held* that '[i]n seeking to do justice between man and man it is at least interesting and sometimes instructive to have some comparative regard to the law of other countries').

80 Act 24 of 1936.

81 See D Kleyn & F Viljoen *Beginner's guide for law students* (2002) 268-270

82 Act 61 of 1973.

83 See HS Cilliers *et al Corporate law* (1992) 6.

84 Act 22 of 2003. C Visser *et al Gibson South African mercantile and company law* (1997) 60.

85 Schulz (n 24 above) 192.

86 R Zimmerman *et al Mixed legal systems in comparative perspective* (2004) 3; HJ Erasmus 'Roman law and common law in Southern Africa: Past and future' in JE Spruit *et al* (eds) *Roman law at the crossroads* (2000) 43, 44.

87 AB Edwards *The historical background of South African law: An outline* (1996) 3: '[T]he historical method of teaching law has assumed considerable importance at most South African universities'.

It is typical of superior courts in Namibia to consider foreign or comparative law in constitutional and controversial equality cases. Former Namibian Chief Justice Strydom remarked in *Mwilima* that comparative studies of the constitutional law of other countries are 'always helpful' and have 'more or less become the norm' in matters concerning the interpretation of fundamental rights and freedoms.[88] Effectively, many of the Namibian Supreme Court's decisions on constitutional law and human rights resemble treatises on comparative constitutional law.[89] In *Frank,* the Court referred to comparative jurisprudence extensively. On constitutional interpretation, the Court quoted a book on the constitutional law of India,[90] referred to case law from Botswana, England, Canada, South Africa, the United States, and Zimbabwe. On the interpretation of the right to equality, the Court referred to the South African and Zimbabwean constitutions and the cases based on them.

5. Constitutional interpretation and preferences

5.1 Constitutional preferences

In order to operationalise the preference concept, this chapter conceives of comparative law and international law as distinct legal systems rather than as different levels of law. Furthermore, the chapter disaggregates comparative law into individual national legal systems as and when relevant for analytical purposes.

'Preference' occurs during the interpretation of laws. 'Preference' in the context of this chapter refers to the weight and role that the Namibian courts attach to legal positions in legal systems other than the Namibian legal system (ie comparative law or international law) in the final outcome of the cases before the courts. Courts would be said to have preferred international law if, in a given case, the outcome is more in line with international law than comparative law. Likewise, to say that the Namibian courts prefer comparative law over international law means that the Namibian courts attach more weight to comparative law than to international law in deciding cases before them. Further, a court would

---

88 *Government of the Republic of Namibia and Others v Geoffrey Kupuzo Mwilima and Others*, Case No SA 29/2001 (Sup Ct) (*Mwilima*).

89 *Kauesa* (n 1 above) (where the Supreme Court analysed Canadian, American and Indian constitutional law); *Ex parte Corporal Punishment* (n 1 above) (British, German, Botswana, Zimbabwean and South African constitutional law); and *Ex parte Attorney General: In re Constitutional Relationship between the Attorney-General and the Prosecutor-General* (n 1 above) (British law, German constitutional law and an impressive study of the different models of prosecutorial functions in the various jurisdictions around the world); *Mwandinghi* (n 1 above) (South African, Australian, and Indian constitutional law, and British Privy Council jurisprudence); and *Myburg* (n 1 above) (South African constitutional law).

90 *Frank* (n 5 above) 83.

be said to have preferred one particular legal system over other legal systems if, in a given case, the outcome is more in line with that particular legal system than other legal systems.

'Preference' does not relate to a quantitative but a qualitative reference. That means that a given court will not be said to have preferred a certain legal position in a foreign legal system because it has referred several times to that legal position, but because it has heavily relied on that position in rendering a judgment. Constitutional preferences are inescapable because most questions posed to the Constitution are not answered by its visible text but by the 'invisible Constitution', which tells which meaning as well as how much force to ascribe to that text.[91] In the end, Namibian legislators would wisely invest in the semantic clarity of the equality clause of the Constitution if they enact an equality-specific legislation, more or less like the South African Promotion of Equality and Prevention of Unfair Discrimination Act.[92]

5.2 Interpretation of the Namibian Constitution

There are in theory at least six models of constitutional interpretation,[93] namely doctrinal (based on judicial precedents), textual[94] (based on the constitutional text), value-oriented (based on social norms), prudential[95] (based on a cost-benefit analysis), historical and structural[96] (based on rules coming out of structures created by the Constitution). Depending on the models adopted, interpretation may result in the extension, restriction or modification of the meaning of a constitutional provision. More precisely, interpretation may extend, restrict or modify the meaning of the equality clause of the Namibian Constitution so as to include or exclude 'sexual orientation' in or from the prohibition to discriminate on the basis of 'sex'.[97]

---

91 LH Tribe *The invisible constitution* (2008) 7.

92 Act 4 of 2000. Cf DP Zongwe 'The South African Equality Act: Lessons for Namibia' unpublished LLB dissertation, University of Namibia, 2006.

93 CJ Roederer 'Mapping the jurisprudential terrain in the search for truth in law' in C Roederer & D Moellendorf (eds) *Jurisprudence* (2004) 1-24; PC Bobbitt *Constitutional fate: Theory of the Constitution* (1982) 12-13. See also SE Finer *et al Comparing constitutions* (1995) 4-5; LM Du Plessis 'The jurisprudence of interpretation and the exigencies of a new constitutional order in South Africa' in G Bradfield & D van der Merwe (eds) *'Meaning' in legal interpretation* (1998) 8-20. These six models are an attempt to make sense of a sometimes confusing mass of court materials and have not received judicial endorsement in Namibia.

94 This model is the point of departure of constitutional interpretation in Namibia.

95 This model is very rare in Namibia.

96 In Namibia for instance, the parliament, the Ombusdman, and the National Planning Commission.

97 *Frank* (n 5 above) 113 O'Linn AJA (quoting from the Oxford Advanced Learners Dictionary) distinguished sex and sexual orientation as follows: 'Whereas the word "sex" can be defined as "being male or female," or "males or females as a group",

The value-oriented and purposive model is frequently employed in Namibian courts and the most representative of Namibian constitutional jurisprudence. Namibian judges see the Constitution as a 'mirror reflecting the national soul', the 'identification of the ideals and aspirations of a nation', and the 'articulation of the values bonding its people and disciplining its government'.[98] The 'spirit' of the Namibian Constitution is to 'preside and permeate judicial processes and judicial discretion'.[99] The leading case is *Ex parte Attorney-General: In re Corporal Punishment by Organs of State*, where the Court held that the purposive approach to interpretation requires a value judgment. In that case, Mahomed AJA, in a national anthem of constitutional interpretation, said:[100]

> The question as to whether [a certain act] can properly be said to [violate the Constitution] is however a value judgment which requires objectively to be articulated and identified, regard being had to the *contemporary norms, aspirations, expectations and sensitivities of the Namibian people* as expressed in its national institutions and its Constitution and further having regard to the *emerging consensus of values in the civilised international community* (of which Namibia is a part) which Namibians share.

In a similar vein, O'Linn AJA in the *Frank* case, which also used the value-oriented model of constitutional interpretation, summarised the interpretation of the Constitution as follows:[101]

> The guideline that a Constitution must be interpreted 'broadly, liberally and purposively' is … anchored in the provisions of the Namibian Constitution, the language of its provisions, the reality of its legal history, and the *traditions, usages, norms, values and ideals of the Namibian people* … [W]hether or not they are 'liberal', 'conservative' or a mixture of the two, does not detract from the need to bring this reality into the equation when interpreting and applying the Namibian Constitution'.

In *Minister of Defence v Mwandinghi,* the Supreme Court held that the Namibian Constitution must be interpreted purposively to avoid the 'austerity of tabulated legalism' and any 'narrow and pedantic' interpretation.[102] O'Linn AJA convincingly linked the value-oriented interpretative model to the principle of popular sovereignty in the Constitution,[103] which stipulates that '[a]ll power shall vest in the people of Namibia who shall exercise their sovereignty through the democratic institutions of the State.'[104]

"sexual orientation" could encompass in theory "any sexual attraction of *anyone* or *anything*."'

98 *S v Acheson* 1991 (2) SA 805 (Nm).

99 As above.

100 *Ex parte In Re Corporal Punishment* (n 1 above) 20. Emphasis added.

101 *Frank* (n 5 above) 87. Emphasis added.

102 *Mwandinghi* (n 1 above) 12.

103 *Frank* (n 5 above) 98.

104 Namibian Constitution art 1(2).

The above holdings of the Supreme Court of Namibia represent the value-oriented model that prevails in constitutional and equality cases in Namibia. In terms of article 81 of the Namibian Constitution, these holdings are binding on all other courts and all persons in Namibia until reversed by the Supreme Court itself or by legislation.[105] From these holdings, it is evident that the sources of constitutional interpretation are the constitutional text and its language, the legal history of the Constitution, the values of the Namibian people and the values of the international community. Interestingly, Mahomed AJA identifies as sources of constitutional meaning the 'values and ideals of the Namibian people' and the 'emerging consensus of values in the civilized international community of which Namibia is a part'. The 'values in the civilized international community' may refer to values as expressed in either international law or comparative law,[106] or in both. Put another way, the learned judge identifies comparative law and international law as sources of constitutional interpretation.

It is easy to see why Namibian judges adopted a teleological, value-based, ethical model, given Namibia's pre-independence history, when courts served as the oppressive arms of the apartheid regime. The judiciary in Namibia has carried some of the legacy of Namibia's apartheid and colonial past and is the least transformed state institution.[107] VonDoepp emphasises that:[108]

> [J]udicial decisions that have favored elements of the previous order have sometimes been met with hostility as ruling party stalwarts have singled out the institution as a holdover from the previous era. In turn, popular support for the courts, viewed by some as critical for judicial independence,has paled in comparison to that for majoritarian institutions, which reflect the aspirations of the independence movement.

In order to earn legitimacy in their own society, Namibian judges, shortly after the country's independence in 1990, opted for an 'apologetic' value-oriented model that derives its substance from the moral and political choices of the majority.[109] The majority Court in *Frank* resorted to this model and found no violation of the respondents' constitutional rights to equality, non-discrimination, family, privacy or freedom of movement. In reaching that conclusion, the Court relied

---

105 Namibian Constitution art 81: 'A decision of the Supreme Court shall be binding on all other courts of Namibia and all persons in Namibia unless it is reversed by the Supreme Court itself, or is contradicted by an Act of Parliament lawfully enacted.'

106 It is instructive that the phrase 'civilized international community' is similar in its wording to the phrase 'general principles of law recognized by civilized nations', found in art 38(1)(c) of the Statute of the International Court of Justice. This similarity suggests that both phrases might refer to comparative law.

107 P VonDoepp 'Context-sensitive inquiry in comparative judicial research: Lessons from the Namibian judiciary' (2007) 20 *Comparative Political Studies* 7.

108 As above.

109 Cf M Du Plessis 'Between apology and utopia – The Constitutional Court and public opinion' (2002) 18 *South African Journal on Human Rights* 1-40.

heavily on comparative law, in a controversial judgment that reveals the inherent weaknesses of the value-based model in harmonising municipal law and international law.

6. Explaining the preference for comparative law

6.1 Legitimacy and the value-based interpretive model

The central argument in this chapter is that Namibian courts prefer comparative law because in controversial cases international values cannot sustain the legitimacy of a national judiciary where these values contradict local values. The search for legitimacy by the courts feeds on the value-based nature of constitutional interpretation in equality cases. By 'legitimacy' is meant the liberal idea that links the authority of the state to the consent of the governed. In particular, it is the assumption that only laws that are based upon arguments and reasons to which no member of society has a rational reason to object are politically acceptable, and as such can be applied coercively even to those who actually disagree with them.[110]

The legitimacy hypothesis reconciles all the major controversial equality cases (*Müller, Kauesa and Frank*). The argument that in controversial equality cases courts give precedence to local values where these conflict with international and comparative law explains the outcome of most controversial equality cases. More specifically, the judgments reveal that Namibian courts do in fact prefer local values and selectively use comparative law to support local values.[111] The hypothesis's heuristic value lies in its ability to explain variations in judicial preferences, for example it explains why in the *Frank* case the Supreme Court preferred Zimbabwean constitutional jurisprudence over South African constitutional law. In one of the 'most Christianized' countries in Africa,[112] it is small wonder that churches have been shoring up the Namibian government's anti-homosexual attitude and concurring with the Supreme Court decision in *Frank*.[113] A failure to incorporate the moral and political choices of the majority of the Namibian people into the constitutional interpretative process would 'strengthen the perception that the courts are imposing foreign values on the Namibian people.'[114]

---

110 Sadurski (n 12 above) 28.

111 *Frank* (n 5 above) 115.

112 N Horn 'Religion and human rights in Namibia' (2008) 2 *African Human Rights Law Journal* 409. See FJ Bold 'Vows to collide: The burgeoning conflict between religious institutions and same-sex anti-discrimination laws' (2009) 158 *University of Pennsylvania Law Review* 179, 187 (showing that in the US, for example, marriage is not only a social institution in which religious actors play a part but also as an intrinsically religious concept with deep theological significance).

113 Bold (n 112 above) 427.

114 Frank (n 5 above) 98.

The characteristic value-based interpretative model adopted by Namibian courts invites judges to consider both comparative law and international law. Nevertheless, that model does not justify the judicial propensity to favour comparative law over international law. In actual fact, the model – which draws from the 'traditions, usages, norms, values and ideals of the Namibian people' – may occasionally contravene international law by embracing an interpretation of human rights not warranted by international law. More particularly, the UN Human Rights Committee (HRC) in *Müller* disavowed the value-based model,[115] and instead employed a gender-based model and ruled that the tradition-centred reason for the differential treatment of men and women for the purposes of name changes is insufficient to outweigh a gender-based approach.[116]

Had the Supreme Court of Namibia employed a gender-based approach in *Frank*, it could have found a violation of the constitutional prohibition to discriminate against anyone on the basis of sex. However, to arrive at that probable conclusion, the court must first determine that non-recognition of same-sex relationships constitutes sex discrimination or gender discrimination. Although the Namibian Constitution does not enumerate gender as a prohibited ground of discrimination, Namibia is obliged, as a member of the Southern African Development Community (SADC) by the SADC Treaty[117] not to discriminate against any person on the ground of gender.[118]

Another downside of the pro-majoritarian value-based model as an interpretative approach and a guide for constitutional preferences is that it weakens the protection of unpopular minorities in constitutional democracies like Namibia. Unpopular minorities are not adequately represented in the national parliament in Windhoek. In the same vein, their rights, interests and claims are not always adequately protected in national laws and policies. When laws do not sufficiently protect their interests and claims, they increase the disadvantage of and further marginalise unpopular minorities,[119] who thereby become vulnerable

---

115 *Müller and Engelhard v Namibia* (n 7 above) para 6.8: 'In view of the importance of the principle of equality between men and women, the argument of a long-standing tradition cannot be maintained as a general justification for different treatment of men and women, which is contrary to the [ICCPR].'

116 As above: '[T]he reason for the distinction has no sufficient importance in order to outweigh the generally excluded gender based approach.'

117 Treaty of the Southern African Development Community 32 ILM 116. Namibia ratified the SADC Treaty on 17 August 1992.

118 SADC Treaty art 6(2); see also the SADC Protocol on Gender and Development.

119 P de Vos 'Gay and lesbian legal theory' in C Roederer & D Moellendorf (eds) *Jurisprudence* (2004) 328, 331: '[L]egal discourse and practice may operate to hide and/or legitimize the violence imposed on society by these [social] institutions, rather to protect gay men and lesbians and other marginalized people against such violence'.

political constituencies as they cannot secure for themselves favourable legislation.[120]

The protection of minorities is one of the reasons why courts check and counter-balance the powers of the other two branches of government.[121] As Doyle puts it in the context of Irish constitutional law, 'constitutional equality' is equality enforced by an 'unelected judiciary against the electorally accountable organs of government.'[122] The importance of the right to equality is that it serves as a counter-balance so that the majority does not subsume the minority or individual.[123] Without such guarantee of equality, minorities and individuals are left to rely upon the will of the majority to project their rights.[124]

Marginalisation and vulnerability imply that unpopular minorities are in need of greater protection and special treatment. The protection of unpopular minorities is premised upon the axiom that, regardless of who they are, how they think and what they do, the humanity and dignity of members of these minorities are inviolable[125] and insulated from 'political bargaining' and the 'calculus of social interests'.[126] In view of the fact that unpopular minorities are not participants in the legislative process, the courts in Namibia can shield these minorities by endorsing a more assertive, if not counter-majoritarian, interpretation of the equality clause. A more assertive interpretation of the equality clause may result in a more important influence of and increased references to international law in controversial equality cases.[127] This robust interpretation could be achieved by making public opinion or the views of the majority an important but no longer a decisive factor in judicial decisions.[128]

6.2 Other plausible explanations

Another plausible explanation of why Namibian courts prefer comparative law is that in controversial cases there exists no real international society to which Namibia can be compared. The fact that the Court in the *Frank* case was only comparing the Namibian society with the Zimbabwean and South African societies while ignoring the international community, supports this hypothesis. Notwithstanding the differences in the wording of the equality clauses in the constitutions of Namibia, Zimbabwe and South Africa, the fact remains that each of

---

120 D Johnson *et al Jurisprudence: A South African perspective* (2001) 240.
121 *Makwanyane* case (n 51 above).
122 O Doyle *Constitutional equality law* (2004) 24.
123 Cooper (n 15 above) 41.
124 As above.
125 See J Rawls *A theory of justice* (1971) 3: 'Each person possesses an inviolability founded on justice that even the welfare of society as a whole cannot override'.
126 Rawls (n 125 above) 4: '[t]he rights secured by justice are not subject to political bargaining or to the calculus of social interests'.
127 *Makwanyane* case (n 51 above).
128 This is the approach taken by the Constitutional Court of South Africa in *Makwanyane*.

those clauses drew inspiration from international standards,[129] which are deemed universal. It is thus a bewildering conundrum that these Southern African countries come up with diverse and diametrically opposed interpretations of the concept of equality. Actually, the phrasing of the right to equality in international legal instruments is general, vague and ambiguous; and so is the notion of 'international community' and the values attributed to it. However, courts in *Frank* and other controversial equality cases do not expressly state the comparability explanation in their judgment, probably because it is intuitive and therefore there is no need to expressly articulate it.

Namibian courts prefer comparison with societies with enough commonalities. The fact that the Court referred more to the constitutional law of countries located in the same geographical region (ie South Africa and Zimbabwe) and with similar experiences, historical development, cultural and ethnic outlook, further supports this hypothesis. This explanation would account for the Court's references in *Frank* to South African and Zimbabwean constitutional law more than it did to cases from England, Canada, and the US. In addition, the Court's references in *Frank* to the constitutional jurisprudence of common law countries and none from civil law countries support this explanation, which justifies judicial preferences in terms of commonalities between two legal systems.

Finally, it is also possible that Namibian courts prefer comparative law because Namibian higher courts are increasingly asserting local identity and autonomy vis-à-vis the South African constitutional jurisprudence. Namibian constitutional law is replete with references to South African constitutional cases. However, in a few cases, Namibian higher courts have expressed their autonomy from the South African jurisprudence. In *Müller,* Chief Justice Strydom said that the decisions of the South African courts, and more particularly that of the Constitutional Court, are

> very relevant and in the past this Court and the High Court of Namibia, have frequently applied these decisions but this must always be done with due recognition of the differences that may exist between our two Constitutions.[130]

In *Frank*, O'Linn AJA was careful to hold that Namibian and South African trends, contemporary opinions, norms and values tend in opposite directions.[131] The autonomy hypothesis seems a plausible explanation of the decision in *Frank.* The majority Court in *Frank* held that, with respect to sexual orientation, the South African cases are irrelevant to Namibia. This was because the Namibian Constitution,

---

129 Ie UDHR and ICCPR.

130 *Müller* (n 7 above) 12.

131 *Frank* (n 5 above) 114.

unlike the South African Constitution,[132] does not expressly forbid discrimination on the ground of sexual orientation.[133] The Court felt that South Africa's inclusion of sexual orientation in its constitution reflected a difference of values between the two nations.[134] But, on closer look, the autonomy hypothesis does not support the Namibian court preference for comparative law in equality cases that do not involve sexual orientation. Indeed, nothing in the judgments of *Müller and Kauesa* indicates the desire to assert autonomy or independence from the South African constitutional influence.

6.3 The influence of international law

International law offers a comfortable shelter to unpopular minorities in Namibia in controversial equality cases because the treaties binding on Namibian courts cover most grounds of discrimination not listed in the Namibian Constitution. This is so notwithstanding the fact that pragmatism would not concern itself so much with identifying which ground or 'badge' of discrimination applies, but with whether an individual has been discriminated against in relation to a substantive right.[135]

Particularly, international law could only be of limited assistance to the complainants in *Frank* because those treaties do not cover sexual orientation. Solace for the complainants in *Frank* and similar cases in the future come in the form of the rejection by the UN Human Rights Committee of 'long-standing tradition' as a justification for differentiating between married men and married women in *Müller*. Most importantly, in *Toonen v Australia,*[136] the HRC held that homosexuality (a ground of discrimination not expressly enumerated in the ICCPR) was covered by the reference to 'sex' in article 26 (on equality) of the ICCPR. Even though the views of the HRC are only of persuasive authority, litigants in *Frank* and similar litigants could take *Müller* and *Toonen* to their next logical step and argue against the type of value-based constitutional theory practiced in Namibia.

Grounds that are not explicitly protected in the Namibian Constitution are gender, pregnancy, language, national origin, property, birth, culture, ill health, HIV/AIDS, disability, and sexual orientation. Fortunately, for most of these grounds unpopular minorities can find redress by relying

---

132 Constitution of Republic of South Africa of 1996 art. 1(1)(xxii)(a): '"prohibited grounds" are race, gender, sex ... sexual orientation ...' [hereinafter South African Constitution].

133 *Frank* (n 5 above) 113.

134 *Frank* (n 5 above) 114.

135 Cooper (n 15 above) 53.

136 *Toonen v Australia,* CCPR/C/D/488/1992.

on Namibia's obligations under international law,[137] through article 144 of the Namibian Constitution. But such advocacy and litigation strategies will not adequately solve the problem of unpopular minorities in general because by definition the values, claims and interests of these minorities contradict those of political majorities. It is therefore easy for some members of society to discriminate against certain minorities in subtle ways and on new grounds not protected under the Namibian Constitution and international law.

The rub is not the new or unlisted grounds of discrimination as such but a system of judicial decision-making that resolves the competing claims of social groups in favour of the majority in controversial equality cases. Namibian courts should not adopt an anti-majority or uncritical counter-majoritarian stance. Rather, courts should embrace an interpretive philosophy that consecrates human autonomy as the real source of the right to equality and not the state, as implied by the decision in *Frank* to defer to the parliament on the recognition of sexual orientation. Indeed, albeit democratic, the current constitutional interpretation model based on the values of the majority subverts human rights orthodoxy that holds that human beings are equal by virtue of being human.

7 Conclusion

The chapter discussed the judicial preference for comparative law over international law in controversial equality cases. It first defined controversial equality cases in Namibia, presented the *Frank* case, listed the attractions of international and comparative law in judicial decisions, unpacked the concept of preference, and developed a theory to explain the judicial preference for comparative law over international law in controversial equality cases in Namibia. From the foregoing discussion, it appears the most plausible explanation of preferences in controversial equality cases in Namibia is the legitimacy thesis because it not only explains the Namibian preference for comparative law but it also indicates which national legal system is nearest to guiding court decisions. Moreover, the legitimacy thesis appears to be the most plausible explanation of judgments in favour or against unpopular minorities in Namibia. It is the best story of why, despite being connected to international law by a constitutional umbilical cord, Namibian courts have developed an interpretive practice that prefers to learn from the legal position in sister states – a matricidal interpretive practice that may threaten the already fragile human rights protection of unpopular minorities.

---

137 See eg Charter of the United Nations art 1(3), UDHR art 2, CCPR art 2(1), International Covenant on Economic, Social and Cultural Rights art 2(1), SADC Treaty art 6(2).

9

Litigating the right to health in Nigeria: Challenges and prospects

Ebenezer Durojaye*

Summary

This chapter examines the meaning of the right to health under international law and its main content. It argues that the right to health is one of the most fundamental rights, which interlinks with several other rights such as life, dignity and non-discrimination. It then discusses the importance of litigating the right to health generally; paying attention to HIV-related litigation. The chapter notes that despite the recognition given to the right to health under national and international documents, litigating this right has met with different challenges. Thus, the chapter discusses barriers to litigating the right to health in Nigeria, such as non-recognition of the right to health as an enforceable right, the requirement for *locus standi*, stigma and discrimination associated with HIV-related cases and lack of knowledge on the part of lawyers and judges on international human rights principles and standards. The chapter argues that despite these challenges some opportunities exist for litigating the right to health cases, especially HIV-related cases in Nigeria. In conclusion, recommendations are made that will improve health-related litigation in Nigeria

1 Introduction

Nigeria with about three million people living with HIV (PLWH) has the second highest number of HIV infected persons in Africa.[1] Stigma and discrimination are rife against people living with HIV in the country. Moreover, studies have shown that on a daily basis people living with HIV encounter human rights abuses in employment, housing,

---

* LLD candidate Department of Constitutional Law and Philosophy of law, University of the Free State, South Africa; ebenezer1170@yahoo.com. Thanks go to Prof Charles Ngwena, Prof Akin Oyebode and Nontobeko Ncinitwa for their wonderful support always.

1 Federal Ministry of Health (FMOH) *Report of the national HIV/syphilis sentinel sero prevalence survey* (2005). South Africa, with about 5 million people living with HIV, has the largest number of HIV infected person in Africa.

community, family and health care setting.[2] Yet only few cases have been filed in the courts and decided on this issue.[3]

This chapter discusses the importance of litigating the right to health generally, focusing on HIV-related litigation. It examines challenges to litigating the right to health in Nigeria, such as non-recognition of the right to health as an enforceable right, the requirement for *locus standi* before instituting public interest cases, stigma and discrimination associated with HIV-related cases and lack of knowledge on the part of lawyers and judges on international human rights principles and standards. The chapter finally explores the opportunities which exist for litigating right to health cases, especially HIV-related cases, in Nigeria.

2 The right to health under international human rights law

A clear understanding of the nature of the right to health will help a prospective litigant to frame his or her action in a court of law. Therefore, what follows in this section is a discussion on the recognition of the right to health under international human rights law.

Article 12 of the International Covenant on Economic, Social and Cultural Rights (ICESCR) provides that 'States Parties to the present Covenant recognise the right of everyone to the enjoyment of the highest attainable standard of physical and mental health'. Article 12(2) further contains, among others, important determinants of the right to health such as prevention and treatment of diseases, essential for the enjoyment of the right.

The UN Committee on Economic, Social and Cultural Rights (ESCR Committee) in its General Comment 14, while clarifying the content of the right to health, has noted that the right to health contains both freedoms and entitlements. In other words, an individual should have the right to control his/her body and health, including sexual and reproductive health, and the right to be free from coercive medical treatment and experimentation.[4] On the other hand, the entitlements relate to the right to 'a system of health protection which provides equality of opportunity for people to enjoy highest attainable level of health'.[5] The Committee further advises that the right to health as guaranteed in article 12 of the ICESCR should be construed as an inclusive right limited not only to the provision of timely and appropriate health care services but also intersecting with determinants of health such

2 Center for the Right to Health (CRH*) HIV/AIDS and human rights: Experiences of people living with HIV/AIDS in Nigeria* (2001); see also Journalist against AIDS (JAAIDS) *Behind the Shadow* (2004).

3 So far the only decided case on this issue is *Odafe and Others v Attorney General of the Federation and Others* (2004) AHRLR 205 (NgHC 2004) while other cases are pending in courts across the country.

4 'The right to the highest attainable standard of health' UN Committee on Economic, Social and Cultural Rights, General Comment 14, UN Doc E/C/12/2000/4. para 8.

5 As above.

as access to safe and potable water and sanitation, adequate supply of food, nutrition and housing, healthy environmental condition and access to health-related information and education.[6]

The ESCR Committee has noted that the right to health intersects with other human rights such as the rights to life, non-discrimination, dignity, equality and liberty.[7] In the same manner, the Human Rights Committee in its General Comment 6 on article 6 of the Covenant on Civil and Political Rights (ICCPR) has noted that the right to life should not be construed narrowly, but should be broadly interpreted to embrace other rights such as right to housing, food and medical care.[8] This position of the Committee has been echoed by other commentators.[9]

The ESCR Committee has identified the essential elements of the right to health to include, availability, accessibility, acceptability and quality. According to the Committee, health care goods and services should be made available to all in sufficient quantity. Accessibility relates to four important elements namely, non-discrimination, physical, economic and information accessibility. In summary the Committee is of the view that health care services should attend to the needs of all categories of people in society, especially the vulnerable and marginalised groups such as women, children, people with disability and people living with HIV.[10] Acceptability implies that health care services must be culturally and scientifically acceptable to all, especially vulnerable and marginalised members of the society.

With regard to states parties' obligations regarding the right to health under the Covenant, the Committee opines that like all other human rights, states have the obligations to respect, protect and fulfil the right to health. Although the Committee admits that the Covenant provides for progressive realisation of the right to health, however, this should not be interpreted as 'depriving states parties' obligations of all meaningful content'.[11]

The Committee has explained that certain obligations are not subject to progressive realisation, but must be realised immediately. Thus, the Committee identifies obligations relating to core content of the right to health as those obligations which a 'state party cannot under any circumstances whatsoever, justify its non-compliance'.[12]

---

6 General Comment 14 (n 4 above) para 11.

7 General Comment 14 (n 4 above) para 3.

8 'The right to life', UN Human Rights Committee General Comment 6.

9 V Leary 'The right to health in international human rights law' (1994) 1(1) *Health and Human Rights* 27; see also, AE Yamin, 'Not just a tragedy: Access to medication as a right under international law' (2003) 21 *Boston University International Law Journal* 125.

10 General Comment 14 (n 4 above) para 12.

11 General Comment 14 (n 4 above).

12 General Comment 14 (n 4 above) para 47. The Committee has identified the following as the core content of the right to health: (a) To ensure the right of access to health facilities, goods and services on a non-discriminatory basis, especially for vulnerable or marginalised groups; (b) To ensure access to the minimum essential food which is

The ESCR Committee has observed that the obligation on states to prevent, treat and control diseases and epidemic, requires them to establish prevention and education programmes for behaviour-related health concerns such as sexually transmitted infections generally, and HIV/AIDS in particular.[13] The Committee has also explained that the provision on non-discrimination in the ICESCR applies to people living with HIV. In the same vein, the Committee established under the Convention on the Elimination of All Discrimination against Women (CEDAW) has noted that the issues of HIV/AIDS and other infectious disease are central to a woman's enjoyment of her right to health including sexual health. The Committee therefore, requires states to report on the steps they have taken to address the threats posed by HIV/AIDS and other diseases to women's health.

The International Guidelines on HIV/AIDS and Human Rights[14] contains a number of important provisions addressing the nexus between human rights and HIV/AIDS. For instance, the Guidelines urge states to respect and protect the human rights of all vulnerable groups including those infected and affected by HIV. The Guidelines also require states:

> to establish effective programmes to address HIV/AIDS;
>
> to develop laws and policies to address human rights concerns raised by HIV/AIDS;
>
> to review criminal law and correctional law so as to ensure that these laws are not misused in the context of HIV/AIDS;
>
> to enact and strengthen anti-discrimination laws in the context of HIV/AIDS;
>
> to enact law and legislation that will ensure access to HIV-related goods and services including access to treatment.

Furthermore, the UN General Assembly Special Session on HIV/AIDS recognised that HIV/AIDS has a gender dimension and that respect for the rights of women will go a long way in reducing the

---

nutritionally adequate and safe, to ensure freedom from hunger to everyone; (c) To ensure access to basic shelter, housing and sanitation, and an adequate supply of safe and potable water; (d) To provide essential drugs, as from time to time defined under the WHO Action Programme on Essential Drugs; (e) To ensure equitable distribution of all health facilities, goods and services; (f) To adopt and implement a national public health strategy and plan of action, on the basis of epidemiological evidence, addressing the health concerns of the whole population; the strategy and plan of action shall be devised, and periodically reviewed, on the basis of a participatory and transparent process; they shall include methods, such as right to health indicators and benchmarks, by which progress can be closely monitored; the process by which the strategy and plan of action are devised, as well as their content, shall give particular attention to all vulnerable or marginalised groups.

13 General Comment 14 (n 4 above) para 16.

14 Adopted at the Third International Consultation on HIV/AIDS and Human Rights (Geneva 25 July 2002), organised by the Office of the UN High Commissioner for Human Rights and Joint United Nations Programme on HIV/AIDS.

prevalence of HIV infection in the world.[15] The General Assembly also affirmed that access to medicines in the context of HIV/AIDS is a fundamental right.[16]

Under regional human rights instruments the right to health is guaranteed under article 16 of the African Charter on Human and Peoples' Rights (African Charter). Article 16 states that everyone has the right to enjoy the best attainable state of physical and mental health. The African Commission on Human and Peoples' Rights (African Commission) in the *Purohit* case held that the 'Enjoyment of the human right to health as it is widely known is vital to all aspects of a person's life and well-being, and is crucial to the realisation of all the other fundamental human rights and freedoms.'[17] The Commission stated further that the right includes the right to health facilities and access to goods and services be guaranteed to all without discrimination of any kind

Article 14 of the Protocol to the African Charter on the Rights of Women (African Women's Protocol)[18] contains detailed provisions recognising the right to health. Under article 14 states are required to 'ensure that the right to health of women, including sexual and reproductive health of women, is respected and promoted'. The Protocol is the first human rights treaty that clearly recognises women's reproductive health as human rights and contains specific provisions on women's protection in the context of HIV/AIDS.[19]

It should be noted that Nigeria has ratified most of the above mentioned instruments[20] and has even incorporated the African Charter into its domestic law. However, as this article will show later, the mere fact of ratification does not guarantee effective implementation of these instruments within domestic law. Indeed, in most countries of the world the enforcement of the right to health has remained a subject of controversy. This is sometime due to the claim that the right to health is vague or insufficiently clarified.[21]

Furthermore, there are some non-binding regional statements and declarations, which are relevant in the realisation of individuals' right to health in the context of HIV/AIDS. These include the Abuja Declaration

---

15 UN General Assembly Special Session on HIV/AIDS Resolution A/S-26/L2 June 2001 para 15.

16 As above.

17 *Purohit and Another v The Gambia* (2003) AHRLR 96 (ACHPR 2003) para 80.

18 Adopted by the AU Assembly in July 2003, entered into force 25 November, 2005.

19 Centre for Reproductive Rights *The Protocol on the Rights of Women in Africa: An instrument for advancing reproductive and sexual rights* (2005); see also E Durojaye 'Advancing gender equity in access to HIV treatment through the Protocol on the African Charter on the Rights of Women' (2006) 4 *African Human Rights Law Journal* 187; F Banda *Women, law and human rights: An African perspective* (2005) 80.

20 For instance, Nigeria ratified the ICESCR in 1993, African Charter in 1983, CEDAW in 1985 and the Women's Protocol in 2004.

21 See DP Fidler *International law and infectious diseases* (1999) 12.

on HIV/AIDS, tuberculosis, malaria and other related diseases,[22] the Maputo Declaration on Women and HIV/AIDS,[23] the Solemn Declaration on Gender Equity[24] and the Resolution on HIV/AIDS of the African Commission on Human and Peoples' Rights.[25]

3 Importance of litigating the right to health

Litigation generally, and public interest litigation in particular provides an avenue for individuals or groups to redress human rights violations. Although litigation is by no means the only avenue for realising the right to health, it remains one of the most important tools of achieving change in society.[26] Litigation provides a catalyst for change in law so that its application can reach beyond the individual case in such a way that its outcome affects a large number of people. Equally, litigation can easily generate public awareness over an issue. This is true in the case of class action where a case is brought on behalf of a large number of people on a particular issue. By taking such matter before the court it may generate publicity and gain the attention of the public on a hitherto unnoticed issue. This may lead to public support or sympathy on such an issue or matter.[27]

With regard to the right to health litigation, Gloppen has argued that such litigation can be used to hold a government accountable for its failure to realise the right to health.[28] Her argument is based on the ground that people and institutions entrusted with powers and responsibilities have the obligation to justify that those powers and responsibilities have been used appropriately.[29] While she observes that elections remain the most vital and legitimate means of holding a government accountable in a democracy, Gloppen nevertheless notes that because of their infrequent nature, and the fact that they may be subject to manipulation, particularly in Africa, reliance on them is uncertain. Therefore, litigation can provide an alternative means of holding governments accountable to their responsibilities with regard to

---

22 April 2001, OAU/SPS/ABUJA/3. It was agreed that African governments should commit at least 15% of their annual budget to the health sector.

23 Assembly/AU/Decl. 6(II) 2003.

24 Adopted by the AU Assembly, July 2004.

25 'Resolution on the HIV/AIDS pandemic - Threat against human rights and humanity' adopted at the 29th ordinary session of the African Commission, ACHPR Res.53/(XXIX)01.

26 Center for Reproductive Rights *Reproductive Rights in European Court of Human Rights* (2004) 3.

27 See for example, the American case of *Brown v Board of Education of Topeka* 347 US 483 (1954). Beyond the fact that the case addressed discrimination in relation to the right to education, it also sends out a strong statement in condemnation of racial discrimination in America.

28 S Gloppen 'Litigating as a strategy to hold governments accountable for implementing the right to health' (2008) 10 *Health and Human Rights* 21.

29 As above.

the right to health. This position has been echoed by Hogerzeil *et al* as follows:[30]

> Skilful litigation can help to ensure that governments fulfil their constitutional and international treaty obligations. Such assurances are especially valuable in countries in which social security systems are still being developed.

A good example of a case where a government has been held accountable for its obligation to realise the right to health is the South African case of *Minister of Health and others* v *Treatment Action Campaign.*[31] In that case, the South African government argued that providing Nevirapine in public hospitals to prevent transmission of HIV from pregnant women to their children was too expensive and that there was no medical proof guaranteeing the safety and efficacy of the drug. In its judgment, the Constitutional Court of South Africa rejected the government's excuse of lack of resources and found that refusal on the part of the government to make the drugs available in public health institutions contravened the right to health guaranteed under section 27 of the Constitution of South Africa. The Court then ordered the government to ensure that these drugs were made available in public health institutions. In the words of Forman, the decision in *Treatment Action Campaign* 'broke the deadlock on a social struggle where political debates had consistently failed to achieve satisfactory outcome'.[32] It needs to be stated here, however, that the Constitution of South Africa remains exceptional, being one of the few to explicitly recognise socio-economic rights, particularly the right to health, as enforceable rights in Africa.[33]

It has also been argued, with regard to access to medicines, that litigation on the right to health has the potential to redistribute wealth in the society, particularly from the rich to the poor.[34] This can particularly be so as regards litigating on the high prices of drugs. It has been noted that litigation combined with other strategies to bring down prices of ARVs drugs in South Africa during the early 2000s led to a substantially reduced cost of paying for drugs and prevented unnecessary expenses by the government.[35] Thus, litigation led to positive results for both

---

30 HV Hogerzeil *et al* 'Is right to essential medicines as part of the fulfilment of the right to health enforceable through the courts?'(2006) 368 *Lancet* 305.

31 *Minister of Health and ors v Treatment Action Campaig*n (TAC) (2002) 10 BCLR 1033 (CC).

32 L Forman 'Ensuring reasonable health: rights, the judiciary, and South African HIV/AIDS Policy' (2006) *Journal of Law, Medicine and Ethics* 711-724 719.

33 Other countries which recognise socio-economic rights as justiciable rights in Africa include Algeria, Caper Verde, Benin and Burkina Faso; see F Viljoen *International Human Rights Law in Africa* (2007) 573.

34 See M Heywood 'South Africa's Treatment Action Campaign: Combining law and social mobilisation to realise the right to health' (2009) 1 *Journal of Human Rights Practice* 24.

35 As above (The author argues that the various success recorded in cases such as the *Treatment Action Campaign* case (n 31 above) and *EN and others v The Government of South*

individuals who needed to purchase these drugs and government who would need to allocate resources to ensure the availability of these drugs.

4 Barriers to litigating the right to health in Nigeria

In a country like Nigeria where the judicial system is charaterised by corruption and undue delay in the administration of justice, resorting to litigation can be frustrating. This situation is exacerbated by weak infrastructure and exorbitant cost of litigation. It is a well known fact that filing of cases and securing the services of competent lawyers can be very challenging for the underprivileged. The result is that many vulnerable groups who have experienced violations of their rights tend to avoid using the courts as a means for redress.

The ability to litigate on right to health issues in any society will depend on the recognition given to this right under the domestic constitution. In other words, where the right to health is explicitly recognised in a national constitution it becomes relatively easy for cases to be filed on it. On the other hand, if the right to health, as in Nigeria, has not been explicitly recognised as an enforceable right in the national constitution, litigating on it may become very difficult. Therefore this section of the paper considers some of the barriers to litigating the right to health, especially HIV-related cases in Nigeria. These include non-justiciability of the right to health under the Constitution, negative attitudes of judges, and lack of access to justice to vulnerable groups.

4.1 The non-justiciability argument

The 1999 Constitution of Nigeria, like other previous constitutions, does not contain a specific provision recognising the right to health as an enforceable right in the country. The provision that makes reference to health in the Constitution is found in section 17 in chapter II of the Constitution. While section 17(1) of the Constitution provides for 'freedom, equality and justice', section 17(3)(d) places an obligation on the state to ensure that there are 'adequate medical and health facilities for all persons'. However, this section is under chapter II of the Constitution, which is captioned 'Fundamental Objectives and Directive Principles of State Policy', and which according to the Constitution is not justiciable.[36]

In *Okogie and others v Attorney General of Lagos State*[37] the applicant challenged the policy of the Lagos state government to abolish private

---

Africa and others unreported case 4576/06, 28 August 2006 available at http://www.alp.org. combined with intense activism and advocacy serve as a catalyst to reduction in prices of ARVs by pharmaceutical companies in South Africa.

36 See s 6(6)(c) of the Nigerian Constitution 1999, which provides that all rights, including the right to health, listed in chapter 2 of the Constitution, shall not be made justiciable.

37 *Archbishop Okogie and others v The Attorney-General of Lagos State* (1981) 2 NCLR 350.

schools within the state claiming that it was in violation of the right to education guaranteed under section 16 (chapter II) of the 1979 constitution, which is similar to the provision of the 1999 Constitution. The Court held that by virtue of section 6 of the 1979 Constitution (similar to section 6 of the 1999 Constitution) the provisions of chapter II of the Constitution were not enforceable and that it was not in the power of the Court to make any pronouncement on them. Rather this should be done by either the executive or the legislative arm of government. If ever there was any hope of litigating on socio-economic rights (contained in chapter II of the Nigeria Constitution) prior to *Okogie* case, this hope was dealt a deadly blow by the Court in that case. Although this case was decided before Nigeria incorporated the African Charter into its domestic law (as discussed below), subsequent decisions by the courts have not differed so much as Nigerian courts have continued to shut the door to prospective socio-economic rights litigants.[38]

The reluctance to recognise the right to health and other socio-economic rights as justiciable rights is hinged on the fact that adjudicating on these rights may erode the principle of separation of powers. It is often assumed that courts are not in the best position to make decisions intersecting with governments' policies and allocation of resources as this responsibility is best left to the executive arm of government.[39] Consequently, health-related issues have been viewed as largely political rather than legal matters, leading to a situation where domestic courts 'have been relatively reluctant to review health policies from human rights perspective', believing that doing so may exceed the appropriate democratic functions of the judiciary.[40] An-Na'im, however, has contended that to leave the matter of policy to the 'unfettered discretion of governments, however democratic without the possibility of judicial guidance and supervision', defeats the whole purpose of recognising social and economic rights as international human rights.[41]

Some commentators have argued that the provision of section 6 of the Nigerian Constitution, which provides that the socio-economic rights contained in chapter II of the Constitution are non-justiciable, should not deter prospective litigants from bringing cases relating to the right to health before the courts. For instance, Nnamuchi has noted that the argument that the right to health is non-justiciable in Nigeria because of

---

38 See for instance, the subsequent decision of the Court of Appeal in *Badejo v Federal Minister of Education* [1990] LRC (Const) 735. The Court held that the right to education was not a justiciable right under the Nigerian Consitution of 1979, which is in *pari materia* with the 1999 Constitution; see also S Ebobrah 'The future of economic, social and cultural rights litigation in Nigeria' (2007) 1 *Review of Nigerian Law and Practice* 109 116.

39 L Lester & C O'Cinneide 'The effective protection of social-economic rights' in Y Ghai & J Cottrell (eds) *Economic, social & cultural Rights in practice* (2004) 17 at 19.

40 See Forman (note 32 above) 711.

41 AA An-Na'im 'To affirm the full human rights standing of economic, social & cultural rights' in Ghai & Cottrell (n 39 above) 7.

resource implications is exaggerated as the country can at least provide basic primary health care services to the people.[42] He argues further that the Nigerian Constitution has described the primary purpose of the government as ensuring 'the security and welfare of the people'. Therefore, ensuring the availability of health care for the population is an essential obligation of the government and this can only be discharged by providing adequate health care and other social services.[43] In Nnamuchi's view, the problem with realising the right to health of the citizens in Nigeria is not one of lack of resources but rather act of kleptomania on the part of the rulers.[44]

Ebobrah has argued that section 6(6)(c) does not in any way debar courts from entertaining cases on socio-economic rights.[45] His argument is premised on the fact that chapter II of the Constitution is not exclusively dedicated to socio-economic rights, but rather is made up of conglomerates of rights, plans and programmes. According to him, the clause making chapter II non-justicable in not directly targeted at socio-economic rights. He further argues that the legislature can translate the contents of chapter II of the Constitution into enforceable laws.

The African Charter was enacted into law through the African Charter (Ratification and Enforcement) Act.[46] The relationship between the African Charter and national law was spelled out by the Supreme Court in *Abacha v Fawehinmi*[47] In that case Mr Fawehinmi had filed an application before a lower court challenging his unlawful arrest by armed security agents of the state and subsequent detention without trial, claiming that it violated his rights to liberty and dignity guaranteed under chapter IV of the Nigerian Constitution and the provisions of the African Charter.

One of the issues before the Supreme Court was the status of the African Charter in relation to the Constitution. The Supreme Court held that the African Charter had become part of Nigerian law and therefore enforceable in the country like any other statute. Moreover, the Court held that the African Charter has become a binding law in Nigeria and that in the event of its conflict with other statutes, the Charter will prevail. However, the Court noted that where there is a conflict between the provisions of the African Charter and the Constitution of Nigeria the latter will take precedence.

The implication of the *Abacha* judgment is important taking into consideration that the African Charter contains enforceable socio-economic rights which are classified as Directive Principles of State

---

42 O Nnamuchi 'Kleptocracy and its many faces: The challenges of justicability of the right to health care in Nigeria' (2008) 1 *Journal of African Law* 1 8.

43 As above.

44 As above.

45 Ebobrah (n 38 above) 118.

46 Cap 10, Laws of the Federation 1990.

47 *Abacha v Fawehinmi* (2000) 6 NWLR (Part 660) 228.

Policy under the Nigerian Constitution. As would be expected, the decision has become a subject of debate amongst commentators. For instance, Egede has noted that the position of the Court in coming to the conclusion that the African Charter is not superior to the Constitution is correct and that to hold otherwise would have been absurd considering the provisions of section 1(1) and (3) of the Constitution.[48] In Onyemelukwe's view it would appear that the opportunity to invoke the socio-economic rights provisions contained in the African Charter to cases in Nigeria might have been foreclosed.[49] She therefore, submits that this approach is not only restrictive but also problematic in that it prevents the African Charter the full force it deserves as a duly incorporated law within Nigeria.[50]

Nigerian courts have referred to the provisions of the African Charter in a number of cases,[51] mostly in relation to civil and political rights. It is only on a few occasions that courts have applied the provisions of the African Charter to socio-economic cases in general and the right to health in particular. For example the Court of Appeal[52] and a High Court[53] held article 24 of the African Charter (Ratification and Enforcement) Act (right to clean environment) to be justiciable. A good example of the reliance on the African Charter to advance the right to health is the *Festus Odaife* case.[54] In that case four HIV positive prisoners who were denied access to HIV treatment when they suffered from opportunistic infections filed an action for the enforcement of their fundamental rights. They claimed among others that the denial of treatment to them amounted to violations of their rights to health, non discrimination and freedom from inhuman and degrading treatment. The Court held that denying treatment to these prisoners as stipulated by law was a violation of article 16 of the African Charter. This is a positive

---

48 The combined reading of these provisions (similar to the 1979 Constitution) is to the effect that the Constitution is the supreme law of the land and that if any law is inconsistent with the Constitution, the Constitution shall prevail and such law shall be declared null and void to the extent of its inconsistency. E Egede 'Bringing human rights home: An examination of domestication of human rights treaties in Nigeria' (2007) 51 *Journal of African Law* 249 254.

49 C Onyemelukwe 'Access to anti-retroviral drugs as a component of the right to health in international law: Examining the application of the right in Nigerian jurisprudence' (2007) 7 *African Human Rights Law Journal* 446 449.

50 As above.

51 *Ogugu v The State* (1994) 9 NWLR (pt 366); *Peter Nemi v State* [1994] 1 LRC 376 (SC); *Agbakova v Director State Security Service* [1994] 6 NWLR 475; *Chima Ubani v Director of State Security Services and Attorney General of the Federation* unreported case no CA/L 260/96 7 July 1999.

52 See *Oronto Douglas v Shell Petroleum Development Company Limited* (1999) NWLR Pt 591 466.

53 *Gbemre v Shell Petroleum Development Company of Nigeria and ors*, First Instance Decision, FHC/B/CS/53/05; ILDC 924 (NG 2005); (2005) AHRLR 151 (NgHC 2005), 14 November 2005.

54 n 3 above.

decision which serves as a good precedent to rely on to advance litigating the right to health generally and HIV-related cases in particular. However, one would still need to interpret this case cautiously in view of the decision of the Supreme Court in *Abacha* case.[55]

In my view, the decision of the Supreme Court in *Abacha* with regard to the status of the African Charter is correct. The mere fact that an international treaty has been incorporated into domestic law does not necessarily elevate the treaty above the Constitution. This is particularly true of a dualist state like Nigeria. As correctly noted by the Supreme Court, the incorporation of the African Charter into domestic law by virtue of the African Charter Act qualifies it as an 'Act' of the National Assembly and can be enforced by the courts like every other legislation in the country. If that be the case, the provision of section 1(3) of the Constitution which provides that the Constitution is the supreme law of the land and that any law that is inconsistent with the Constitution shall be declared null and void according to its incontinency will equally apply to the African Charter Act. While it is noted that essentially, the provisions of the African Charter Act are the same as with the African Charter itself, and that section 1 of the Act provides that states shall give effect to the provision of the African Charter, it is submitted that this must be interpreted in line with section 1(3) of the Constitution.

It should be noted that the recently issued Fundamental Rights Enforcement Procedure Rules enjoins Nigerian courts to 'expansively and purposely' apply the provisions of the Nigerian Constitution and the provisions of the African Charter in matters relating to human rights violations in the country.[56] The purport or intent of these provisions is unclear. However, the expansive and purposive interpretation of the African Charter must be done *in tandem* with the provisions of the Constitution. In other words, such an interpretation must be consistent and not conflict with the provisions of the Constitution. This will tally with the position of the Nigerian Supreme Court on this issue.[57]

4.2 Section 12 of the Constitution

Another important obstacle to litigating the right to health and HIV-related cases in particular is the provision of section 12 of the Constitution relating to the status of ratified international human rights treaties before Nigerian courts. As mentioned earlier, Nigeria has ratified most of the international human rights instruments relating to the right to health. Despite this, courts have been very reluctant to invoke these instruments as a result of section 12(1) of the Constitution. This section

---

55 n 47 above.

56 Fundamental Rights Enforcement Procedures Rules (2009) issued pursuant to section 46(3) of the Nigerian Constitution, 1999.

57 In the *Abacha* case, the Court affirmed that in the event of any conflict between the Constitution and the African Charter the former will take precedence.

provides that '[n]o treaty between the Federation and any other country shall have the force of law to the extent to which any such treaty has been enacted into law by the National Assembly.'

Unless a treaty has been enacted into domestic law by the legislature it cannot be enforced in Nigeria. This coincides with the reasoning of the dualist school of thought.[58] Nigerian courts have often construed this section restrictively to refuse application of international human rights treaties to cases before them.

It may be argued that the mere fact that Nigeria has ratified international human rights treaties recognising the right to health makes it possible for the provisions of these instruments to be invoked before Nigerian courts. While it is noted that international treaties are enforceable in Nigeria only if they have been incorporated into domestic law, there is nothing preventing the courts from relying on principles and standards relating to the right to health under international law. For example, in *Mojekwu*[59] the Nigerian Court of Appeal held that a cultural practice violated women's rights to non-discrimination and cited provisions in CEDAW to support its finding.

The use of international law has received further support from the Chief Justice of the Federation in the Fundamental Rights Enforcement Procedure Rules issued in December 2009.[60] The preamble to these Rules provides as follows:

> For the purpose of advancing but never for the purpose of restricting the applicant's rights and freedoms, the Court shall respect municipal, regional and international bills of rights cited to it or brought to its attention or of which the Court is aware, whether these bills constitute instruments in themselves or form parts of larger documents like constitutions. Such bills include;
>
> (i) The African Charter on Human and Peoples' Rights and other instruments (including protocols) in the African regional human rights system.[61]
>
> (ii) The Universal Declaration of Human Rights and other instruments (including protocols) in the United Nations human rights system.

The import of this provision is that Nigerian courts should consider international law standards and principles contained in binding human rights treaties or instruments when handling cases relating to human rights violations of the citizens. This readily provides an avenue for the courts in the country to invoke international law standards and principles relevant to advancing the right to health in general and human rights violations in the contest of HIV/AIDS in particular. But this can only happen if civil society groups in conjunction with human rights lawyers file test cases in courts to challenge violations relating to the right to health. It will also be important for NGOs to embark on human rights

---

58 J Dugard *International law: A South African perspective* (2005) 47.

59 *Mojekwu & Others v Ejikeme & Others* (2000) 5 NWLR 402.

60 Fundamental Rights Enforcement Procedures Rules (2009) (n 56 above).

61 See para 3(b).

training for lawyers and judges on the relevance of international human rights standards to domestic cases.

There is nothing preventing an applicant's lawyer, in a case involving denial of access to treatment due to HIV positive status, from referring to for example the International Guidelines on HIV and Human Rights. Though these Guidelines are not legally binding, they nevertheless, lay down important norms and standards.

4.3 Stigma and discrimination associated with HIV/AIDS

HIV/AIDS remains a highly stigmatised disease in Nigeria. Whilst it is agreed that there has been an appreciable improvement in the level of awareness among the people about HIV/AIDS, this has not necessarily translated to behavioural change. Thus, in many parts of the country people living with HIV still encounter stigma and discrimination in their daily lives. Studies have shown that discrimination against people living with HIV is manifested in the form of denial of access to treatment, denial of employment, denial of housing or right to found a family.[62] Members of the legal profession including lawyers and judges who ought to protect the rights of people living with HIV sometimes also exhibit discriminatory practices against them.[63] A good example is the *Georgiana Ahemefule* case.[64] This was a case of a woman living with HIV whose employment was terminated because she tested positive to HIV. She decided to challenge her termination of employment in court. The Court requested expert evidence to prove that HIV is not transmissible through casual contact, before she could be allowed to enter the Court and testify in her own case. This kind of an attitude on the part of the court can send negative signals to the public with regard to HIV. In actual fact, it can fuel stigma and discrimination associated with the epidemic and can discourage people living with HIV who have suffered human rights violations from seeking redress in the court of law.

At present there is no law specifically addressing discrimination related to HIV in the country. This, in itself, is a gap in the law. Although the provisions of the National Policy on HIV/AIDS of 2003 forbid discrimination against people living with HIV, discrimination continues to thrive in the country since the provisions of the Policy are not legally enforceable. It would be recalled that during the UN Declaration of Commitments[65] in 2001 it was agreed that countries of the world should by 2003, enact legislation specifically addressing HIV-related discrimination in their countries. Nigeria is yet to keep up to this

---

62 Center for the Right to Health (n 2 above).

63 As above.

64 *Georgina Ahamefule v Imperial Medical Centre and other* unreported suit no ID/1527/2000 (HC).

65 UN General Assembly Special Session on HIV/AIDS Resolution A/S-26/L2 June 2001.

promise. Section 42 of the Constitution forbidding discrimination has been interpreted narrowly by a Federal High Court in one of the very few cases decided on HIV in the country.[66] The Court reasoned that section 42 of the Constitution does not prohibit discrimination based on health or disease status. It has been argued elsewhere that this interpretation of the Court is not only restrictive but also falls short of principles of international human rights law.[67] It is therefore, imperative that an enabling environment is created where the rights of all the people, including HIV positive persons, are respected and where discriminatory practices against people living with HIV are addressed. Stigma and discrimination associated with HIV fuel fear about the disease and may discourage infected or affected persons from seeking legal remedy for the violations of their rights.

4.4 Lack of knowledge of international human rights law

One other barrier to litigating the right to health in Nigeria is the negative attitudes of judges to issues relating to human rights of people living with HIV. Often lawyers and judges are not aware of international human rights law especially with regard to issues relating to the right to health, including HIV/AIDS. The implication of this is that most lawyers are unable to cite relevant and appropriate international human rights instruments to advance their cases. Equally, most judges are unable to apply relevant human rights instruments or draw examples from other jurisdictions on similar issues to come to a logical conclusion as regards cases before them.

Most lawyers are unwilling to litigate on HIV-related cases either because they are not interested or because they lack the necessary skills and knowledge on the human rights issues relating to HIV. Commenting on some of the constraints militating against good performance of the courts in Nigeria, Ogowewo opines as follows:[68]

> Another constraint that is often ignored is the quality of the Bar. If legal training in Nigeria is poor and mandatory continuing legal education is non-existent, judges will increasingly have to grapple with the constraint imposed on them by the poor forensic skills and the slender legal knowledge of a significant number of barristers.

At present very few non-governmental organisations are concerned with issues relating to human rights violations of people living with HIV in the country. From the discussion above, it is clear that unless lawyers and judges are well equipped on issues relating to international human

---

66 *Odafe* (n 3 above).

67 See E Durojaye 'Discrimination based on HIV/AIDS status: A comparative analysis of the Nigerian Court's decision in *Festus Odaife and others v Attorney General of the Federation and others* with other Commonwealth jurisdictions' (2007) 11 *Law, Democracy ad Development* 133-151.

68 T Ogowewo 'Self-inflicted constraints on judicial government in Nigeria' (2005) 49 *Journal of African Law* 49.

rights law in general and the right to health in particular, jurisprudence on HIV in the country will not develop. It will, therefore, be necessary for civil society groups, particularly NGOs to provide human rights training for lawyers and judges in the country. It is believed that good knowledge of international human rights law will go a long way in enhancing the development of jurisprudence on the right to health in the country.

4.5 The requirement of *locus standi*

Public interest litigation on the right to health in general and HIV/AIDS in particular is threatened by the requirement of *locus standi* by Nigerian courts. This rule is viewed by Nigerian courts as fundamental to confer rights of action on a plaintiff in a case. The *locus standi* rule follows from section 46 of the Nigerian Constitution which provides: 'Any person who alleges that any of the provisions of this Chapter has been, is being or likely to be contravened in any State in relation to him may apply to a High Court in that State for redress.'

According to the court in *Thomas and others v Olufusoye*[69] in order for an applicant to establish *locus standi,* he or she must demonstrate a sufficient interest in the case which must be a personal interest that is over and above that of the general public who may likely be affected by the action he or she is challenging. This principle of law is well entrenched in Nigerian legal system. Ever since the decision of the Supreme Court in *Adesanya v President of the Federal Republic of Nigeria*[70] the courts have requested that an applicant filing a case on constitutional matters which may affect other members of the public must display an interest in the case before he or she can be heard. Even a moderation of this principle in *Fawehinmi v Akilu*[71] has not changed the attitudes of the courts with regard to the principle. This has become a stumbling block to public interest litigation in the country. There is no doubt that it can also limit access to court and justice to people living with HIV, especially if public interest litigation is contemplated

The argument often adduced in support of *locus standi* is that it saves the court from being turned into a meeting arena for 'busybodies' who do not have genuine business to do with the court. The *locus standi* rule, it is believed, will not only save the precious time of the court but will also protect its integrity. However, while it is necessary to ensure that it is only those who have genuine business with the court that can bring cases

69 *Thomas and others v Olufusoye* (1986) 1 NWLR part 18 669.

70 *Adesanya v President of the Federal Republic of Nigeria* (1981) 1 All NLR 1.

71 *Fawehinmi v Akilu* (1987) 4 NWLR 797. In that case the Supreme Court held that the lawyer of a slain journalist could initiate a criminal proceeding to determine who killed his client. According to the Supreme Court, the lawyer had *locus standi* since in Africa we are all our brothers' keepers. It must be noted that the Supreme Court decision in this case is limited to private initiation of criminal proceedings. Therefore, the decision did not overrule *Adesanya* case.

before it, a restrictive adherence to the principle of *locus standi* can prevent vulnerable groups such as women, children and people living with HIV from obtaining justice.

As Ogowewo correctly suggests the application of the *locus standi* rule must be tempered by the courts so as to ensure justice for those who have experienced violations of their rights.[72] Ogowewo is of the view that the *Adesanya* case never laid down any requirement for *locus standi* before a constitutional action can be brought before the court.[73] No doubt the requirement for *locus standi* by Nigerian courts can restrict access to court for many people who have suffered violations of the rights. It does not serve the interest of justice and therefore it should be done away with.

This may finally become true with the new Fundamental Rights Enforcement Rules, which clearly state in paragraph 3(e) as follows:[74]

> The Court shall encourage and welcome public interest litigations in the human rights field and no human rights case may be dismissed or struck out for want of *locus standi*. In particular, human rights activists, advocates, or groups as well as any non-governmental organisations, may institute human rights application on behalf of any potential applicant. In human rights litigation, the applicant may include any of the following:
> (i) Anyone acting in his own interest;
> (ii) Anyone acting on behalf of another person;
> (iii) Anyone acting as a member of, or in the interest of a group or class of persons;
> (iv) Anyone acting in the public interest, and
> (v) Association acting in the interest of its members or other individuals or groups

Undoubtedly, the purpose of this provision is to relax the *locus standi* rule to allow for public interest litigation. This is a welcome development and will surely go a long way in improving access to justice. By this provision, Nigerian courts should be able to interpret the provision of section 46 of the Constitution broadly so as to diminish the negative effect of the requirement for *locus standi* in class action relating to the violations of the rights of HIV positive persons in the country. In this regard, Nigerian courts can draw inspiration from decisions of Ugandan courts. For instance, in the case of *The Environmental Action Network Ltd (TEAN) v Attorney- General and National Environment Authority*[75] the Ugandan Supreme Court overruled an objection by the counsel to the defendants stating that the petitioners should have brought a representative action under Civil Procedure Rules. The application in question was brought on behalf of the non-smoking public pursuant to article 50 of the Ugandan Constitution dealing with the right to a clean and healthy environment, right to life and for the general good of public health of Ugandans. In its judgment, the Court noted that an

---

72 T Ogunwewo 'The problem with standing to sue in Nigeria' (1995) 39 *Journal of African Law* 14.

73 As above 15.

74 n 56 above.

75 *The Environmental Action Network Ltd (TEAN) v Attorney-General and National Environment Authority* Misc App 39 of 2001.

organisation can bring public interest litigation on behalf of groups or members of the public even where the applying organisation has no direct interest or has not been directly affected by action it seeks to redress.

Furthermore, the recent decision of the ECOWAS Court of Justice in the *Registered Trustee of SERAP* case is very instructive on this liberal approach to the *locus standi* rule. In that case, the Court in response to Nigerian government's objection to the suit based on lack of *locus standi* said as follows:[76]

> Public international law in general is in favour of promoting human rights and limiting the impediments against such a promotion, lends credence to the view that in public interest litigation, the plaintiff need not show that he has suffered any personal injury or has a special interest that needs to be protected to have standing. Plaintiff must establish that there is a public right which is worthy of protection which has been allegedly breached and that the matter in question is justiciable. This is a healthy development in the promotion of human rights and this court must lend its weight to it, in order to satisfy the aspirations of citizens of the sub-region in their quest for a pervasive human rights regime.

Though the decisions cited above are not binding on Nigerian courts, nonetheless, they serve as a good reference point in mitigating or relaxing the negative impact of the *locus standi* rule.

5 Prospects for litigating the right to health in Nigeria

An important opportunity for litigating the right to health in the country is the fact that under chapter IV of the Nigerian Constitution some fundamental rights such as rights to life, dignity, liberty and privacy have been guaranteed which can have implications for the enjoyment of the right to health. As earlier mentioned, the ESCR Committee has observed that the right to health is dependent on the enjoyment of other rights.[77] The implication of this is that when a person is denied access to treatment, solely based on his or her HIV status, his/her rights to life, dignity and equality will equally be affected. Rather than filing an action to challenge the violation of the right to health of the affected person (which may face the hurdle of non justiciability), an action can be brought based on chapter IV of the Constitution.

This interdependence and interrelatedness of rights approach has received judicial approval in some countries, notably India. For instance, in the case of *Olga Tellis v Bombay Municipal Corporation*[78] the Indian Supreme Court held that the eviction of the petitioners from their dwellings amounted to a deprivation of their livelihood. This decision provides an avenue for courts to imply violation of civil and political

---

76 *Registered Trustee of SERAP v Federal Government and another,* suit ECW/CCJ/APP/0808, 27 October 2009.

77 General Comment 14 (note 4 above).

78 *Olga Tellis v Bombay Municipal Corporation* (1985) 3 SCC 545.

rights in a case dealing with social and economic rights. Similarly, in *Majoor Samity*[79] the Supreme Court held that a denial of emergency medical treatment to an individual violated the right to life under article 21 of the Indian Constitution. In *Kesavananda Bharati v State of Kerala*[80] the Supreme Court noted that although section 37 of the Indian Constitution specifically provides that Directive Principles of State Policy are not legally enforceable, they should nonetheless, enjoy equal status with traditional fundamental rights.

It should be noted that India shares a similar legal system with Nigeria. As in Nigeria, the socio-economic rights provisions in the Indian Constitution are classified under the Directive Principles of the State Policy. As shown above the Indian courts have ingeniously linked the violation of non-justiciable socio-economic rights with justiciable civil and political rights. This is a welcome development that is worthy of emulation.

Although Nigerian courts have yet to apply this approach to cases before them, there is no reason to suggest that they should not. Indeed, an attempt to explore this approach by the Centre for the Right to Health (CRH) in one of the cases filed before a Lagos High Court failed not because the Court was opposed to this approach but rather due to technical reasons. In *X v Attorney General of Lagos State and others*[81] a 39 year old woman living with HIV, who was denied treatment due to her HIV status by a state hospital when she was critically ill, filed an action against the government of Lagos State for the enforcement of her fundamental rights. In her application she claimed that the denial of access to treatment was in violation of her fundamental rights to life, dignity and non discrimination, all guaranteed under the Nigerian Constitution and the African Charter. However, during the hearing of the case, a preliminary application was brought by the respondent claiming that the claims of the applicant were essentially tied to the violation of her right to health, which is not enforceable before the court. Unfortunately, this application could not be argued on its merit as it was later abandoned by the respondent thereby forcing the Court to strike it out.

With regard to the substantive case, the Court held that the applicant's case was meritorious and in line with the provisions of the Constitution of Nigeria. However, since there were contradictions in affidavits of the applicant and that of the respondent, the Court was unable to resolve the case in favour of the applicant. Implicit in the decision is that a denial of a person's right to treatment due to his or her HIV status can be challenged by relying on provisions of chapter IV of the Nigerian Constitution. This indeed provides a window of opportunity to challenge

---

79 *Paschim Banga Khet Majoor Samity v State of West Bengal* [1996] AIR (SC) 2426.

80 *Kesavananda Bharati v State of Kerala* (1973) 4 SCC 225.

81 *X v Attorney General of Lagos State and others* unreported suit no LD/M/2002.

violation of the right to health by creatively relying on legally enforceable rights such as rights to life, dignity, liberty and non-discrimination.

The Indian approach above provides one way to overcome the non-justiciability argument. However, the greatest opportunity to realising the right to health in Nigeria through litigation is the fact that the African Charter has been incorporated into the domestic law of the country as discussed above.[82]

6 Way forward

One of the important steps that will need to be taken to encourage litigating the right to health and HIV-related cases is to create a conducive environment for victims to be confident of securing redress. Therefore, the present condition where people living with HIV are still made subject of discrimination does not augur well for litigation on this issue. It is long overdue for the country to enact legislation that will address discrimination, including HIV/AIDS-related discrimination. A bill is before the legislature since 2004 and it is unclear when it will be enacted. However, when enacted the law will not only encourage people living with HIV to seek legal redress for the violation of their rights but will also provide solid foundation for them to rest their cases. As earlier pointed out, the provision of section 42 of the Nigerian Constitution on non-discrimination has been construed narrowly by Nigerian courts to exclude prohibition of discrimination on health or HIV status. This confusion can be overcome with a specific anti-discrimination law in the country.

As seen from above, despite barriers to litigating the right to health, including HIV-related cases in Nigeria opportunities still exist for litigation on this right. One of the ways by which jurisprudence on right to health can be developed in the country is through human rights education for lawyers and judges. The Bangalore Principles of Judicial Conduct state that judges should continuously undergo training on issues relating to international law in general and human rights law in particular.[83] Training of judges and lawyers on human rights issues related to HIV can lead to positive jurisprudence on the right to health in the country. It will provide judges and lawyers with important information and knowledge on HIV and prepare them to better respond to human rights violations experienced by people living with HIV. For example, after the ruling in *Georgiana* case,[84] the Centre for the Right to

---

82 See F Viljoen 'Application of African Charter on Human and Peoples' Rights by domestic courts in Africa' (1999) 49 *Journal of African Law* 1-18; see also Ebobrah (n 38 above).

83 See the Bangalore Principles of Judicial Conduct adopted by the Judicial Group on Strengthening Judicial Integrity, as revised at the Round Table Meeting of Chief Justices held at the Peace Palace, The Hague, 25-26 November 2002) paras 6.3-6.6.

84 n 64 above.

Health (CRH), an NGO based in Lagos, commenced sensitisation seminars on HIV and human rights for judges and lawyers in Lagos, Abuja and Enugu. These series of seminars were well attended and responses thereafter were very encouraging. Most of the judges and lawyers were learning in details for the first time issues relating to the science of HIV/AIDS and the likely human rights violations which the epidemic may raise. People living with HIV were invited to share their experiences and the nature of violations they have suffered.

At the end of each seminar invitation was extended to interested lawyers to join the Legal Action Committee Initiatives (LACI). This is a diverse body of well experienced practicing lawyers, health practitioners, social scientists and academia that conducts research on laws and policies relating to human rights of people living with HIV in the country. It also gives expert opinion and advice on cases relating to the violation of human rights of people living with HIV. The Committee recommends possible cases to be filed in court. This multi disciplinary approach to litigating HIV-related cases is important and necessary in an environment like Nigeria, where mobilisation for right to health litigation is still unpopular. It must be noted that an important aspect of the success story of health rights litigation in South Africa is that civil society groups from different backgrounds and disciplines have been able to forge a formidable alliance to advance the right to health in the country. Heywood has noted that 'without an accompanying social mobilisation, the use of the courts may deliver little more than pieces of paper, with a latent untapped potential'.[85]

One of the positive outcomes of the seminar series is the *X v Attorney of Lagos*[86] case. In that case, the applicant after filing the court papers but before commencement of hearing, brought an application to protect her identity by requesting that her real name be substituted with a pseudonym. After listening to the submission of the counsel to the applicant to the effect that stigma and discrimination associated with HIV is rife in the country and that the applicant's action to sue a state government may draw negative attention to her, this application was graciously granted. Thus, the real name of the applicant was substituted with 'X'. This was one of the very few cases where such a request had been granted. It is a positive development and shows willingness on the part of the Court to address HIV-related stigma and discrimination and advance the rights of people living with HIV in the country. This will no doubt encourage more HIV positive persons to seek redress in court for the violations of their rights.

Beyond organising seminars for judges and lawyers on human rights issues raised by HIV, it will be important to incorporate issues on the right to health and reproductive health in the curricula of law faculties

---

85 See Heywood (n 34 above) 22.

86 *X v Attorney General of Lagos and others* (n 81 above).

across the country. As earlier noted, a large number of lawyers pass through university and law school without any opportunity to learn about human rights issues. Although some universities now offer human rights as a course, this subject is optional for students. As the training ground for future lawyers and judges, the Nigerian law school should consider including human rights training including issues relating to health law and reproductive health as part of its curriculum for law training in the country.

In the 21st century where globalisation is the order of the day and nearly every area of human endeavour speaks the language of rights, it is justifiable to advocate for the inclusion of human rights standards and principles (including principles and standards on the right to health) in the curriculum for law students. After all, lawyers are trained to become 'learned' in all areas of human endeavours. This will go a long way in building capacity of students and prepare them to be better advocates of citizens' rights to health. A good example in this regard is the recent initiative by the Women AIDS Collective (WACOL), an NGO based in Enugu in the Eastern part of Nigeria, in collaboration with other partners (both local and international) to incorporate health law and reproductive health into curriculum of law faculties across the country.[87] This initiative has won the approval of the National Universities Commission and may soon become a reality. This is encouraging and provides hope for a more conducive environment for litigating on the right to health and HIV cases in particular.

Furthermore, Nigerian courts should adopt the 'practical measure'[88] approach, which allows the courts to critically evaluate steps taken by the government realising the rights of the citizens in the context of HIV/AIDS. Whenever the court is faced with a case dealing human rights violations in the context of HIV/AIDS, they should draw inspiration from international norms or standards and from the experiences of courts in other jurisdictions to ask the following questions:

- To what extent do policy and budgetary measures respect, protect and fulfil the right to access health care services, particularly for vulnerable groups?
- Do these measures prioritise access to HIV treatment?
- How justified or reasonable are the measures in question?

7 Conclusion

This chapter has discussed some of the benefits of human rights litigation in general and rights to health litigation in particular. It has also

87 A series of meetings and workshops have been organised to this effect the last being an International Colloquium on Teaching Health Law and Reproductive Rights, 13-14 November 2008 in Abuja, Nigeria.

88 See B Twinomugisha 'Exploring judicial strategies to protect the right to access to emergency obstetrics care in Uganda' (2007) 7 *African Human Rights Law Journal* 298.

identified certain barriers to litigating the right to health and HIV-related cases in Nigeria, which include the non-recognition of the right to health as a justiciable right, the need for international human rights treaties to be domesticated before being enforceable, lack of knowledge on international human rights law on the part of lawyers and judges and stigma and discrimination associated with HIV. However, these barriers are not insurmountable. The chapter has identified opportunities for litigating the right to health in the country such as the domestication of the African Charter, the provisions of chapter IV of the Constitution and the increasing activism on the right to health by civil society groups.

The chapter suggested that there is need for lawyers and judges to develop the culture of health rights litigation in the country. This can only be achieved by incorporating human rights teaching, including health law into curriculum of the Nigerian Law School and law faculties in the country. Moreover, there will be need for continued education or training by way of seminars and workshops for senior lawyers and judges so as to update them on human rights issues relating to health in general and HIV in particular.

10

The role of international law in the development of children's rights in South Africa: A children's rights litigator's perspective

Ronaldah Lerato Karabo Ngidi*

Summary

Section 28 of the South African Constitution provides for what could be termed 'children's human rights', aimed to provide special protection for children in recognition of their vulnerability. While the provisions of section 28 assures one of the commitment of South Africa to provide the best for children, realising children's rights does not end there but requires taking steps to make these rights a reality. One of the effective tools in holding the state accountable and making sure that they deliver on children's constitutional rights in South Africa has been litigation. This chapter aims to review some of the decisions of the South African courts in which, in the process of protecting and developing children's constitutional rights, international child law was used as an interpretative tool, in order to attain a higher standard of protection for children's rights. The chapter also highlights the South African courts' willingness to adhere to constitutional rights and international law obligations in this regard. The conclusion is that while there may be challenges in protecting and developing children's rights, the positive legal developments assures one that there is fertile ground for a further coherent children's rights jurisprudence in South Africa which in turn can lead making the paper rights a reality for children.

1 Introduction

Litigation has been an effective tool in holding the state accountable and making sure that they deliver on children's rights in South Africa. All the tiers of the South African courts, with the Constitutional Court being the highest, take seriously the obligations placed on them by section 39(1)(b)

* LLB LLM (UP); Attorney at Centre for Child Law, University of Pretoria; ronaldah.ngidi@up.ac.za.

and 233 of the Constitution.[1] It is interesting to note that the international law that have been considered and applied in children's rights matters range from treaties, guidelines and general comments. The application of the provisions of international law has been used by child rights lawyers' to enhance arguments before the courts. This has produced profound judgments, some of which detail what role international law plays in South African child law and the development of children's rights.

Section 28 of the Constitution provides for what could be termed 'children's human rights' aimed to provide extra protection for children in recognition of their vulnerability. These are rights that children enjoy in addition to all the other rights provided for in the Bill of Rights in the Constitution. Section 28 was largely influenced by the United Nations Convention on the Rights of the Child (CRC), which provides extensively for the protection, care and development of children.[2] The CRC was followed by the African Charter on the Rights and Welfare of the Child (ACRWC), which is Africa's regional treaty on the protection of children.[3] The ACRWC aims to provide for the protection of children relevant to the African continent and for some matters that were not addressed by the CRC.[4] Both the CRC and the ACRWC are clear on the rights of children and responsibilities of member states in ensuring that what is on paper becomes a reality for children. In addition to the CRC and the ACRWC there are other children's rights instruments that South Africa has ratified which place an obligation on the state to aim for the highest standard of protection of children's rights.[5]

This chapter aims to review some of the decisions of the South African courts in which international law was used as an interpretative tool within which children's constitutional rights operate and how the courts have met the obligations arising from international law in the process of developing children's rights. This will be done with particular focus on how litigants craft their arguments to bring any relevant provisions of international instruments relating to children to the attention of the courts in order to elevate children's rights. The role of lawyers litigating for the protection of children's constitutional rights requires that they apply their minds to how to make strategic arguments using whichever of the instruments that is applicable on a particular issue that is before a court, in this way drawing the courts' attention to interpretative tools that could enhance the standard afforded to children's rights.

---

1 Act 108 of 1996.

2 South Africa ratified the CRC on 16 June 1995.

3 South Africa ratified the ACRWC on 7 January 2000.

4 F Viljoen 'The African Charter on the Rights and Welfare of the Child' in T Boezaart (ed) *Child Law in South Africa* (2009) 335.

5 The Hague Convention on the Civil Aspects of International Child Abduction and the Hague Convention on the Protection of Children and Cooperation Respect of Inter-country Adoption are some of the other conventions that South Africa has ratified.

The chapter will first consider the operation of international law in the South African context specifically with reference to section 39(1) and 233 of the Constitution. Attention will be paid to how the courts have interpreted their obligations under the auspices of these provisions. Secondly, it will assess how children's rights lawyers use international law arguments to persuade the courts to interpret children's rights within the context of international law and in this way advocate for the optimal protection of children's rights. This will be through an assessment of arguments presented to the courts, how the courts interpret these arguments and whether these arguments are reflected in the judgments of the courts. In conclusion, some thoughts on the significant role that international law has played in the development and protection of children's rights and child law in South Africa.

2 The application of international and foreign law in terms of section 39(1) and 233 of the Constitution

The application of international law, as an interpretive tool, within the South African legal system is provided for in section 39(1)(b) of the Constitution which provides that courts *must* consider international law and 39(1)(c) that courts *may* consider foreign law when interpreting the Bill of Rights. Section 233 of the Constitution further provides that when interpreting any legislation, every court *must* prefer any reasonable interpretation of the legislation that is consistent with international law over any alternative that is inconsistent with international law.

The predecessor to the Constitution, the Interim Constitution,[6] provided that in interpreting the provisions of the Bill of Rights a court of law shall, amongst others, have regard to public international law applicable to the protection of the rights entrenched in the Bill of Rights, and may have regard to comparable foreign case law.[7] This provision is not similar to section 39(1) and 233 of the Constitution, and the courts had to determine the meaning of the role of international law as an interpretive tool within the South African legal system. The judgments in relation to the Interim Constitution remain relevant under the operation of the Constitution and deserve to be mentioned as they provide clarity on the position and the type of international law the courts consider binding.

In one of the first landmark cases of the Constitutional Court, *S v Makwanyane and Another*,[8] the Court addressed the question of the applicability of international law in the interpretation of the Bill of

6 Act 200 of 1993.

7 S 35(1).

8 *S v Makwanyane and Another* 1995 3 SA 391 (CC).

Rights. In the judgment, Chaskalson P said the following with regard to the applicability of international law:[9]

> The international and foreign authorities are of value because they analyse arguments for and against the death sentence and show how court of other jurisdictions have dealt with this vexed issue. For that reason alone they require our attention. They may also have to be considered because of their relevance to section 35(1) of the Constitution

With regard to the types of international law that the courts could consider, the Court stated that in the context of section 35(1), public international law would include non-binding as well as binding law.[10] In *S v Williams*[11] judicially imposed corporal punishment as a sentence for children who are found guilty of criminal offences, was declared unconstitutional. The Constitutional Court found that the provision that prescribed such punishment was not in line with the Constitution and that judicially imposed corporal punishment was an inhuman, cruel, degrading and unusual punishment. In its judgment, the Constitutional Court used international law and foreign case law to interpret what 'inhuman and degrading punishment' meant.[12] After the substantial analysis of international and comparative law, the Constitutional Court concluded that the words still needed to be interpreted within the historic context of South Africa.[13][14]

It has been said that section 35(1) of the Interim Constitution strengthened the role of international law in the interpretive process as it obliged courts to apply international law where it was applicable, and since 'virtually every provision in the South African Bill of Rights has some counterpart in an international human rights convention or is governed by general principles of international law', it is difficult to imagine situations where public international law would not be applicable.[15]

---

9 *Makwanyane* (n 8 above) para 34.

10 The court stated that 'they may both be used under the section as tools of interpretation. International agreements and customary international law accordingly provided a framework within which chap 3 [the Bill of Rights] can be evaluated and understood, and for that purpose, decisions of tribunals dealing with comparable instruments, such as the United Nations Committee on Human Rights, the Inter-American Court of Human Rights, and the European Court of Human Rights and, appropriate cases, reports of special agencies such as the International Labour Organisation, may provide guidance as to the correct interpretation of particular provisions of [the Bill of Rights]'. *Makwanyane* (n 8 above) paras 35 & 39.

11 *S v Williams* 1995 7 BCLR 861 (CC).

12 *Williams* (n 11 above) para 50.

13 *Williams* (n 11 above) para 51.

14 *Williams* (n 11 above) paras 21 & 23.

15 J Dugard 'The role of international law in interpreting the Bill of Rights' (1994) 10 *South African Journal on Human Rights* 208 at 212. See also *Azapo & Others v The President of the Republic of South Africa* 1996 4 SA 671 (CC) at 688 paras 26-32.

The 1996 Constitution separated the provisions relating to the interpretation of the Bill of Rights and changed the language to emerge as section 39(1) which provides as follows:

> 39(1) When interpreting the Bill of Rights, a court, tribunal or forum (a) must promote the values that underlie an open and democratic society based on human dignity, equality and freedom; (b) must consider international law; and (c) may consider foreign law.

Section 233 of the Constitution provides that:

> When interpreting any legislation, every court must prefer any reasonable interpretation of the legislation that is consistent with international law over any alternative interpretation that is inconsistent with international law.

Section 233 makes it is clear that the use of international law as an interpretive tool is not only confined to the interpretation of the constitutional rights contained in the Bill of Rights, but also applies with regard to the interpretation of any other domestic law. It is from this premise that the South African courts should utilise international law as an integral part of the South African law and as an aide in the interpretation of human rights.[16]

In *Government of the Republic of South Africa & Others v Grootboom & Others*[17] reference was made to the role of international law in the interpretation of Constitutional rights, as laid down by the Court in *S v Makwanyane.*[18] Yacoob J stated that:[19]

> The relevant international law can be a guide to interpretation but the weight to be attached to any particular principle or rule of international law will vary. However, where the relevant principle of international law binds South Africa, it may be directly applicable.

It is clear that international law does have an intrinsic role within the South African law, but with the emphasis on the fact that as an interpretive tool it has to be applied within the context of the South African legal system, in particular the supreme law that is the Constitution.[20]

---

16 See *Kaunda & Others v President of the Republic of South Africa & Others* 2004 10 BCLR 1009 (CC) 1017 at paras 33-35 & 151-171.

17 *Government of the Republic of South Africa & Others v Grootboom & Others* 2001 1 SA 46 (CC).

18 *Grootboom* (n 17 above) para 23.

19 *Grootboom* (n 17 above) para 26. Section 231(4) of the Constitution states that '[a]ny international agreement becomes law in the Republic when it is enacted into law by national legislation; but a self-executing provision of an agreement that has been approved by Parliament is law in the Republic unless it is inconsistent with the Constitution or an Act of Parliament.'

20 See Dugard (n 15 above) 211, where he states even if there had been no reference to the international law in the Constitution, South African courts would have been obliged to turn to international human rights law for guidance.

3 Developing child law and protecting children's rights through litigation

The development of child law by courts, under the constitutional dispensation, was one of the earliest tasks of the Constitutional Court when it found judicially imposed corporal punishment for child offenders unconstitutional in *S v Williams*.[21] We now turn to examine the role of international law in the development of children's rights jurisprudence, in three tiers of the South African courts: the High Court, Supreme Court of Appeal and the Constitutional Court. The discussion will be with particular reference to the cases undertaken by the Centre for Child Law (CCL)[22] and cases where the CCL entered as *amicus curiae* using international law as part of the arguments to uphold children's rights. This discussion will highlight the international and foreign law arguments advanced as well as the influence thereof on the judgments of the courts.

3.1 Inter-country adoption

The matter of *AD and Another v DW and Others (Centre for Child Law as amicus curiae; Minister of Social Development as intervening party)*[23] was concerned with the issue of the correct procedures for inter-country adoption in South Africa. The Constitutional Court judgment was the final in the trilogy of judgments, as this matter was initiated in the High Court, was appealed to the Supreme Court of Appeal, before it came to the Constitutional Court for a final say.

The applicants had approached the High Court for an order for sole custody and guardianship of a minor child referred to as R. The order sought by the applicants further indicated their clear intention to remove R from South Africa and adopt her in the USA. The High Court, per Goldblatt J, concerned about the overall aim of the application, invited the *amicus curiae* to make submissions on the proper procedure that should be followed under the circumstances. The *amicus curiae* made written and oral submissions to the Court. With regard to the international law, the *amicus curiae* advanced the following arguments:

> That South Africa had ratified the UNCRC and acceded to the Hague Convention on the Protection of Children and Co-operation in Respect of Inter-Country Adoption and is bound to act in accordance with the obligations in terms of such Conventions;
>
> That by granting an order for sole guardianship and custody over South African children to foreign couples, South Africa's obligations under the UNCRC and the

21 n 8 above.

22 The Centre for Child Law is a non-governmental organisation and registered law clinic which undertakes children's impact- or test litigation.

23 *AD and Another v DW and Others (Centre for Child Law as amicus curiae; Minister of Social Development as intervening party)* 2008 3 SA 183 (CC).

> Hague Convention are overlooked and the constitutional rights of children may be prejudiced;
>
> That the granting of sole guardianship and custody to foreign couples over South African children bypasses the practice and procedure being widely adhered to- even by potential adopters in non-Hague Convention countries;
>
> That the practice of utilising the route of sole guardianship and custody orders in the place of the adoption procedures in terms of the Child Care Act was contrary to the intention of the Constitutional Court in the case of *Minister of Welfare and Population Development v Fitzpatrick and Others* 2000 (3) SA 422 (CC) BLCR 713; and
>
> That once the *Fitzpatrick* case had found that inter-country adoption procedures would be sufficiently protective of children if carried out in terms of the Child Care Act, the procedures set out in that Act for local adoptions within South Africa are also applicable to inter-country adoptions, in keeping with art (e) of the UNCRC.

The arguments advanced by the *amicus curiae* were not directly quoted in the High Court judgment, but what is clear from it is that the Court was alive to the role of international law in the process of interpretation of the rights in the Bill of Rights and children's rights in particular. The Court affirmed the position of international law in the process of the interpretation of the Bill of Rights and also that of other domestic legislation.[24] Having been provided with substantial information on international law, Goldblatt J commented specifically on what article 21 of the CRC expects of state parties.[25] Article 21 of the CRC provides that a child considered for inter-country adoption must enjoy safeguards and standards equivalent to those existing in the case of national adoptions.[26] The article also provides that inter-country adoption may be considered as an alternative means of child-care if the child cannot be placed in a foster or an adoptive family or cannot, in any suitable manner, be cared for in the child's country of origin.[27] The CRC has a particularly important role within the South African law and can be said to have been constitutionalised in section 28 of the Constitution.[28] Therefore its provisions had a great influence on the Court's decision. The Court dismissed the application as it considered itself bound by the *Fitzpatrick* judgment with regard to the procedure to be followed where non-South Africans wished to adopt South African children.[29] The applicants,

---

24 *De Gree and Another v Webb and Others (Centre for Child Law, University of Pretoria, Amicus Curiae)* 2006 (6) SA 51 (W) paras 20-22.

25 *De Gree* (n 24 above) para 24.

26 As above.

27 This refers to what is termed the subsidiarity principle and had a profound effect on the judgments of the Supreme Court of Appeal and the Constitutional Court. See also J Sloth-Nielsen 'Children's rights in the South African courts' (2002) 10(2) *The International Journal of Children's Rights* 137 at 141-142.

28 Sloth-Nielsen (n 27 above) 139.

29 In *Minister of Welfare and Population Development v Fitzpatrick and Others* 2000 (3) SA 422 (CC), which was the case where the Court ruled that inter-country adoptions should be allowed, the Court found that inter-country adoption procedures would be sufficiently protective of children if carried out in terms of the Child Care Act in the Children's Court.

dissatisfied with the outcome, pursued an appeal to the Supreme Court of Appeal.

In the Supreme Court of Appeal, the CCL applied and was admitted as *amicus curiae*.[30] The applicants amplified their arguments and contended that there was no proper procedure available for inter-country adoptions in the Children's Court and therefore they should be granted an order for sole custody and guardianship. The *amicus curiae* argued that there was a proper procedure and that inter-country adoptions have been conducted in the Children's Court and therefore the applicants should approach this court for an inter-country adoption. The provisions of the CRC and the ACRWC remained relevant and were referred to in the majority judgment.[31]

In the majority judgment, Theron AJA, stated that one of the objectives of the Hague Convention was to establish safeguards to ensure that inter-country adoption takes place in the best interest of the child and with respect of the child's fundamental rights as recognised in international law.[32] She acknowledged that in terms of section 231 of the Constitution an international treaty shall not have effect until enacted into domestic legislation. However, since the Children's Act[33] will bring the Hague Convention into operation the provisions thereof could not be ignored. According to Theron AJA:[34]

> The fundamental principles which underlie the Hague Convention are drawn from the UNCRC, particularly article 21, which South Africa has ratified ... Despite the fact that the principle of subsidiarity has not been expressly provided for in domestic legislation, our Courts are obliged, in terms of s 39(1)(b) of the Constitution to take this into account when assessing the best interests of the child, as it is a well-established principle of international law. The principle of subsidiarity is also enshrined in article 24(b) of the African Charter, but in somewhat stronger terms inter-country adoption should only be considered as 'the last resort'.

In conclusion the majority of the Court dismissed the appeal stating that in the light of the Hague Convention and other international law the right procedure which safeguards the interests of the child was an application for adoption in the Children's Court.[35]

---

30 The fact that the CCL was *amicus curiae* in the High Court did not make it entitled to enter as such in the Supreme Court of Appeal. The CCL had to apply to be admitted as provided for in rule 16 of the Supreme Court of Appeal Rules.

31 The court was split two to three. The majority dismissed the appeal, while the minority wrote two separate judgments wherein they stated that the appeal should be allowed and that they would have granted the applicants the order for sole custody and guardianship.

32 *De Gree and Another v Webb and Others (Centre for Child Law, University of Pretoria, Amicus Curiae)* 2007 (5) SA 184 (SCA) para 11.

33 Act 38 of 2005 came into operation on 1 July 2007. However, the sections that incorporate the Hague Convention into domestic legislation were not in operation at the time of hearing of the matter and only came into operation on 1 April 2010.

34 *De Gree* (n 32 above) para 12.

35 *De Gree* (n 32 above) para 15.

The applicants approached the Constitutional Court insisting that they should be allowed to obtain sole custody and guardianship in order to remove the child from South Africa as this was in the best interests of the child.[36] The central questions that arose in the Constitutional Court was whether the High Court should have jurisdiction to make an order for sole custody and guardianship, where the intention was to remove a child from South Africa, as well as whether the subsidiarity principle[37] overrides the best interests principle.[38] The *amicus curiae* maintained their position and argued that article 21 of the CRC and article 24 of the ACRWC made it clear that the subsidiarity principle had to be adhered to before a child could be adopted in terms of inter-country adoption. The gist of the *amicus curiae*'s submissions was that international law, with particular reference to inter-country adoption, required that the subsidiarity principle be complied with as it safeguards the best interests of children and that the correct procedure for inter-country adoption be followed.[39] Also, the *amicus curiae* contended that the procedure in terms of which the inter-country adoption takes place is important for the protection of children. The aspect of upholding the best interests of one child *vis-à-vis* that of children in general, through ensuring that a wrong precedent is not set with regard to the procedure for inter-country adoption, required a delicate balance in the arguments of the *amicus curiae*.

The Constitutional Court, per Sachs J, found that the subsidiarity principle was important; however it was subsidiary to the paramount principle of the best interests of a child.[40] The Court went through a process of articulating how the subsidiarity principle had to be balanced with the best interest principle.[41] In the words of Sachs J:[42]

> Rigorous procedural mechanisms are put in place to reduce possible abuse. In these circumstances the framers [of the Hague Convention] appear to have felt it would be permissible to reduce the relatively autonomous effect of the subsidiarity principle, as expressed in the CRC and the African Charter on the Rights and Welfare of the Child ... and bring it into closer alignment with the best interests of the child principle

36 *AD v DW* (n 23 above).

37 The origin of the subsidiarity principle is traced originally from article 17 of the United Nations Declaration on Social Development and Legal Principles Relating to the Protection and Welfare of Children adopted by the General Assembly in 3 December 1986.

38 *AD v DW* (n 23 above) para 18. At paras 31 and 34 the Court stated that the High Court as upper guardian of all children had the jurisdiction to make orders for sole custody and guardianship in relation to foreigners, however bypassing the Children's Court procedures .would only be justified under exceptional circumstances.

39 The submissions also made reference to the particular aims of the Hague Convention and the CRC and ACRWC.

40 *AD v DW* (n 23 above) para 55.

41 *AD v DW* (n 23 above) para 47.

42 As above.

The Court found that the Supreme Court of Appeal was correct to dismiss the appeal, as the correct procedure for inter-country adoptions was through the Children's Court.[43] However, the Court held that the Supreme Court of Appeal could have made an order to refer the matter to the Children's Court for speedy resolution and to protect the best interests of the child.[44] The parties concluded a settlement agreement and this was made an order of court, which included that the applicants were to approach the Children's Court with their application for an inter-country adoption and that the Children's Court should make an order for such adoption within 30 days from the date of the order.[45]

The courts agreed on the correct procedure, as prescribed by the CRC, the ACRWC and the Hague Convention required that an inter-country adoption takes place with the necessary safeguards for the child concerned. The Constitutional Court's and the majority judgment of the Supreme Court of Appeal illustrate the fact that even where the relevant international law is not yet operative in South Africa, the provisions thereof cannot be ignored and that the decisions of the court should aim to uphold the objectives of the said international law.[46]

3.2 Sentencing of a primary care-giver of minor children

Another recent profound judgment of the Constitutional Court in the area of child law is *S v M (Centre for Child Law as amicus curiae).*[47] This matter concerned the sentencing of a mother of children aged between 8 and 16 years who had been convicted of fraud. The mother was the primary care-giver of the children. She was sentenced by the High Court to four years imprisonment. On appeal to the same court, the sentence was converted to a sentence which had the effect that she would have to serve eight months in prison before she became eligible for release under correctional supervision.

The mother petitioned the Supreme Court of Appeal to appeal against the order of imprisonment, but her application was dismissed. The mother then approached the Constitutional Court for leave to appeal the sentence meted by the High Court. The Chief Justice issued directions inviting any interested person or organisation to enter as *amicus curiae*,

---

43 *AD v DW* (n 23 above) para 55.

44 As above.

45 The agreement was concluded in the light of the fact that the paramouncty of the best interests of the child in this matter required that she adopted by the applicants without any further delays.

46 See *K v K* 1999 4 SA 691 (C), where the Cape Provincial Division of the High Court found that, where the Hague Convention on the Civil Aspects of International Abduction was not yet incorporated into South African Law when the dispute concerning a child abduction arose, the best interests of the child required that the principles of the Hague Convention be applied to the extent that they indicated what was normally in the interests of such a child.

47 *S v M (Centre for Child Law as amicus curiae)* 2008 3 SA 232 (CC).

and also ordered that the court papers be served on the CCL. In the directions three issues were identified as being at the heart of the matter.[48] The first one was the duties of a sentencing court in the light of section 28(2) of the Constitution, and of any relevant statutory provisions, when the person being sentenced was a primary care-giver of minor children; secondly whether these duties had been observed *in casu* and, thirdly if these duties had not been observed, what order, if any, the Court should make.

CCL as *amicus curiae* made substantial written and oral submissions to the Constitutional Court with particular attention to what the best interest of children required from the sentencing courts when a primary care-giver is convicted and stands to be sentenced to a prison term. Section 28(2) provides that in every matter concerning a child, the best interest of the child are the paramount consideration and section 28(1)(b) provides for the children's right to parental care. These provisions, according to the *amicus curiae,* had the effect that the duties of the sentencing court include a duty to properly consider the rights of a child or children when considering imprisonment as a sentence to be imposed on their primary care-giver. The *amicus curiae*'s submission was that the sentencing court failed to properly consider the rights of the children concerned in this matter.

The *amicus curiae*'s further submissions were that section 28(2) and 28(1)(b) had to be interpreted within the context of international and regional instruments that South Africa has ratified. The international law arguments advanced by the *amicus curiae* can be summarised as follows:

> That the South African Constitution provides a stronger wording with regard to the best interests of the child in that it states that they are the paramount consideration - thus stronger than the CRC and the ACRWC;
>
> That the Convention on Elimination of all Forms of Discrimination Against Women, article 16(1)(f) also uses the word 'paramount' with regard to the duties of parents towards their children;
>
> Article 3(1) of the CRC provides that 'In all actions concerning children, whether undertaken by public or private social welfare institutions, courts of law, administrative authorities or legislative bodies, the best interests of the child shall be a primary consideration';
>
> Article 9(1) and 9(2) of the CRC provide that 'a child has a right not to be separated from his or her parents and, where this is necessary for the protection of the child's best interests, to remain in direct contact when separated from a parent'.
>
> Article 4 of the ACRWC provides that 'in all actions concerning the child undertaken by any person or authority the best interests of the child shall be the primary consideration.'
>
> Article 30 of the ACRWC states that 'States parties to the present Charter shall undertake to provide special treatment to expectant mothers and to mothers of infants and young children who have been accused or found guilty of infringing the penal law and shall in particular: (a) ensure that a non-custodial sentence will

48 The parties had to address the Court only on the three identified issues.

> always be the first consideration when sentencing such mothers; (b) establish and promote measures alternative to institutional confinement for the treatment of such mothers; (c) establish special alternative institutions for the holding of such mothers; (d) ensure that a mother shall not be imprisoned with her child; (e) ensure that a death sentence shall not be imposed on such mothers; (f) the essential aim of the penitentiary system will be the reformation, the integration of the mother to the family and social rehabilitation.

It was the *amicus curiae*'s contention that article 30 of the ACRWC contains a requirement for states to ensure that a non-custodial sentence will always be the first consideration when sentencing a primary care-giver of children. This does not prevent courts, which have discretion when it comes to sentencing, from imposing imprisonment in cases where the need to protect society is found to be compelling. But it must be factored in to the sentencing exercise in order to determine whether it is reasonable and justifiable to limit the child's rights as provided for in section 28(2) and 28(1)(b) of the Constitution.[49]

The *amicus curiae* referred to other case law[50] that dealt with the issue of children being deprived of parental care as a result of action of the state or as result of orders of the courts. In all these matters the courts saw it fit to consider children's constitutional rights and how they would be affected by the actions that were directed at their parents. The *amicus curiae* contended that the court was correct in those matters as these matters did concern children and that this was also the case with regard to the matter before the court.

The Constitutional Court was divided in its decision, with the majority finding that it would not be in the interests of the children for their mother to be imprisoned. The dissenting judgment, which in principle agreed with the majority that constitutional rights, in this case children's constitutional rights, had to be scrupulously observed, dismissed the application.[51] Writing for the majority, Sachs J made reference to the CRC and the ACRWC and stated that:[52]

---

49 In South African criminal law there is what is termed the Zinn-triad principle which guides the courts when sentencing an accused. This principle entails that the nature of the crime, the personal circumstances of the accused and the interests of the community be considered as the relevant factors determinative of an appropriate sentence. Part of the *amicus curiae's* argument was that in the light of the Constitution and international law obligations, the sentencing courts also have to consider the best interests of children, within the Zinn-triad matrix, when sentencing a primary care-giver.

50 *Patel and Another v Minister of Home Affairs and Another* 2000 2 SA 343 (D); *S v Howells* 1999 1 SACR 675 (C) and *S v Kika* 1998 2 SACR 428 (W).

51 *S v M* (n 47 above) para 121.The dissenting judgment appears at 269 and is not discussed herein as it makes no particular reference to international law. The crux thereof was that taking into account the fact that M was a re-offender, that her sentence had already been reduced, that the court *a quo* had taken into account the best interest of the children and that sentencing has to have the interests of society in sight, consequently that M's appeal should be dismissed.

52 *S v M* (n 47 above) para 16 & 17.

> [S]ection 28 must be seen as responding in an expansive way to our international obligations as a state party to the United Nations Convention on the Rights of the Child (the CRC) ... Regard accordingly has to be paid to the import of the principles of the CRC as they inform the provisions of s 28 in relation to the sentencing of a primary care-giver. The four great principles of the CRC which have become international currency, and as such guide all policy in South Africa in relation to children, are said to be survival, development, protection and participation. What unites these principles, and lies at the heart of s 28, I believe, is the right of a child to be a child and enjoy special care.

The judgment refers, directly, to the submissions of the *amicus curiae* with regard to South Africa's obligations under international law, which underscored the special requirement to protect children's interests as far as possible.[53] The Constitutional Court went on to refer to the obligations, under article 30(1) of the ACRWC, when considering imprisonment as a sentence for mothers of young children.[54] The Constitutional Court set aside the order of the High Court and replaced it with an order which, amongst others, suspended the prison term in its entirety for four years and placed the mother under correctional supervision. She was also ordered to do community service, undergo counselling and repay all persons or entities that she had defrauded.[55]

The ability to use international law and in particular article 30 of the ACRWC undoubtedly influenced the Court's interpretation of section 28(1)(b) and 28(2) of the Constitution. Although the ACRWC was ratified after the Constitution, its provisions have a profound impact on children's rights within the African context and the protection of children's constitutional rights in South Africa.

3.3 Socio-economic rights

In the *Centre for Child Law and Another v Minister of Home Affairs and Others*[56] the applicants approached the High Court for an order to assert the rights of unaccompanied foreign children. The application arose from a situation where unaccompanied foreign children, awaiting deportation, were accommodated with adults at the detention camp. The applicants had, in the initial application, sought an order that a *curator ad litem* be appointed for the children; that the children be moved to a place of safety and that Children's Court inquiries[57] should be held with regard to each child. The order was granted but the respondents did nothing to facilitate

---

53 *S v M* (n 47 above) para 31.

54 *S v M* (n 47 above) para 31.

55 *S v M* (n 47 above) para 77.

56 *Centre for Child Law and Another v Minister of Home Affairs and Others* 2005 6 SA 50 (T).

57 In terms of section 12 of the Child Care Act 74 of 1983 a Children's Court inquiry was held for each child who is found to be in need of care and at the conclusion of such an inquiry the court makes a suitable order of placement. The Children's Act, section 150, now provides for circumstances under which a child can be found to be in need of care and protection and it is our view that these provisions apply to unaccompanied foreign children.

the Children's Court inquiries and the Court was faced with a further application to compel the respondents to take steps to protect the concerned children. In handing down her judgment, De Vos J, elaborated on South Africa's international obligations with regard to the protection of children and stated as follows:[58]

> South Africa is also a signatory to certain relevant conventions. These are the United Nations Convention on the Rights of the Child, which affords every child the right to health, the right to social security and to education. Second, the African Charter on the Rights and Welfare of the Child, which similarly affirms every child's right to education and health care. Thirdly, there is the United Nations Convention Relating to the Status of Refugees, which requires States to provide compulsory primary education for refugee children of standard equivalent to that provided to its own nationals.

The intention of the Court, with this judgment, was to ensure that unaccompanied minors' are treated as individuals and that circumstances of each one of them are investigated before a suitable order, be it an order that they be returned to their home country or that they remain in the South African care system, is made.[59] This is in accordance with the rights of the concerned children to have their best interests be the primary consideration, which the CRC, the ACRWC and the Constitution require. To emphasise the obligations on South Africa with regard to the protection of children's rights De Vos J stated that:[60]

> We subscribe to the principles contained in the international treaties already mentioned. We claim to enforce the laws put in place to protect the rights of illegal immigrants, and especially those pertaining to children. Yet all these lofty ideals become hypocritical nonsense if those policies and sentiments are not translated into action by those who are put in positions of power by the State to do exactly that; who are paid to execute these admirable laws, and yet, because of apathy and lack of compassion, fail to do so.

In the recent judgment of *S v M* Sachs J summarised it in the following resounding words:[61]

> No constitutional injunction can in and of itself isolate children from the shocks and perils of harsh family and neighbourhood environments. What the law can do is create conditions to protect children from abuse and maximise opportunities for them to lead productive and happy lives. Thus, even if the State cannot itself repair disrupted family life, it can create positive conditions for repair to take place, and diligently seek wherever possible to avoid conduct of its agencies which may have the effect of placing children in peril.

---

58 *Centre for Child Law and Another v Minister of Home Affairs and Others* (n 56 above) para 24.

59 Article 20 of the CRC provides that state parties shall, in accordance with their national laws, ensure alternative care for a child who has been temporarily or permanently deprived of his or her family environment or in whose own best interest cannot be allowed to remain in that environment. Article 23 and 25 of the ACRWC respectively provide for the protection of refugee children and children separated from their parents.

60 *Centre for Child Law and Another v Minister of Home Affairs and Others* (n 56 above) para 30.

61 *S v M* (n 47 above) para 20.

The facts of *S v M* have already been dealt with above, and although the words of Sachs J were stated in a different context, the relevance thereof to matters concerning the situation of unaccompanied minors is self evident. In an ideal world, the clear law and jurisprudence would eliminate the problems that the case of the *Centre for Child Law v Minister of Home Affairs and Others* aimed to resolve. However the challenges on the ground remain, thus requiring the children's rights litigants to continue to seek better protection for unaccompanied minors through further litigation and monitoring, and in this way uphold international law.[62]

3.4 Child justice

The Constitutional Court recently, in *Centre for Child Law v Minister of Justice and Constitutional Development and Others (NICRO as amicus curiae),*[63] ruled in favour of the Centre for Child Law (the CCL) and found that the application of what is termed 'minimum sentences' on children aged 16 and 17 years at the time of commission of offences is unconstitutional. The minimum sentences first came into operation in 1998, introduced by the Criminal Amendment Act 105 of 1997 (the CLAA). The effect of the CLAA was that a person convicted for certain identified serious crimes, had to be sentenced to specified periods of imprisonment ranging from 10 years to life imprisonment.[64]

Section 51(3)(b) of the CLAA provided as follows with regard to 16 and 17 year olds:

> If any court referred to in subsection (1) or (2) decides to impose a sentence prescribed in those subsections upon a child who was 16 years of age or older, but under the age of 18 years, at the time of the commission of the offence in question, it shall enter the reasons for its decision on the record of the proceedings.

The provision did not mandate minimum sentences for children aged 16 and 17 years and it was clear that the court had discretion to sentence this group of children to any sentence. But where the court sentenced a child to a minimum sentence, it had to state reasons thereof.

In December 2007 an amendment act to the CLAA passed. The Criminal Law (Sentencing) Amendment Act 38 of 2007 (the Amendment Act) came into operation in December 2007. Section 51(2) of the Amendment Act lists the different minimum sentences that are to be

---

62 Recently Lawyers for Human Rights brought an application to the High Court in Pretoria seeking the protection of the rights of adult foreigners awaiting deportation and requesting the Court that in the case of unaccompanied foreign children the judgment of *Centre for Child Law v Minister of Home Affairs and Others* should be given effect. *Lawyers for Human Rights v Minister of Safety and Security and 17 Others* 5824/2009 in the North Gauteng High Court, unreported).

63 *Centre for Child Law v Minister of Justice and Constitutional Development and Others (NICRO as amicus curiae)* 2009 6 SA 632 (CC).

64 S 51(1) and 51(2) of CLAA.

imposed in instances where specified offences are committed.[65] Section 51(6) states that 'this section does not apply in respect of an accused person who was under the age of 16 years of at the time of the commission of an offence contemplated in subsection (1) or (2).' The effect of the section was that children aged 16 and 17 years could clearly now receive a minimum sentence of 10 years imprisonment.[66] The Amendment Act removed the court's discretion to impose any sentence other than the prescribed minimum sentence.

In its challenge to the Amendment Act the CCL argued that the minimum sentencing regime infringed children's constitutional right, that is section 28(1)(g) and section 28(2).[67] In the High Court and the Constitutional Court the CCL's submissions were, to a substantial extent, supported by international law. The CCL argued, amongst others, that article 37(a) of the CRC states that no child should be subjected to capital punishment or life imprisonment without the possibility of parole, and article 37(b) provides that imprisonment of a child shall be in conformity with the law and shall be used only as a measure of last resort and for the shortest appropriate period of time. This is the article that had an influence on section 28(1)(g) of the Constitution.

In addition to including the principle of imprisonment as a measure of last resort article 17(1)(c) of the United Nations Standard Minimum Rules for the Administration of Juvenile Justice (Beijing Rules)[68] states that:

> [D]eprivation of personal liberty shall not be imposed unless the juvenile is adjudicated of a serious act involving violence against another person or of persistence in committing other serious offences and unless there is no other appropriate response.

A further argument was that the fundamental principle is that any reaction to child offenders must always be in proportion to the circumstances of the child and the offence.[69] The CCL also contended that the United Nations Rules for the Protection of Juveniles Deprived of their Liberty[70] require that imprisonment should be limited to exceptional cases and that the sanction imposed on the child should not preclude the possibility of early release.[71]

---

65 The offences are listed in Schedule 2 to the Amendment Act.

66 See section 51(1) and 51(2) of the Amendment Act.

67 The CCL was successful in the High Court and had to bring an application to the Constitutional Court to confirm the unconstitutionality finding of the High Court. Section 28(1)(g) of the Constitution states, amongst others, that every child has the right not to be detained except as a measure of last resort and only for the shortest appropriate period of time and section 28(2) which states that the best interests of the child are of paramount importance in every matter that concerns the child.

68 General Assembly Resolution 40/33 adopted on 29 November 1985.

69 Rule 17(1)(a) of the Beijing Rules.

70 Resolution 45/113 adopted on 14 December 1990 at the 68th Plenary Session.

71 Fundamental Perspectives, rule I(1) to (3).

Rule 18(1) of the Beijing Rules embodies the principles of individualisation, proportionality and imprisonment as a last resort: 'A large variety of disposition measures shall be made available to the competent authority, allowing for flexibility so as to avoid institutionalisation to the greatest extent possible.' Therefore a system of prescribed minimum sentences falls foul of the sentencing principles set out above because a prescribed minimum by its very nature prevents consideration of other alternative sentences and the well-being of the individual child as the starting point during sentencing. A prescribed minimum sentence is also incompatible with the principle of proportionality. When a prescribed minimum sentence of imprisonment is imposed on a child it cannot be said that deprivation of liberty was the last resort, nor is it for the minimum necessary period. To sum up, the CCL's argument was that the aim of child justice necessarily requires that a sentencing court is free to consider a wide range of sentencing options and to craft a sentence which will suit the needs of the individual child.

The Constitutional Court was split in its judgment with the majority finding that the application of the minimum sentences regime to 16 and 17 year olds was unconstitutional.[72] Cameron J, writing for the majority, made reference to international law and foreign law as provided in the CCL's written submissions.[73] In contextualising the international law principles Cameron J stated as follows:[74]

> It is plain that the Bill of Rights in our Constitution amply embodies these internationally accepted principles. Its provisions merely need to be given the intended effect. This leads to the conclusion that no maintainable justification has been advanced for including 16 and 17 year olds in the minimum sentencing regime.

In addition to international law, the submission made reference to comparative law, which included legislation and case law of countries where a 'minimum sentences regime' is in place and applies to child offenders.[75] Foreign case law also received attention in the judgment and in the words of Cameron J 'the general considerations mitigating the treatment and punishment of child offenders find resonance with comparable system of justice.'[76]

---

72 The Constitutional Court is made up of 11 judges and was split 7 to 4 in this judgment.

73 In *Centre for Child Law v Minister of Justice and Constitutional Development and Others* (n 63 above) para 61 specific reference is made to the CRC, the United Nations Rules for the Protection of Juveniles Deprived of their Liberty, the Beijing Rules and the Riyadh Guidelines, with particular attention to the sentencing principles that can be distilled from these instruments. See also n 61, 62 and 63 of the judgment.

74 *Centre for Child Law v Minister of Justice and Constitutional Development and Others* (n 63 above) para 63.

75 Reference was made to Canada, the United States, Australia, United Kingdom and Germany. A comparison was also drawn between South Africa and other African countries such as Kenya, Uganda, Ghana and Zambia.

76 *Centre for Child Law v Minister of Justice and Constitutional Development and Others* (n 63 above) para 33. Reference was made to *Roper v Simmons* 543 US 551 (2005) at 567,

The majority judgment illustrates an interpretation of children's constitutional rights within an international context and how the treatment of children should be brought in line with the aims of international law.[77] This highlights, not only the progressive nature of children's jurisprudence in South Africa, but also an understanding of how international and comparative law should be utilised for the better treatment and protection of children.

4 Conclusion

The South African Constitution is hailed as one of the best in the world. However, this cannot be celebrated in isolation. Children's rights, as contained in the Constitution, were largely influenced by the provisions of the CRC.[78] The ACRWC has also become an important instrument from which provisions with regard to specific issues relating to children in Africa can be drawn from. The case of *S v M* discussed herein highlights one area where the ACRWC stands out and provides for better protection than the CRC and the Constitution, that is for children whose mothers stand to be sentenced to imprisonment.[79] The ACRWC has also influenced provisions of the Children's Act 38 of 2005[80] with regard to the protection from cultural practices that can be harmful to children.[81] This is another aspect which the Constitution does not directly provide for and hence the provisions of the Children's Act and the ACRWC are essential in matters concerning harmful social and cultural practices.

This chapter has touched on some of the developments of children's rights influenced by the use of international law in the arguments presented to courts. A recent profound statement made in relation to children's rights is that the most formidable challenge that confronts African child rights activists and groups is, and should be, the modalities for bridging the gulf between law and practice - between the text of the

---

which is the case from the United State wherein the death penalty was found unconstitutional for offenders younger than 18 years.

77 The minority judgment makes no particular reference to international law arguments advanced by the CCL and finds that the application of the minimum sentencing regime on 16 and 17 year old is not unconstitutional as it does not take away the court's discretion to depart where substantial and compelling circumstances exist.

78 J Sloth-Nielsen and B Mezmur '2+2=5? Exploring the domestication of the CRC in South African jurisprudence (2002-2006)' (2008) 16(1) *The International Journal of Children's Rights* 1.

79 Art 30 ACRWC, as discussed in *S v M* (n 47 above).

80 Section 12(a) provides that every child has the right not to be subjected to social, cultural and religious practices which are detrimental to his or her well-being.

81 Article 21(1) provides that states party to the ACRWC shall take appropriate measures to eliminate harmful social and cultural practices effecting the welfare, dignity, normal growth and development of the child and in particular (a) those customs and practices prejudicial to the health or life of the child and (b) those customs and practices discriminatory to the child on the grounds of sex or status.

ACRWC and the everyday reality of millions of children.[82] This paper not only highlights the importance of litigation as a tool to realise children's rights, but also how litigation is an essential step in bridging the aforementioned gulf. While challenges remain, great strides have been made in South Africa through the litigation for the development and protection of children's international and constitutional rights. There is undoubtedly fertile ground for further positive development of a coherent children's rights jurisprudence.

---

82 D Olowu 'Protecting children's rights in Africa: a critique of the African Charter on the Rights and Welfare of the Child' (2002) 10 *The International Journal of Children's Rights* 127 at 132.

11

The role of National Human Rights Institutions in promoting international law in domestic legal systems: Case study of the Uganda Human Rights Commission

Kenechukwu C Esom*

Summary

More than 100 countries have established National Human Rights Institutions. Although with varying mandates, these institutions charged mostly with the promotion of human rights, present a potential for promoting international law and international human rights standards in their respective domestic systems. The Uganda Human Rights Commission (UHRC) is an example of one such institution which has demonstrated this potential. By examining the mandate of the UHRC and the challenges it has faced in the implementation of the same, this chapter argues that National Human Rights Institutions, whatever their mandate, can play a pivotal role in promoting international law standards in the domestic legal system.

1 Introduction

This chapter examines the mandate of National Human Rights Institutions (NHRIs) and the potential these present for promoting international law and human rights standards in domestic legal systems. By examining the mandate of the Uganda Human Rights Commission (UHRC) in light of the Principles Relating to the Status of National Institutions for the Promotion and Protection of Human Rights (Paris Principles), the chapter outlines ways in which the UHRC promotes international law and human rights. The chapter begins by tracing the evolution of NHRIs; it then examines the mandate of NHRIs as provided by the Paris Principles; next, the chapter goes on to examine the mandate of the UHRC and how it fulfils its mandate. Finally the chapter

* Head, Legal and Psychosocial Department and coordinator, Child Rights and Protection Programme, Refugee Law Project, Faculty of Law, Makerere University, Uganda; kene.esom@gmail.com.

highlights some of the challenges of implementing the mandate of the UHRC.

2 Evolution of National Human Rights Institutions

The term 'National Human Rights Institutions' represents a variety of bodies – constitutional, statutory and otherwise, which are mandated to promote and protect human rights in the countries in which they are found. NHRIs are 'occupying a unique place between the judicial and executive functions of the state, and where these exist, the elected representatives of the people.'[1]

The idea of national human rights institutions was first mentioned in 1946 when the United Nations (UN) Economic and Social Council (ECOSOC) advised member states to consider setting up information cells or human rights institutions in their various countries. These institutions would liaise with ECOSOC in the furtherance of its human rights mandate.[2] In a 1960 resolution ECOSOC recognised the 'distinctive role that national institutions could play in the protection and promotion of human rights' and invited governments to 'encourage the formation and continuation' of NHRIs.[3] Over the next three decades, standard-setting in the field of human rights led to discussions on how the UN could assist NHRIs in the effective implementation of international human rights standards culminating in the UN International Workshop on National Institutions for the Promotion and Protection of Human Rights held in Paris in 1991.[4] The workshop led to the drafting of a set of guiding principles for NHRIs adopted by the UN Commission on Human Rights in 1992 as the Principles Relating to the Status of National Institutions for the Promotion and Protection of Human Rights (Paris Principles).[5] Today around 100 NHRIs have been established.[6]

---

1 Amnesty International *Amnesty International's recommendations on national human rights institutions,* IOR 40/007/2001 1.

2 International Council on Human Rights Policy *Performance and legitimacy: National human rights institutions* (2000).

3 R Kumar 'National Human Rights Institutions: Good governance perspectives on institutionalization of human rights' (2003) 19 *American University International Law Review* 259 260.

4 Office of the High Commissioner for Human Rights, *Fact Sheet No 19, National Institutions for the Promotion and Protection of Human Rights* http://www.unhchr.org/html/menu6/2/fs19.htm (accessed 10 July 2009).

5 Resolution 1992/54.

6 UN High Commissioner for Human Rights *Survey on National Human Rights Institutions* (2009) http://www.nhri.net/ (accessed 8 April 2010).

3 Mandate of NHRIs

The Paris Principles provides that NHRIs should 'be given as broad a mandate as possible'.[7] The mandate of NHRIs as prescribed by the Paris Principles is discussed below.

3.1 Commenting on existing and draft laws

NHRIs should have the mandate to examine current national legislations and administrative provisions, as well as bills proposed to or before parliament, to ensure that these are in compliance with international human rights standards.[8] This includes the power to monitor laws on their own initiative.

3.2 Monitoring domestic human rights situation

NHRIs are mandated to monitor the human rights situation in their respective countries and may draw the attention of the government to violations as well as make proposals on how to stop such violations. NHRIs may also express opinions on government's positions.[9] NHRIs may monitor civil and political rights as well as economic, social and cultural rights and may monitor human rights compliance by both private and public bodies (including police, military and other security agencies).

NHRIs, in fulfilling this mandate, should have the authority to compel the attendance of witnesses and production of evidence; visit prisons and other places of detention; and to initiate inquiries into human rights violations and publish reports from such inquiries.[10]

3.3 Advise on international human rights standards

NHRIs should encourage the ratification of or accession to international human rights treaties and instruments by their respective states and ensuring their implementation in the domestic systems. NHRIs also have the mandate to promote the harmonisation of national legislations, regulations and practices with international instruments to which the state is party. They should encourage the fulfilment of treaty reporting obligations by contributing to state reports and submitting parallel reports where necessary.[11]

---

7 Paris Principles (n 5 above) part A, para 2.

8 Paris Principles (n 5 above) part A, para 3(a)(i); see also International Council on Human Rights Policy (n 2 above) 18.

9 Paris Principles (n 5 above) part A, para 3(a)(ii)-(iv).

10 See International Council on Human Rights Policy (n 2 above) 18-19.

11 Paris Principles (n 5 above) part A, para 3(b)-(e).

3.4 Education and information dissemination on human rights

As part of their human rights education mandate, NHRIs should take part in the review of school, universities and professional curricula to ensure that human rights education is included. This mandate also includes general human rights awareness, education and training of members of the public as well as officials of agencies most likely to be liable for human rights violations such as the police and other security agencies.[12] The NHRIs' educational mandate should also specifically target marginalised groups such as ethnic, religious and linguistic groups.[13]

3.5 Receiving complaints and petitions on human rights violations

Part D of the Paris Principles provides a quasi-judicial mandate for NHRIs:[14]

> [N]ational institutions may be authorized to hear and consider complaints and petitions concerning individual situations. Cases may be brought before it by individuals, their representatives, third parties, non-governmental organizations, associations of trade unions or any other representative organizations.

This mandate envisages the ability to receive complaints against public as well as private bodies which carry out public functions; the power to receive complaints from individual or bodies not directly affected by the violations; the power to act on its own initiative on individual or collective issues without the prior filing of a complaint and the power to compel the appearance of witnesses, the submission of evidence and to conduct on-site visits. NHRIs may also recommend reparations to victims of human rights violations, take their recommendation to courts for enforcement; and refer complaints outside its mandate to other authorities and appropriate bodies.[15]

3.6 Making recommendations to government and monitoring compliance with its recommendations and advice

In order to give effect to the mandate of the NHRIs to make recommendations to governments on human rights issues, the NHRIs should also have the authority to monitor governments' compliance with their recommendations and advice.[16] This may include the powers to apply to court to compel the enforcement of the recommendations of the NHRIs.

The above are guidelines on the mandate that NHRIs should be given to ensure that they effectively promote and protect international human

12 Paris Principles (n 5 above) part A, para 3(g).

13 International Council on Human Rights Policy (n 2 above) 20.

14 Paris Principles (n 5 above) part D.

15 See International Council on Human Rights Policy (n 2 above) 21 -22.

16 See Paris Principles (n 5 above) part A para 3(a)(iv).

rights standards in their various domestic systems. Although not all NHRIs have mandates broad enough to include the abovementioned entirely within their competence, the implementation without interference of any of the above mandates has the potential to promote international law and human rights standards in domestic legal systems.

4 Uganda Human Rights Commission

4.1 Background on the establishment of the UHRC

The decision to establish the Uganda Human Rights Commission (UHRC) as a permanent body to protect and promote human rights in Uganda was informed by the country's violent and turbulent history. This history was characterised by massive violation of human rights, including extrajudicial killings, torture, rape and defilement, arbitrary arrests, detention without trial, suppression of expression, curtailment of political and religious choice, and deprivation of property. Put simply, a culture of impunity pervaded the country.[17]

In 1986, the National Resistance Movement (NRM) government of President Yoweri Museveni appointed a Commission of Inquiry into the Violation of Human Rights to probe into the various human rights violations that occurred from the time of independence, 9 October 1962 to 26 February 1986 when the NRM took power. The Commission of Inquiry, among other things, recommended that a permanent body be established to monitor human rights protection in the country, and to promote and protect the rights of people in Uganda.

The Paris Principles provide that the mandate of NHRIs should be clearly set out in a constitutional or legislative text.[18] The necessity of the establishment and provision of the mandate of NHRIs in constitutional or legislative text is important to guarantee the independence of the NHRIs from the executive as well as to make it more difficult to abolish them or limit their powers, as may be the case where the NHRIs are established by presidential decrees.[19] Thus in compliance with the Paris Principles, article 51 of the Constitution of the Republic of Uganda 1995 establishes the UHRC with its functions and powers set out in articles 52 and 53 of the Constitution. The Uganda Human Rights Commission Act[20] (UHRC Act) makes further provisions on the appointment, composition, functions and procedure of the UHRC, among others.

---

17 See the website of the Uganda Human Rights Commission http://www.uhrc.ug/index.php?option=com_content&view=article&id=162&ltemid=26 (accessed 25 October 2009).

18 Paris Principles (n 5 above) part A, para 2.

19 Amnesty International (n 1 above) 2-3.

20 Cap 24, Laws of Uganda 2000.

4.2 Mandate of the UHRC

The UHRC is mandated: [21]

> To investigate, at its own initiative or on a complaint made by any person or group of persons against the violation of any human right;
> To visit jails, prisons, and other places of detention or related facilities with a view of assessing and inspecting conditions of the inmates and make recommendations for improvement;
> To establish a continuing programme of research, education and information to enhance respect of human rights;
> To recommend to Parliament effective measures to promote human rights, including provision of compensation to victims of violations of human rights;
> To create and sustain within society the awareness of the provisions of the constitution as the fundamental law of the people of Uganda;
> To educate and encourage the public to defend the constitution at all times against all forms of abuse and violation;
> To formulate, implement and oversee programmes intended to inculcate in the citizens of Uganda awareness of their civic responsibilities and appreciation of their rights and obligations as free people;
> To monitor the Government's compliance with international treaty and convention obligations on human rights; and
> To perform such other functions as may be provided by law.

Article 52(2) of the Constitution requires the Commission to publish periodic reports and submit annual reports to parliament on the state of human rights in the country.

4.3 Implementation of the mandate of the UHRC

This section will examine the implementation of the UHRC mandate. The discussion of the interpretation and implementation of the mandate of the UHRC will highlight how NHRIs in general can maximize their operation by a more generous interpretation and implementation of their mandate. The following are some of the practical ways through which the UHRC implements it mandate.

4.3.1 Commenting on existing and draft laws

The UHRC embarks on analysis of existing and draft laws in order to advise government and parliament on the compliance of the laws or draft bills with international law and human rights standards. These comments and recommendations are usually sent through the relevant government department[22] and to parliament via reports that are published annually and made available to members of the public.[23] In its 11th Annual Report, covering the year 2008, the UHRC made recommendations to

---

[21] See the Constitution of the Republic of Uganda, 1995, art 52(1)(a)-(i).

[22] UHRC's comments on existing laws are sent through the Office of the Attorney-General under the Ministry of Justice and Constitutional Affairs, Uganda.

[23] The UHRC publishes an annual report of its activities of the preceding year. The report contains reports on thematic areas and recommendation to government and parliament in this regard.

parliament on the reform of the Uganda Penal Code Act's provisions on sedition, criminal libel and sectarianism, which provisions impinge on the freedom of the press, in order to make the Act 'consistent with international instruments on freedom of expression and on freedom of the press'.[24]

The UHRC in the same report expressed its position on three bills before parliament. These were the Anti-Corruption Bill, the Regulation of Interception of Communications Bill, 2008, and the International Criminal Court Bill. The report highlighted aspects of the bills which were in violation of international law and human rights standards and made recommendations on their amendment. For instance, the report analysed the Regulation of Interception of Communications Bill 2008 and concluded that 'the Bill in its current form ... threatens the right to privacy as contained in the article 17 of the International Covenant on Civil and Political Rights (ICCPR) which Uganda has ratified'.[25]

The reports of the UHRC contain a synopsis of the draft laws under consideration highlighting both the positive and negative aspects of the bill and then make recommendations such as the one quoted above on various provisions of a draft law. One practical effect of this, other than informing parliament of the aspects of the law which do not conform with international standards, is that the reports also inform the public of the human rights dimensions of bills being debated in parliament and form a basis for the public to monitor the implementation of the UHRC's recommendation in relation to the bills. Other bills which the UHRC has successfully contributed to include the Disability Act, the Equal Opportunity Act, the Refugee Act and the Dual Citizenship Act.

4.3.2 Monitoring domestic human rights situation

The UHRC has eight regional offices across the country. In 2006, the UHRC in conjunction with the Ministry of Local Government undertook a joint venture which aims at establishing human rights desks and committees across the administrative districts of Uganda. Since then, human rights desks have been established in 31 of 61 local government districts.[26] The human rights desks are intended to liaise with the UHRC on human rights issues at the district level, facilitate human rights work, refer complaints and facilitate the realisation of human rights based approaches to development at the local government level. The UHRC's presence at the regional and district levels facilitate its monitoring of the human rights situation across the country and enhance coordination of response to these issues.

---

24 Uganda Human Rights Commission *11th Annual report of the Uganda Human Rights Commission to the Parliament of the Republic of Uganda* 2008 119, http://www.uhrc.ug (accessed 19 May 2010).

25 Uganda Human Rights Commission (n 24 above) 127.

26 Uganda Human Rights Commission (n 24 above) 12–13.

It is pertinent to note that the rights monitored by the UHRC under this mandate are not limited to civil and political rights but also include economic, social and cultural rights. The UHRC's reports have covered such economic, social and cultural rights as the rights to food, shelter, clean and safe water, education, health and others. Although the Constitution of the Republic of Uganda 1995 does not include economic, social and cultural rights within the Bill of Rights chapter but rather within the National Objective and Directive Principles of State Policy,[27] the UHRC's approach in the monitoring of the human rights situation in the country is to treat all human rights as 'universal, indivisible and interdependent and interrelated' according to international standards.[28]

The Constitution of Uganda expressly provides that the UHRC shall have the power to 'visit jails, prisons, and places of detention or related facilities with a view to assessing and inspecting conditions of the inmates and make recommendations'.[29] The UHRC visits places of detention in line with this mandate. In 2008 the UHRC inspected a total of 543 places of detention comprising of prisons, police stations, police posts and military detention centres[30] and made recommendations to government on a variety of issues including the detainees' rights to food, education, work and rehabilitation services, health and others.

4.3.3 Advise on international human rights standards

This mandate obligates the UHRC to encourage government to ratify or accede to international human rights instruments as well as ensure compliance with these instruments within the domestic system. As noted above the UHRC makes recommendations to parliament on existing laws and draft bills with a view towards ensuring that laws comply with international instruments to which Uganda is party. Moreover, the UHRC lobbies government to ratify international human rights instruments to which Uganda is not yet party such as the Optional Protocol to UN Convention Against Torture (CAT).

The UHRC also initiates the drafting of bills to domesticate international treaties to which Uganda is party. One such bill is currently underway: the Prevention and Prohibition of Torture Bill 2009. This bill is an attempt to domesticate CAT. The annual reports of the UHRC show that freedom from torture, cruel, inhuman and degrading treatment and punishment is the most violated right as reported to the Commission.[31] Flowing from this and a number of reports from

---

27 See the Preamble of the Constitution of the Republic of Uganda 1995.

28 See Vienna Declaration and Programme of Action adopted by the World Conference on Human Rights in 1993, UN General Assembly Conference 157/23.

29 Art 52(1)(b) Constitution of the Republic of Uganda 1995.

30 Uganda Human Rights Commission (n 24 above) 37 & 53.

31 According to the 10th and 11th annual reports of the UHRC, between 2006 and 2008, the UHRC received 888 complaints on the violation of the right to freedom from torture, cruel, inhuman and degrading treatment and punishment representing 28.3% of

international NGOs such as Human Rights Watch, the UHRC and the Civil Society Organisation (CSO) Coalition Against Torture set up a task force to draft a bill criminalising torture in Uganda. It was the opinion of CSO stakeholders that the absence of a law making torture a crime in Uganda was responsible for the high incidence of torture in the country and the repeated resort to torture by security operatives in Uganda. Not only does the bill domesticate the provisions of CAT, it further incorporates contemporary international law jurisprudence in the area of torture. As will be seen later in this chapter, the UHRC relies on international law in its tribunal decision and these decisions informed some of the provision of the Prevention and Prohibition of Torture Bill 2009.

The definition of torture in the bill widens the definition in CAT and includes torture committed by private persons which is in line with the contemporary international definition of torture.[32] The bill also widens the criteria of the act[s] of torture to include 'intimidating or coercing the person or any other person to do, or to refrain from doing, any act; or any reason based on discrimination of any kind of the person'.[33] The bill goes further to provide for circumstances aggravating the offence of torture as follows:[34]

> offender uses or threatens to use a deadly weapon;
> offender uses or used sex as a means of torture;
> victim was a person with a disability;
> victim was pregnant or becomes pregnant;
> offender causes death;
> the victim was subjected to medical experiments;
> victim acquires HIV/AIDS;
> victim was under the age of 18 years;
> the victim is permanently incapacitated; or
> the act of torture is recurring

Some of these grounds listed above reflect the decisions of the UHRC on individual complaints in particular the reasoning of the Commission with regard to compensation.

The bill mentioned above is an example of ways in which the UHRC directly promotes the application on international law in Uganda.

---

all complaints received during the period, See generally Uganda Human Rights Commission *10th Annual Report 'A decade of human rights reporting in Uganda'* (2007) 15 and Uganda Human Rights Commission (n 24 above) 16.

32 See Human Rights Committee, General Comment No. 20 concerning prohibition of torture and cruel treatment or punishment, para 13 states that 'States parties should indicate when presenting their reports the provisions of their criminal law which penalize torture and cruel, inhuman and degrading treatment or punishment, specifying the penalties applicable to such acts, whether committed by public officials or other persons acting on behalf of the State, or by private persons.' The responsibility of state parties for torture committed by private persons was considered by the UNCAT in *Dzemajl and Others v Yugoslavia*, communication 161/2000, 21 November 2002.

33 S 3(1)(c) and (d), Prohibition and Prevention of Torture Bill 2009.

34 S 6, Prevention and Prohibition of Torture Bill.

The UHRC continues to lobby parliament and relevant government departments with a view to exerting sufficient pressure on government to ensure compliance with its recommendations and decisions.

4.4 Challenges to the implementation of the mandate of UHRC

The implementation of the mandate of the UHRC is not without challenges. Many of these challenges are not unique to the UHRC but are also faced by other NHRIs. The challenges mentioned below were presented by the then Chairperson of the UHRC to the Conference for Commonwealth National Human Rights Institutions in February 2007.[48]

Wide mandate and resource implication
The wide mandate of the UHRC presents resource challenges both in terms of personnel and finances. This is particularly acute since budgetary allocations are not sufficient to finance the mandate of the UHRC.

Human rights protection in conflict areas
There is also the challenge of monitoring and protection of human rights in conflict areas particularly in northern Uganda where due to years of conflict, the culture of impunity is rife and institutional infrastructure is still lacking.

Implementation of the decisions and recommendations of the UHRC
As mentioned above, government does not comply fully with the decisions and recommendations of the UHRC. Settlement of awards from the decisions of the tribunal is one of the most challenging aspects in this regard, resulting in greater hardship to victims of human rights violations.

External funding
Due to the insufficiency of budgetary allocations from government, the UHRC has to rely on external funding for many of its activities. The problem is that such external sources of funding are not always guaranteed.

Human rights values v cultural traditions
The challenge of cultural relativism *vis-a-vis* international human rights standards continues to pose a problem especially on issues such as polygamy, female genital excision, rights of sexual minorities, and payment of bride price. The cultural perceptions of these issues pose a

48 'Experiences of the Uganda Human Rights Commission in fulfilling its mandate', a paper presented by Ms Margaret Sekaggya, Chairperson of the UHRC to the Conference of the Commonwealth NHRIs in London 26–27 February 2007.

challenge for the UHRC in its human rights awareness and education campaigns.

Instilling a culture of democracy

The challenge of building a culture of democracy and respect of the rule of law remains. This is particularly difficult in a jurisdiction which has recently come out of conflict and where the vestiges of a culture of impunity are still evident. Similarly, Uganda is still finding its feet in the area of multi-party democracy having recently transitioned from a one-party system. The need to inculcate respect for democratic processes and institutions remains a major concern of the UHRC. For an NHRI which exercises quasi-judicial mandate and yet is not publicly perceived as a court of law, the challenge is evident in the difficulty associated with executing and ensuring respect of its summon and in enforcing its decisions, among others.

Appointment of commissioners

The manner of appointment of the commissioners also raises its own challenges. For instance, in Uganda the President of the Republic appoints the commissioners of the UHRC with the approval of parliament. There is no constitutional requirement as to the qualifications of the commissioners except that they must be persons of high moral character and proven integrity.[49] The commissioners are often persons with no background or experience in human rights.

4.5 Recommendations

The following are some recommendations to strengthen the capacity of NHRIs to fulfil their mandate and promote international law and human rights standards in domestic legal systems. Some of these are responsible for the success the UHRC has achieved while others would strengthen the ability of the UHRC to continue and sustain the achievements made.

Constitutional or legislative establishment

As mentioned earlier in this chapter, entrenching the NHRI within a constitutional or legislative text ensures to a great degree its independence. It also guarantees that the work of the NHRI will not be subject to the whim of the executive. Similarly, where the mandate of the NHRI is clearly spelt out and qualification to and tenure of its officers are provided for, the NHRI is better equipped to pursue its mandate.

---

[49] Constitution art 51(4).

Broad mandates

The Paris Principles provides that the mandate of the NHRI should be made as broad as possible.[50] However, the mandate should be as broad in its jurisdiction as it is in its activities. A NHRI which has a broad mandate with respect to activities but which has no jurisdiction over certain organs and agencies of government may not be very successful.

Sufficient and secure resources

The funding for the budget of the NHRI should be sufficient to cover the activities under the mandate of the NHRI. The funding should also be secure to ensure that it is not subject to executive downward review which may easily become a tool for crippling the activities of the NHRI if government is uneasy about its activities. The NHRI should be sufficiently staffed in order to successfully implement its mandate.

Regional presence and ease of access

The NHRI should have sufficient presence in all parts of the country to adequately promote and protect human rights. Additionally, access to the NHRI should be as easy as possible and not unnecessarily clogged by formality. As was mentioned in the case of the UHRC, the lack of unnecessary legal formality is one of the advantages and reasons for its popularity. Access to the NHRI should not inadvertently preclude people on the basis of level of education, economic status and so on.

Government compliance with decisions and recommendation

Government's delay or failure to comply with the decisions and recommendations of the NHRI will frustrate the very basis for its establishment. It will also make the public lose confidence in the work of the NHRI. Conversely government's compliance with the decisions and recommendations of the NHRI will foster a culture of respect for human rights and the effect will be visible to government agencies and the public.

Qualification and tenure of members

The qualification and tenure of the members of the NHRI should be clearly provided for and guaranteed by law. Also the means of appointing, selecting or electing the members should be transparent enough to inspire public confidence in the mandate of the NHRI. A situation where unqualified members are appointed to the NHRI or the members hold their office at the pleasure of the executive will greatly undermine the mandate of the NHRI.

Publicity of the activities of the NHRIs

The mandate and activities of the NHRI should be sufficiently publicised in order to make the public aware of its presence and its mandate. It is

[50] Paris Principles (n 5 above) part A para 2.

also important for the NHRI to make public its decisions and recommendations. This way the public will be able to follow the activities of the NHRI and government's responses to them. This will also give the public an avenue to judge the commitment of its government to democratic ideals and respect for human rights.

Vigorous human rights education
Knowledge of human rights is a prerequisite for individuals and groups to reasonably expect and demand respect for their rights and freedoms. The mandate of promoting and protecting human rights is much more difficult where people have not been informed or educated about them.[51] The mandate of the NHRI should therefore include a human rights education component. This human rights education should also include the training of government agencies such as the police, the military, prison officials and other security agencies which are common violators of human rights.

5 Conclusion

By highlighting the mandate and *modus operandi* of the UHRC, this chapter demonstrated that the mandate of NHRIs, broad or narrow, presents a potential for the promotion of international law and human rights standards in domestic legal systems. Despite the challenges associated with the implementation of their respective mandates, NHRIs have a great potential for inculcating and promoting international law and human rights standards in domestic legal systems and therefore their capacity must be strengthened to achieve this.

51 Uganda Human Rights Commission (n 24 above) 2.

Permissions

All chapters in this book were first published in ILDHRIA, by Pretoria University Law Press (PULP); hereby published with permission under the Creative Commons Attribution License or equivalent. Every chapter published in this book has been scrutinized by our experts. Their significance has been extensively debated. The topics covered herein carry significant findings which will fuel the growth of the discipline. They may even be implemented as practical applications or may be referred to as a beginning point for another development.

The contributors of this book come from diverse backgrounds, making this book a truly international effort. This book will bring forth new frontiers with its revolutionizing research information and detailed analysis of the nascent developments around the world.

We would like to thank all the contributing authors for lending their expertise to make the book truly unique. They have played a crucial role in the development of this book. Without their invaluable contributions this book wouldn't have been possible. They have made vital efforts to compile up to date information on the varied aspects of this subject to make this book a valuable addition to the collection of many professionals and students.

This book was conceptualized with the vision of imparting up-to-date information and advanced data in this field. To ensure the same, a matchless editorial board was set up. Every individual on the board went through rigorous rounds of assessment to prove their worth. After which they invested a large part of their time researching and compiling the most relevant data for our readers.

The editorial board has been involved in producing this book since its inception. They have spent rigorous hours researching and exploring the diverse topics which have resulted in the successful publishing of this book. They have passed on their knowledge of decades through this book. To expedite this challenging task, the publisher supported the team at every step. A small team of assistant editors was also appointed to further simplify the editing procedure and attain best results for the readers.

Apart from the editorial board, the designing team has also invested a significant amount of their time in understanding the subject and creating the most relevant covers. They scrutinized every image to scout for the most suitable representation of the subject and create an appropriate cover for the book.

The publishing team has been an ardent support to the editorial, designing and production team. Their endless efforts to recruit the best for this project, has resulted in the accomplishment of this book. They are a veteran in the field of academics and their pool of knowledge is as vast as their experience in printing. Their expertise and guidance has proved useful at every step. Their uncompromising quality standards have made this book an exceptional effort. Their encouragement from time to time has been an inspiration for everyone.

The publisher and the editorial board hope that this book will prove to be a valuable piece of knowledge for researchers, students, practitioners and scholars across the globe.

List of Contributors

Magnus Killander and Horace Adjolohoun

J Osogo Ambani

Emmanuel K Quansah

Chacha Bhoke Murungu

Michelo Hansungule

Busingye Kabumba

Armand Tanoh and Horace Adjolohoun

Dunia P Zongwe

Ebenezer Durojaye

Ronaldah Lerato Karabo Ngidi

Fatou Kama Marone

Kenechukwu C Esom

Index